MARY IN THE CATHOLIC TRADITION

Frederick M. Jelly, O.P.

Our Sunday Visitor Publishing Division
Our Sunday Visitor, Inc.
Huntington, Indiana 46750

Imprimi Potest: Rev. Paul Hinnebusch, O.P.
Southern Dominican Province, Order of Preachers
August 2, 1986

Dedication

*To my beloved parents of happy memory,
who were the first to hand on to me
the Catholic Tradition about Mary*

Table of Contents

List of Abbreviations † vi

Introduction † 1

I † A Madonna for Catholics Today † 5

II † Daughter of Sion † 19

III † The Perfect Disciple — Mother of God's Son † 26

IV † The Woman of Faith — Mother of God's People † 56

V † New Eve † 69

VI † Ever-Virgin † 78

VII † Theotokos: the Birth-Giver of God † 90

VIII † Chosen by God to Be the Holy Virgin
Theotokos — the Immaculate Conception † 100

IX † Mother and Son Reunited — Mary's Glorious Assumption † 117

X † Mary in the Theology of the Church's 'Common Doctor' † 131

XI † Mary and Joseph in the Communion of Saints † 148

XII † Mary in the Liturgical Year † 168

XIII † Mary in Private Devotions and Apparitions † 178

XIV † A Madonna for All Christians † 196

Notes † 204

Recommended Reading † 208

Discussion Questions † 211

List of Abbreviations

Documents of the Second Vatican Council:
DV: Dogmatic Constitution on Divine Revelation (*Dei Verbum*)
LG: Dogmatic Constitution on the Church (*Lumen Gentium*)
SC: Constitution on the Sacred Liturgy (*Sacrosanctum Concilium*)
UR: Decree on Ecumenism (*Unitatis Redintegratio*)

Other Abbreviations:
BYM: *Behold Your Mother: Woman of Faith*, Pastoral Letter of the U. S. Bishops
CCSL: *Corpus Christianorum, Series Latina*, Turnhout, 1953 -
CSCO: *Corpus Scriptorum Christianorum Orientalium*, Louvain 1903 -
DS: H. Denzinger - A. Schönmetzer, *Enchiridion Symbolorum Definitionum et Declarationum de Rebus Fidei et Morum*
MC: *Marialis Cultus*, Apostolic Exhortation of Pope Paul VI on Devotion to Mary
MG: J. P. Migne, ed., *Patrologiae cursus completus, series graeca*
ML: J. P. Migne, ed., *Patrologiae cursus completus, series latina*
NCE: *New Catholic Encyclopedia*
PTOL: *Papal Teachings — Our Lady*
ST: St. Thomas Aquinas, *Summa Theologiae*
TCT: *The Church Teaches: Documents of the Church in English Translation*
TH: *Theotokos: A Theological Encyclopedia of the Blessed Virgin Mary*

Introduction

DURING the course of the Catholic Tradition there has been but one Mary, mother of Jesus, and yet there have been many Madonnas. Like her divine Son, Mary is first of all and most of all a mystery. The triune God has engaged her so intimately in the mystery of her Son's incarnation and of our redemption that we must always gaze on her in the light of divine revelation. In God's sight Mary can only be that one person in salvation history uniquely called to be the mother of the Father's only begotten Son, and also uniquely redeemed by the foreseen merits of her own Son. From our point of view, however, there must be many Madonnas or portraits of Mary from the New Testament to the teaching and faith of the Church today. The mystery of Mary, sharing in the infinite richness of divine Truth, can be contemplated by our limited minds only from a great variety of approaches. We are just unable to fit her into one mental picture. Hence the appropriateness of the title for this book: *Madonna* (Italian for "my lady") conjures up in our memories the magnificent paintings of Our Lady over the Christian centuries, each one quite distinct, depending upon what the artist was trying to portray about this fascinating woman in her special relationship to God and us; *Mary in the Catholic Tradition* implies that, no matter how much her image may vary from one culture and generation to the next, our faith keeps us focused upon the authentic Mary of Scripture, Tradition, and the Magisterium or infallible teaching of the Church.

Consequently, the first chapter looks at Mary in light of the contemporary Madonna that the teaching Church assures us is a faithful likeness of what has been handed on to us in the Catholic Tradition from the inspired word of God. This begins our consideration, because

1

we are able to look back at the archives of our faith in sacred Scripture and the witness of the Fathers of the Church only as twentieth-century believers. Without reading into these sources of our faith which communicate God's revealing word to us, we still must be conscious of our contemporary understanding if they are to speak to us. Otherwise, the Tradition will not be meeting our needs in salvation history, and it will not be alive in us as the bearers of that Tradition in our own time.

Chapters II through IV provide a summary of the biblical Madonnas. Out of these inspired portraits of Mary, especially those of Luke and John, we hope to be able to follow the development of Marian doctrine and devotion in the Tradition. Chapters V - IX give special attention to the patristic Madonnas, to the special witness of the great Fathers of the Church to Mary according to the apostolic faith. These chapters consider the main truths about Mary, particularly the Marian dogmas of the *Theotokos*, her virgin motherhood of God, her perpetual virginity, her Immaculate Conception, and her glorious Assumption into heaven. Next, in Chapter X, with St. Thomas Aquinas, the great medieval "Common Doctor" of the Church, as our guide, we reflect upon a synthesis of the best Mariology in that Tradition.

Then in Chapters XI through XIII, we glance at our devotion to Mary as expressed most importantly in our liturgical worship in the Church and in private devotions, especially the Rosary, viewed in relationship to the Eucharist. St. Joseph's place in our Christian life is included in the context of Chapter XI, where he can best be appreciated for his special role in the Communion of Saints. In Chapter XII, we survey the various Marian feasts throughout the liturgical year, in order to see how they enhance the celebration of the mysteries of our redemption on the feasts of her Son and during the special liturgical seasons. A brief consideration is devoted to the place of Our Lady's apparitions in our devotion to her in Chapter XIII.

Finally, the concluding chapter of this book takes an ecumenical look at Mary. Can we Catholics, faithful to the best in our own Tradition, portray a Madonna that our sisters and brothers in the other Christian churches will find acceptable to their faith? Although we apparently have a long way to go in clarifying the ecumenical issues involved in the Marian question, considerable progress has been made during the past two decades. In fact, right now it would seem that the Holy Spirit would have us behold the Madonna as the "Mother of Unity."

For the reader to derive the most benefit from this book, it would be wise for him/her to read it in sequence. Each successive chapter is best understood in light of those that have preceded it. If one chooses to do otherwise, however, each chapter should be clear enough in itself.

I should like to take this opportunity to thank Our Sunday Visitor, Inc., for the invitation to write this book, and also to express my special gratitude to Fr. Paul Hinnebusch, O.P., a member of our Dominican community, who read the manuscript.

CHAPTER I

A Madonna for Catholics Today

HOW is Mary portrayed in Catholic teaching today? What do the faithful believe about her? How do they express their devotion to our Lady in the contemporary Church? Do their beliefs and pious practices regarding our Blessed Mother differ very much from those of Catholic Tradition of the past? To what extent does the modern Madonna resemble the Marian portraits of the New Testament, of the Church of the Fathers, of medieval piety, and of the period following the Protestant Reformation through the first part of the twentieth century?

These are the kinds of questions that we Catholics must be asking during this era after Vatican Council II. And we ought to be raising them not only for the sake of our own faith, but also to offer good reasons for that faith to others, especially to our brothers and sisters in the other Christian churches. It is completely in accord with the ecumenical spirit engendered by Vatican II that we reflect upon our Catholic convictions in the setting of our world, and particularly with due regard for our fellow Christians.

Concerning Mary in the Catholic Tradition, this is a special challenge.

Marian doctrine and devotion have been quite distinctive in the Roman Catholic Church over the ages. And so we are called upon to show that the developments that have taken place are in keeping with the faith of the Apostles. Catholics are to be especially careful today in distinguishing what are precisely the Church's dogmas about Mary from the many beliefs and devotional customs that are not held to be necessary for salvation. Also, as was pointed out in the Introduction to this book, there have been many "Madonnas" in the Catholic Tradition. While there is but a single Mary, Mother of Jesus and of all of us

5

redeemed by her Son, there is a diversity of Marian mosaics, even in the New Testament itself. This rich diversity depends upon the theological purpose of each evangelist and the cultural conditions of the historical period, as well as the basic fact that the infinite depths of divine mystery can never be adequately expressed in human terms. At the same time, amid this pluriformity of images, symbols, thought-forms, credal formulas, liturgical rituals, and other devotional expressions, a profound unity of faith must abide. As will be explained later in this chapter, the source of this unity amid diversity, i.e., truly catholic unity, is always the revealing word of God, ever new and ever rooted in the Word made flesh.

Before contemplating divine revelation regarding Mary, particularly by searching the inspired word of God in the Bible and examining how it unfolded and developed in the Tradition, we should glance at the main features of today's Madonna for Catholics. Only then can we ask the right questions of our forebears in the faith, especially those who were called to be the unique witnesses of our Tradition in the Apostolic Church.

In his calling of the extraordinary general assembly of the Synod of Bishops, Pope John Paul II stated to all Catholics: ". . . with you above all I implore the Immaculate Virgin, Mother of the Church, that she may assist us in this hour and obtain for us that fidelity to Christ of which she is the incomparable model through her readiness to be 'the handmaid of the Lord' and through her constant openness to the Word of God (cf. Luke 1:38, 2:19, 51)."[1] He announced the Synod during Mass on January 25, 1985, the Feast of the Conversion of St. Paul, in the Basilica of St. Paul-Outside-the-Walls, where Pope John XXIII had announced on the very same feast that Vatican II would take place. In his homily preached at the close of the Extraordinary Synod, December 8, 1985, the present Holy Father made many references to Mary on the Feast of her Immaculate Conception, among which he proclaimed: "At the end of the second millennium after Christ, the Church only desires one thing: to be the same Church that was born of the Holy Spirit, when the Apostles devoted themselves to prayer, together with Mary in the Upper Room in Jerusalem (cf. Acts 1:14). For from the very beginning they had within their community the one who 'is the Immaculate Conception.' And they looked to her as their model and figure.''[2]

These rather recent papal pronouncements seem to synthesize the main features of a Madonna for Catholics today. And appropriately they were made in close connection with the event in the Church that was the greatest single influence upon the renewing of Mary's portrait, namely, Vatican II. The Extraordinary Synod of Bishops met not merely to commemorate the Council after twenty years, but to recapture its spirit and to implement further its renewals. The ways in which John Paul II referred to Mary, as cited above, portray the Christocentric (centered upon Christ) and the ecclesiotypical (Mary as prototype of the redeemed Body of Christ, the Church) characteristics of Vatican II's Marian teaching. Let us consider briefly some of the more significant historical influences that helped bring about this renewed emphasis from the earliest Catholic Tradition.

The Renewed Portrait of Mary from Vatican II

The Marian doctrine of the Council is contained principally in Chapter VIII of the *Dogmatic Constitution on the Church* or *Lumen Gentium* (LG 52-69).[3] It was issued November 21, 1964. But considerable debate among the conciliar fathers had preceded the very close decision on October 29, 1963, to make their teaching on Mary a part of the document on the Church instead of a separate *schema*. During the debate, it was carefully pointed out that doctrine about Our Lady and devotion to her were not the issue, but in what context of the Council's teaching would she most effectively be portrayed. Those who were of the opinion that the cult of Mary in the Church had too often been unduly separated from the mystery of Christ and the Church argued in favor of making the Council's Marian doctrine an integral part of LG. The title finally chosen for the chapter was: "The Blessed Virgin Mary, Mother of God, in the Mystery of Christ and the Church," which clearly expresses their position.

In the perception of most Catholic Mariologists, or theologians of Mary, the decision has proven providential. Although it has frequently been misinterpreted, as though the Council were minimizing Mary's role in the Church, the results have generally been salutary. Doctrinally, it has helped place the truths of our faith or the dogmas about Mary in their proper perspective, i.e., in intimate relationship with the mystery of Christ and the Church. Devotionally, the portrait of the modern Madonna in Chapter VIII of LG has drawn Catholics away from a "privilege-centered" Mariology toward one that is more "sharing-oriented." In other words, instead of beholding Mary's special graces and privileges as isolating her from us, we see them as revealing what God intends ultimately for all who have been redeemed by Christ. Theologically, therefore, this renewed emphasis or rediscovery of the best about Mary in our Catholic Tradition gives us greater enlightenment and inspiration concerning the very core of our faith in Christ and his redeemed-redeeming Body, the Church.

Ecumenically, this Madonna for Catholics today is also more pleasing for our fellow Christians to behold. Our sisters and brothers of the other churches have traditionally considered that we practically make Mary a substitute for Christ and the Holy Spirit in our salvation and sanctification. We should concede that, often enough in the course of history, grounds for such suspicions are found, especially in the superstitious beliefs and practices of popular piety. More, however, will be said about this in the proper context of a later chapter of this book. Suffice it to say here that a previous Mariology which tended to place Mary at the side of Christ, looking downward upon us, distorted her relationship both to him and to us. And so the ecclesiotypical emphasis — which sees her as *one of us redeemed* and a member of her Son's Body, the Church, albeit an extraordinarily favored one — is much less likely to distort the mystery of her unique role in salvation history.

At the same time, this approach is completely compatible with the Christocentric emphasis in contemporary Catholic Mariology. The ecclesiotypical is mutually complementary with the Christocentric emphasis.[4] All authentic teaching about Mary, as well as any true devotion to her, is based upon her unique relationship with Christ. And, just as Christ cannot be understood and revered apart from the ecclesial Body or Church that he received through his redemptive activity, so neither can the Madonna be properly contemplated and venerated as though she were not in solidarity with that same Body. She is, after all, the first fruits of her Son's redemption, and so the prototype or primary example of what it means to be a faithful member of her Son's Church.

There is a certain parallel between what Catholic theologians have been trying to do in Christology and their efforts in Mariology. From the beginning, the mystery of Christ has been a challenge to the human understanding's ability to preserve the divinity of Christ without disparaging his humanity and vice-versa. Similarly, the intelligence of the believer finds it very difficult to keep in harmony Mary's unique relationship with the Word made flesh and her special role in salvation history with the truth of revelation that she is our sister in faith and one of us redeemed members of the Church. Just as there are current attempts at maintaining our relationship with Christ as both Other (truly Son of God) and as brother (truly Son of Mary), so too the Madonna for Catholics today tries to portray her as the only Mother of God, the spiritual mother of us all, as well as our sister in the Church. In the case of both mysteries, the balance is a very delicate one indeed. And to miss it about Mary means misconceptions in our faith about Christ and the Church.'

Other Characteristics of Contemporary Mariology

Vatican II's teaching about Our Lady has proven to be an excellent impetus to the cultivation and development of an ecclesiotypical approach to Mary, but not at the expense of the Christocentric. Chapter VIII of LG treats in a balanced way both Mary's motherhood of Christ and of Christians in the order of grace. The divine favor of her full and firm faith intimately affects both of her maternal relationships. And, as will be made manifest throughout the course of this study, this fact has been very influential on Mariological writings after the Council.

Another characteristic beginning to emerge in postconciliar Mariology is the renewed emphasis upon the special relationship between Mary and the Holy Spirit. Although the relationship is not very clear and explicit in the Marian doctrine of Vatican II, still the seeds were sown there. Once she is more intimately related to both the Head and members of the Church, then the rediscovery of her close bond with the Pentecostal Spirit cannot be too far behind. Thanks to a reawakening of devotion to the Holy Spirit and of Pneumatology (theology of the Holy Spirit) generally among the Christian churches of the West, the Third Person of the Blessed Trinity has become more evident in our lives of faith and worship. And the Spirit of our risen Lord is joined much more intimately with Christ, particularly in the establishment and preservation of the Church. The gifts and charisms of the Holy Spirit within individual believers and in the Church as a whole are being received with a deeper sense of gratitude and responsibility. Keeping faithful to the apostolic traditions of the Church is the work of the Spirit in us.

A Madonna for Catholics today portrays Mary as the new creation of the Holy Spirit without parallel among the redeemed. She is the temple of the indwelling Spirit *par excellence*. Mary may even be called the "icon" of her Son's Holy Spirit. Here we are once again enriched by the great traditions of faith and devotion in the Christian churches of the East, both Orthodox and Catholic. Their rich theology of the Holy Spirit and inspiring use of icons in worship can teach us much. An icon is a pictorial representation of a religious truth or spiritual reality and may be likened to the symbolic signs of the sacraments. As the West has its great Madonnas, so the East has its magnificent icons depicting most often Mary at the birth of the Son. The icon is a very effective medium for helping unite the one beholding it with the spiritual reality expressed in the persons of the painting. And so Mary may fittingly be looked upon as the "icon" of the Holy Spirit — indeed an incarnate icon, one of flesh and blood — who reveals to us what mighty deeds of salvation the Spirit can accomplish in our lives as faithful Christians.

Although it cannot be called a characteristic that is distinctive of contemporary Mariology, since it seems to have more or less perdured throughout the Tradition, there appears to be a new insight into the relationship between Mary and God the Father. She is his most highly favored daughter among all his adopted children. The First Person of the Triune God is the primordial source of all blessings and "every perfect gift" (cf. James 1:17). He sent the Son to save us and with his Son continuously pours forth their Spirit of divine Love to sanctify us. Mary abounds with his gifts of redeeming love and holiness, as his most highly favored daughter. And the grace of her vocation to be the

Mother of his Son as well as to enter so intimately into the mysteries of our redemption was uniquely bestowed upon her by the Father for the good of us all. The renewal of Marian doctrine and devotion during the past twenty-five years or so has not been taking place in a vacuum, isolated from the many other marvelous renewals inspired and encouraged by Vatican II. These include the biblical and liturgical renewals especially. And a rediscovery of the best in the Catholic Tradition of the great Fathers of the Church has also contibuted to all of the renewal movements. Of course, the Council itself did not take place in a vacuum. The foundations for its wonderful work of reform and renewal were laid years before its inception, most proximately,for instance, by the papal encyclicals of Pius XII on scriptural interpretation (*Divino Afflante Spiritu*), the liturgy (*Mediator Dei*), and the nature of the Church as the Mystical Body of Christ (*Mystici Corporis*). While there seems to have been a reciprocal influence of the various renewal efforts — e.g., the interdependence and mutual enrichment of both the liturgical and the biblical — all of them have conspired to gather together those elements in our Tradition which help renew our understanding of the mystery of the Church in the contemporary world. The two focal points of the conciliar documents of Vatican II are: the Church contemplating her own mysterious self in the *Dogmatic Constitution on the Church* (LG); and, the Church looking outside herself, as it were, at the whole world which she is called to serve in her mission of salvation, in the *Pastoral Constitution on the Church in the Modern World*, or *Gaudium et Spes* (GS), issued at the end of the Council on December 7, 1965. We have already glanced at the impact of Vatican II's ecclesiology (theology of the Church) upon contemporary Mariology, i.e., its ecclesiotypical character in which Mary is seen as the prototype or primary exemplar of being a faithful member of the Church. Now let us take a brief look at its mutual relationship with other renewals going on in the Church.

Concentrating upon its sources, contemporary Mariology may be characterized as both biblical and patristic, i.e., greatly influenced by the teaching of the Fathers such as Irenaeus, Augustine, Ambrose, etc. This is not distinctive of Mariology alone, because the other areas of Catholic theology today are also rooting their reflections upon the faith much more carefully and extensively in the uniquely inspired word of God, the biblical revelation, and in the testimony of the Fathers in the ancient Tradition of the Church. It is, however, especially significant for Mariology to do this, since too often in the past insufficient consideration was paid to the Word of God, the theological source of our faith about Mary as well as about Christ, the Church, etc. As a result, a number of beliefs and devotions regarding the Madonna were not always well founded and led to unnecessary confusion among Catholics and conflicts with other Christians. A good part of this book is devoted to the biblical and patristic basis of Marian doctrine and devotion in the Catholic Tradition.

Contemporary Mariology is also liturgical. This characteristic may be understood in two ways, both of which are very significant. One is that the theology of Mary looks to the abiding witness of liturgical celebrations over the ages as a key source of reflecting upon her unique role in the Christian mysteries. And this is done for a very good reason. The liturgy or official public worship of the Church has a special value of giving testimony to the faith of the People of God as well as their devotion. Liturgical prayers and actions are carefully watched over by the bishops or shepherds of the Church to make sure that they truly reflect the apostolic faith. There is an ancient adage from one of the Church's Fathers that sums it up nicely: *Ecclesia orans, Ecclesia credens*, "As the Church prays, so the Church believes." The second sense in which Mariology today is liturgical is that the purest and most effective Marian devotion is that expressed in the liturgy. Since we believe, as part of our divine Catholic faith, that the Holy Spirit guides and inspires the liturgical worship of the Church in a special way, then Marian devotion expressed in the celebrations of the Eucharist and other sacraments as well as the Liturgy of the Hours is most salutary. This conviction will be elaborated in other parts of the book.

Finally, there are three other characteristics of contemporary Mariology that have to do with its impact upon other movements in the Church today. These are its spiritual, pastoral, and ecumenical emphases. And, of course, they are very much interrelated with the other characteristics. Also, all of theology must be spiritual, pastoral, and ecumenical if it is to be of service to the Church. If theology seeks to use reason to make the mysteries of faith more intelligible and meaningful, then it has to have a practical influence upon our spiritual lives of prayer, virtue, etc., upon our ministries, and our share in the quest for greater unity with the other Christian churches. Again, however, we are concentrating upon the special significance of these three characteristics in Mariology today.

Truly to reflect upon Marian dogmas must mean that their relevance to our spiritual lives is so considered. Thus a "sharing-oriented" Mariology views the special graces and privileges of Our Lady as manifestations of the ways in which we are to experience the active presence of the living God in ourselves. To contemplate the mystery of Mary without coming to make this reference to our Christian existence is not really to know her. We may be getting to know many things *about* her, but we really don't come to *know her* personally as our spiritual mother who wishes to help nourish in us the life of her Son. When asked why he thought a decline had taken place in Marian devotion, Karl Rahner replied: ". . . the special temptation that affects Christians today, Catholics and Protestants alike, is the temptation to turn the central truths of the faith into abstractions, and abstractions have no need of mothers."[6] I believe that what is being brought out here is something of what this great theologian of our century had in mind. Certainly he was not belittling the serious intellectual work demanded of theologians, but rather lamenting the fact that too few were penetrating to the spiritual realities behind their abstract ideas. And Mary and Mariology should inspire us to do so.

Drawing out the pastoral implications of a theological consideration of Our Lady is a fairly recent practice and requires much further development. This woman of silence, about whom the Scriptures themselves appear to be quite reticent, has often been proposed as a model for our Christian life of prayer and of contemplation. Now, however, meditation upon the mystery of her Visitation with Elizabeth, and upon her intervention at the wedding feast of Cana, etc., are inspiring more to behold today's Madonna as also a woman of action and generous service.

The ecumenical emphasis in contemporary Mariology has taken many by surprise. Almost from the beginning of the ecumenical movement in the Catholic Church following Vatican II, there have been organized efforts to address the place of Mary in our prayerful striving toward Christian unity. At first, many feared that introducing Mary into the dialogue with our sisters and brothers of the other Christian churches might abort the entire ecumenical movement. Experience, however, has more than testified that, *without* her, the quest for our uniting into the one Church of her Son is inadequate. Not only do we Catholics have to present our Madonna in the clearest light possible, reflecting the best in our Tradition, but we too must learn from our fellow Christians not only their problems with our Marian doctrines and devotions, but also their own traditions about her place in the Church. The questions directly touching upon the mystery of Mary, while not of themselves central to our Christian faith, still are significant in making such basic issues as the relationship between Scripture and Tradition, the way God's grace works in our human freedom, etc., much more concrete in the ecumenical dialogues between our churches.

Mary in Scripture, Tradition, and the Magisterium

In the *Dogmatic Constitution on Divine Revelation, Dei Verbum* (DV) from Vatican II, issued November 18, 1965, we read: ". . . in the supremely wise arrangement of God, sacred Tradition, sacred Scripture, and the Magisterium of the Church are so connected and associated that one of them cannot stand without the others. Working together, each in its own way under the action of the one Holy Spirit, they all contribute effectively to the salvation of souls" (DV 10). A proper understanding of this important conciliar document, particularly its second chapter, "The Transmission of Divine Revelation," is required in order to read this book with profit. And, although it left open to the discussion of theologians a number of questions, such as where the fullness of divine revelation is to be found — whether partly in sacred Scripture and partly in sacred Tradition, or completely in both organs of transmitting the revealing Word of God, or partly in one and totally in the other — the following theological interpretation is entirely in accord with its spirit and letter.

In his eternal Son, Jesus Christ, the Word made flesh, God has revealed himself to us definitively for the sake of our salvation. There can be no other self-disclosure of the triune God that would add anything substantive to the life and teaching of the Savior of the world culminating in the Paschal mystery of his passion, death, and glorification. The unique apostolic witness to this mystery was committed to writing under the special inspiration of the Holy Spirit, the sacred Scripture of both Testaments. These inspired writings came to be within a definite Tradition or living context of faith, worship, and witness or mission. They continue to be, and to be more deeply penetrated in their meaning for the salvation of all generations, within the same Tradition of faith. As a part of that Tradition, and not the whole of it, Christ and his Pentecostal Spirit have endowed the Church with the charism of an infallible teaching authority or Magisterium. Its purpose is to serve the whole Church by teaching all of its members what is necessary to believe and live by in matters of faith and morals. This charism is found in the bishops of the Church, successors to the Apostles.

In light of this, we might say that there is really only one source of revelation, Jesus Christ our risen Lord. As Head of his Body the Church, with the Father, he continuously sends forth his Pentecostal Spirit to keep us faithful to his definitive revelation, which communicates to us not only who God is as our gracious and loving Father, but also what we are to become as his adopted children through grace. Keeping faithful to the true meaning and value of an event that took place over nineteen hundred years ago does not make Tradition static. Rather it is the dynamic process in which all believers are called to have a hand in the transmission of the apostolic faith intact. And preserving the faith intact does not mean a mere repetition of its primordial expressions, as a biblical fundamentalist would hold, but bringing out its real saving significance for the particular time in history. This means development, and the Magisterium of the Church makes bishops, especially the Bishop of Rome, the Pope, primarily responsible to determine what developments are authentic or in keeping with the Word of God. Their special teaching authority is to assist each one of us in his/her own responsibility of transmitting that divine Word faithfully in a form that will be intelligible and meaningful to our contemporaries. And the revealing Word of God is not limited to what is explicitly contained in the sacred Scriptures.

Sacred Scripture and sacred Tradition must be viewed, therefore, as "a single sacred deposit of the Word of God, which is entrusted to the Church" (DV 10). Tradition is not to be considered as though it were an appendix to the Scriptures, making explicit certain truths of salvation not to be found in them. Tradition, rather, is what keeps the whole Bible a living reality and enables its treasures to be uncovered over the ages. The Magisterium serves the Word of God several ways in this dynamic process of development in continuity with the apostolic faith. Infallible pronouncements have been most often made at ecumenical councils, beginning with the first, held in Nicea (325). The most recent, of course, was Vatican Council II (1962-65). When such worldwide gatherings of Catholic bishops, called together and presided over by the Holy Father, the Bishop of Rome, decide to make such pronouncements with papal approval, it is clearly defined in the conciliar documents. These defined dogmas of faith have been relatively rare and usually are in response to heretical misinterpretations of the basic mysteries, such as the Trinity, Incarnation, Redemption, etc., which are explicitly found in the biblical revelation, but must be expressed in a different way to clarify the mystery. Even rarer in the Church's history are infallible definitions of dogmas by Popes apart from ecumenical councils. The two principal instances, particularly for our purposes, are the Marian dogmas of the Immaculate Conception (Pope Pius IX, 1854) and the Assumption (Pope Pius XII, 1950). And both Popes consulted the Catholic Church through their brother bishops before defining these as truths of revelation.

These infrequent occurrences are expressions of the Solemn or Extraordinary Magisterium. There are a few other truths of our divine Catholic Faith which, although never solemnly defined by an ecumenical council or papal pronouncement, are considered to be part of the revealing Word of God. They are a part of what is called the Ordinary Universal Magisterium, or of the constant preaching and teaching of the Church, as well as the expressions of faith from all believers. An example of such a truth of our divine Catholic faith would be Mary's perpetual virginity, as we shall see more extensively in a subsequent chapter.

As the examples cited above indicate, all the dogmas about Mary in the Catholic Tradition, except the definition at the Council of Ephesus (431) that she is the *Theotokos*, the God-Bearer, are without any apparent basis in the biblical revelation. It is particularly important for the Mariologist, therefore, to be able to point out the validity of the development of the dogmas of the Immaculate Conception, the Assumption, and the perpetual virginity of Mary in the Tradition. Are they in any sense to be found in the Scriptures? And, since the testimony of that Tradition is quite late concerning the Immaculate Conception and the Assumption, at least in the precise meanings of their definitions, how are we to hold that they were somehow "insinuated" or implied in the definitive Word of God uttered in Christ? This book will be attending to such questions. They are not solely the concern of us theologians, although we do have a special responsibility to address them. But because the faith grows in a Tradition that belongs to all of us in the Church, then everyone must be more or less concerned.

You will note that this book is dedicated to my parents of happy memory, "who were the first to hand on to me the Catholic Tradition about Mary." This is the case, generally speaking, with all of our convictions as Catholics. I believe that God intends parents to be the primary communicators in our Tradition. They are in the best position to have a profound influence upon the spirits of their own children, and it is an important aspect of the sacramental grace of marriage for them to teach religion in the family. We who are called to teach religion in our schools, or to think theologically, and to write books about our faith, etc., can only build upon such solid foundations in the home. If it is lacking, then there has to be a way of trying to compensate in those unfortunate circumstances where children are denied this education, which goes far beyond intellectual information. A Maryknoll missionary sister told me one time that she and several other religious were trying to teach religion to young children who had been orphaned during the war in Korea. When the sisters, brothers, and priests tried to tell these youngsters about the love of their heavenly Father and their mother Mary for them, they just received blank looks in response. It then dawned upon them that these children had never experienced the love of an earthly mother and father, and so had no basis of understanding the love of the heavenly. The missionaries then endeavored to

do what they could to supply such love and affection. Only then did the
children start to grasp the religious convictions that they wished to
share with them.

One other significant fact that should be underlined about the sacred Tradition is that our faith develops not only through mental activity, but in settings of life that affect our total personalities. The very
language of the Bible abounds with images that inspire our hearts as
well as enlighten our minds. Our liturgical celebrations are so structured that we are more readily motivated to hear God's word as a call
to ministry in actively witnessing to our faith. The affective and con-
ative (active) drives within us are directed along with the cognitive
drive to understand our faith more fully. Our faith grows, therefore, in
a Tradition of devotion and apostolic activity as well as teaching and
learning. In fact, our minds are not being genuinely nourished in the
faith if our religious ideas and images do not translate themselves into
lives of prayerful practices and love of neighbor. And we look back at
the previous moments of our Tradition, especially the unique witness of
the Apostles, not as though it had stopped and we were not continuing
it. Rather, we ponder the past because it is still unfolding in us, and we
are called to shape its further fulfillment in the future.

Everyone who shares in the Catholic Tradition should read these
writings as an active participant in handing on their content — our
faith about Mary. And that faith has deepened and developed especially through the devotion of all the faithful. A Madonna for Catholics
today should reveal the real Mary to everyone sharing that faith.

CHAPTER II

Daughter of Sion

VATICAN Council II begins to paint its biblical Madonna, or portrait of Mary, with the following meditation upon the connection between her and some of the major themes in the salvation history of the Old Testament.

> The sacred writings of the Old and New Testaments, as well as venerable tradition, show the role of the Mother of the Savior in the plan of salvation in an ever clearer light and call our attention to it. The books of the Old Testament describe the history of salvation, by which the coming of Christ into the world was slowly prepared. The earliest documents, as they are read in the Church and are understood in the light of a further and full revelation, bring the figure of a woman, Mother of the Redeemer, into a gradually clearer light. Considered in this light, she is already prophetically foreshadowed in the promise of victory over the serpent which was given to our first parents after their fall into sin (cf. Genesis 3:15). Likewise she is the virgin who shall conceive and bear a son, whose name shall be called Emmanuel (cf. Isaiah 7:14; Micah 5:2-3; Matthew 1:22-23). She stands out among the poor and humble of the Lord, who confidently hope for and receive salvation from him. After a long period of waiting, the times are fulfilled in her, the exalted Daughter of Sion, and the new plan of salvation is established, when the Son of God has taken human nature from her, that he might in the mysteries of his flesh free man from sin. (LG, 55).

The images and themes of the Old Testament which the Catholic Church understands as prophetically foreshadowing the role of Mary in our redemption by her Son probably influenced the New Testament evangelists themselves in their portraits of her, particularly Sts. Luke and John, as we shall see in chapters III and IV. Among these images and themes, many scholars of recent years have come to conclude that the image of Mary as the "Daughter of Sion" is one which is especially rich in its meaning.[1] The original literal meaning of "Daughter of Sion" is based upon the biblical usage of "daughter" to designate the village and rural areas which surrounded and depended upon some central city. So the "daughter of Sion" referred to that district which had a dependency upon Sion or Zion. More precisely it came to signify an area to the north of Jerusalem where those refugees who fled the north after the fall of Samaria had gathered together. They were called "the remnant of Israel," the northern kingdom, which had separated from Judah or the southern kingdom in 922 B.C. and fell to the Assyrians in 721 B.C.. The people were displaced according to the custom of the day. Some of them fled to the district called "Daughter of Zion." The prophet Micah, whose ministry was 714-701, makes reference to it: "And you, O tower of the flock, hill of the daughter of Zion, to you shall it come, the former dominion shall come, the kingdom of the daughter of Jerusalem" (Micah 4:8). In the psalms and the prophets, "Sion" (Zion) becomes synonymous with Jerusalem, which itself, as the capital city, can stand for the whole nation. Thus the "Daughter of Sion" comes to represent the entire people of ancient Israel. Micah's prophecy of hope for restoration refers to the People of God as a whole in the Old Covenant. And the words of another prophet indicate that all of God's people shall benefit by the saving advent of their God: "Say to the daughter of Zion, 'Behold, your salvation comes. . . .' " (Isaiah 62:11). The Old Testament further develops the theme to designate the messianic community, especially that remnant of the chosen people who returned from Babylon to Jerusalem after the Exile, starting in 539 B.C. (cf. BYM, 16). There are many other references to this theme which, in the context of the Old Testament revelation, show forth its meaning as the Church coming to be, or the ancient People of God in their yearning for divine salvation and expectation of Christ.

It is indeed fitting, therefore, that the Church of the New People of God has been inspired to see the fuller meaning of the "Daughter of Sion" in Mary who embodies the mystery of the Church coming to be under its Old Testament expectation of the Savior. As Vatican II put it: "After a long period of waiting the times were fulfilled in her, the exalted Daughter of Zion. . ." (LG, 55). The entire history of salvation is summed up and reaches its highest expression of loving faith in and hope for the Messiah in Mary. God's providential guidance of his people in the Old Covenant made every person, place, and historical event a preparation that would find its fulfillment in her response at the Annunciation. Divine favor had made her *capax Dei*, i.e., capable of receiving God into herself, as we shall consider further in St. Luke's account of this mystery of the dawn of our salvation in Christ.

The inspired Scriptures of the early Church were the books of the Old Testament. The Bible of Christians until about A.D. 150 was the Septuagint, the Greek Old Testament.[2] Of course they understood it in light of the words and deeds of Christ. He brought to fulfillment all that had been foreshadowed in the Law and the Prophets. This earliest stage of our Christian Tradition, therefore, was a preaching and teaching based upon the Old Testament and the apostolic witness to Jesus, handed on by word of mouth. Although this situation gave a certain vitality to the transmission of the Christian message, the oral tradition soon came to be corrupted, especially by the Gnostic heretics. They rejected the Old Testament, setting up a complete opposition between the Jewish and the Christian revelations. This heresy was most clearly taught by Marcion, who flourished in the middle of the second century. He contrasted the good God revealed in Christ with the God of vengeance in the Old Testament, whom he blamed for evil in creation. And so the writing of Christian books was made necessary to offset such heretical misinterpretations. These apostolic writings came to be more urgently needed as the living witnesses to Christ and the Apostles themselves left this earth. Although it took until the fourth century to reach final agreement in the Church about which writings were to be included in the New Testament Canon, they came to be read during liturgical worship, and by A.D. 150 were awarded the authority once given only to the Old Testament. The writings of the Old Covenant, therefore, significantly influenced those of the New Testament.

This brief historical background to the books of the New Testament explains why we are considering some of the more significant Old Testament themes that refer to Mary. Without our being at least basically familiar with them, it is not possible for us to appreciate what is being revealed about her in the Gospels. This is also the case with all the major themes of salvation history and the principal doctrines of our Catholic Tradition. Vatican II clearly taught: "For, although Christ founded the New Covenant in his blood (cf. Luke 22:20; I Corinthians 11:25), still the books of the Old Testament, all of them caught up into the Gospel message, attain and show forth their full meaning in the New Testament (cf. Matthew 5:17; Luke 24:27; Romans 16:25-26; II Corinthians 3:14-16) and, in their turn, shed light on it and explain it" (DV, 16). Let us then turn to a few other Old Testament themes that should help "shed light on and explain" the New Testament revelation regarding Mary.

Daughter of Abraham and of David

As the "exalted Daughter of Sion," Mary has been given a very special place in the tradition of a long line of heroes and heroines in salvation history. Outstanding among them is our father in faith, Abraham, who was raised up by God at the very dawn of the history of our salvation. Filled with a faith in the ancient promises of God, he handed on to all his descendants, including Mary, the hope in the Messiah to come. Of course, it took generations for his primitive beliefs to become explicitly messianic, but he is still the spiritual ancestor of all who place their trust in the saving God revealed only in Jesus Christ. "Now the LORD said to Abram, 'Go from your country and your kindred and your father's house to the land that I will show you. And I will make of you a great nation. . ." (Genesis 12:1-2). Abraham believed God's promise, and it was fulfilled most especially in his daughter Mary, who made him the forefather of Christ and so spiritually the forebear of all the Christian faithful. The American bishops' pastoral teaches: There

> are remarkable likenesses between Abraham and Mary, especially in the accounts of the birth of Isaac, child of promise, and the virginal conception of Jesus, holy Child of Mary. Abraham, Old Testament man of faith, illuminates our understanding of Mary, New Testament woman of faith. Abraham, our father in faith, can teach us much about Mary, our mother in faith. (BYM 30)

One of the most moving accounts of faith, of complete confidence in God, is the story of how Abraham was willing to sacrifice his only son, Isaac. Even though Isaac was the son of God's promise, the only apparent way that it could ever be fulfilled, Abraham was obedient to the Lord's command. We are all familiar with this touching story in the Old Testament (Genesis 22:1-18). Through his heavenly messenger, the "angel of the Lord," God revealed to Abraham how pleased He was with his obedient faith and spared Isaac. In Isaac, the Church beholds a type of Mary's Child of promise. The conceptions of both were miraculous: Isaac, born of Sarah in her barrenness; and Jesus, born of Mary, who became fruitful while still remaining a virgin. Abraham's son carried the wood for his own immolation on a mountain designated by God. Mary's Son bore his cross, the instrument of his own self-sacrifice, up to Mount Calvary. But while God tried Abraham's faith without the death of his son, Mary's faith was tested to the point of watching her Son die upon the cross for our salvation. The heroism of the daughter's faith surpassed even that of her father's. The "exalted Daughter of Sion" embodied and represented the best in the faith of her forefather's people by her obedience to the Father's salvific will at the foot of the cross.

Mary may also be looked upon as the "Daughter of David." When King David conquered the city of Jerusalem, he made it his capital. Although at this time it was only a small town of no importance, he conferred upon it the even greater honor of having the ark of the covenant brought there and installed with much ceremony (cf. II Samuel 6:1-19). At this time David conceived the idea of building a temple to Yahweh. Not only was he prompted by motives of religion and piety, but he also realized that the Temple would become a center for unifying the northern and southern portions of his kingdom more closely. But upon consulting the prophet Nathan about his idea, David learned that it was not God's will at the time. Nathan's prophecy, however, did clearly reveal his messianic plans for the house and family of King David (cf. II Samuel 7:2-16). St. Luke, centuries later, would be inspired to see the fulfillment of this prophecy in his account of the Annunciation: "and the Lord God will give to him the throne of his father David . . . and of his kingdom there will be no end" (Luke 1:32-33).

A deeper insight into the spiritual meaning of Nathan's prophecy about the Davidic dynasty came about during a dark period in the political history of ancient Israel. It was during this time, c. 732 B.C., that another great prophet appears who heralds her liberation through the birth of a royal child who will assume the rule of David his father (cf. Isaiah 8:23; 9:1-3, 5-6). The "Book of Emmanuel" in Isaiah prophesies that the coming of this king will signify a great religious reawakening, when the knowledge of Yahweh will be proclaimed by him and an era of peace will begin. The same great prophet also mentions the mother of this future king: "Hear then, O house of David! . . . Behold a young woman shall conceive and bear a son, and shall call his name Immanuel" (Isaiah 7:13-14). A few years later, the prophet Micah describes the mother of the future king in similar terms (cf. Micah 5:2-3), and the evangelist Matthew sees its fulfillment in the virginal conception of Christ by the power of the Holy Spirit in Mary's womb (Matthew 1:22-23). Vatican II makes reference to these three passages of Scripture (LG 55). As the next chapter will show in greater detail, she who is the "Daughter of David" is the mother of the "Son of David," our divine Savior-King.

Most Highly Favored Daughter of the Father

The *Anawim*, or the poor of Yahweh, were God's favorite children among his chosen people of the Old Covenant. These were "the poor and humble of the Lord, who confidently hope for and receive salvation from him," among whom Vatican II teaches that Mary "stands out" (LG 55). It took much time for ancient Israel to learn from Yahweh that riches and temporal prosperity are not the infallible signs of his blessing. Not only God's Word, but the events in their history interpreted by that prophetic Word, taught his people the true spirit of poverty that is pleasing to him. The prophet Sophonias (Zephaniah) has a special role to play in this spiritual experience of Israel. About 630-625 B.C., after the religious situation had sunk to the lowest depths of impiety during the reign of King Manasseh, Sophonias foretold that the "Day of Yahweh" was coming, a day of divine judgment and wrathful reckoning for the infidelities of his people. This divine judgment, however, as always would not only condemn but purify his people, lovingly calling them back to faithful observance of the covenant. Through his prophlet, Yahweh promises: "For I will leave in the midst of you a people humble and lowly. They shall seek refuge in the name of the LORD" (Zep 3:12). This tiny remnant of the *Anawim*, "a people humble and lowly," will keep alive the hopes of Israel for liberation. Just a verse or two later (Zep 3:14), we hear the prophet calling upon the "daughter of Zion" and the "daughter of Jerusalem" to sing aloud and rejoice heartily over this. And Jeremiah, both by his whole way of life and by his prophetic message, would confirm the Lord's promise to the *Anawim*. "Sing to the LORD; / praise the LORD! / For he has delivered the life of the needy [poor] from the hand of evildoers" (Jer 20:13). The spirit of the poor of Yahweh would sustain the remnant of God's people throughout the Babylonian captivity and return from exile. From this remnant, under the loving inspiration and direction of Yahweh's Spirit and Word, would arise the most highly favored daughter of the Father. In her would be summarized and surpassed the very best in the spirit of the *Anawim*, "the devout believers who counted on God for salvation" (BYM 16). Mary's song of true liberation through the mighty deeds of God our salvation, the *Magnificat* (Luke 1:46-55), rejoices "for he has regarded the low estate of his handmaiden" (Luke 1:48), and, "he has scattered the proud in the imagination of their hearts, / he has put down the mighty from their thrones, / and exalted those of low degree; / he has filled the hungry with good things, / and the rich he has sent empty away" (Luke 51-53). Through the lips of Luke the evangelist, Mary has completely identified herself with the *Anawim*, who were utterly dependent upon Yahweh alone for their salvation and placed all their hopes in him, firmly believing his promises would be kept. In another Old Testament reference (Gen 3:15), Vatican II sees Mary as "already prophetically foreshadowed in the promise of victory over the serpent which was given to our first parents after their fall into sin" (LG 55). "I will put enmity between you and the woman, / and between your seed and her seed; / he shall bruise your head, / and you shall bruise his heel" (Gen 3:15). Frequently in our Tradition of faith this has been called the "*protevangelium*" or first announcement of the Good News about our salvation in Christ. And intimately associated with his redemptive victory over evil is the "woman," his mother. We behold her as the "exalted Daughter of Sion" bridging the Old and New Covenants, expectation and fulfillment (cf. BYM 20).

CHAPTER III

The Perfect Disciple —
Mother of God's Son

THE composite picture of Mary revealed in the New Testament is both Christocentric ("Mother of God's Son") and ecclesiotypical ("The Perfect Disciple"). In their own simple but profound manner, the evangelists paint their Madonnas to portray one or both of these characteristics. Mark and Matthew seem to be mainly concerned with the Christocentric, that Mary of Nazareth is truly the mother of the Lord Jesus our Savior. Luke's Gospel, including his very significant reference to Mary in Acts 1:14, according to which she is at the center of the believing community awaiting Pentecost, nicely combines both emphases in his portrait of Mary, as we shall see in this chapter. And the Madonna according to John's Gospel, while affirming the fact of Mary's motherhood of Jesus, almost presupposes it and concentrates upon the ecclesiotypical or extension of that motherhood to the faithful members of her Son's Church, as the next chapter will consider.

The Second Vatican Council, whose own Marian doctrine is a rediscovery and renewal of these characteristics of the biblical and patristic Mariologies, introduces Chapter VIII of *Lumen Gentium* with a reference to one of the earliest New Testament testimonies to Mary: "Wishing in his supreme goodness and wisdom to effect the redemption of the world, 'when the fullness of time came, God sent his Son, born of a woman . . . that we might receive the adoption of sons' (Galatians 4:4)" (LG 52). Here St. Paul, without mentioning Mary by name, is primarily concerned with giving his apostolic witness to the Christocentric truth that God's own Son truly entered our history. The historical humanity of the crucified and risen Lord whom Paul preached can be real only if Jesus truly became one of us by being born of a woman, a member of the human race descended from Adam.

26

Through this woman, truly the mother of God's Son, sent into the world by him, Jesus Christ, the "New Adam," would restore our race by redeeming or liberating us from the slavery of sin and by bestowing upon us the freedom of the adopted children of the Father in the Holy Spirit.[1] The simple, direct, and forthright testimony of Paul to the role of Mary's motherhood in our redemption by her Son is typical of the sparse witness to her in the first writings of the New Testament. As would also be reflected in Mark's Gospel, it was completely Christocentric, with little or no evidence of concern with Mary's own spiritual qualifications to be a disciple of her Son.

Origin and Development of the Gospel Madonnas

Before examining the Marian portraits of the four Gospels, it is necessary to study the three stages of their formation generally.[2] The earliest stage of Gospel formation consisted of the historic deeds and sayings which were the basis of the narrative in each account of the Good News. During the second stage in the process, traditions about these events were formed based upon the interpretations of the early Christians. The first believers, both communities and individuals, especially the apostolic preachers, selected certain deeds and sayings in accord with their different spiritual needs and concerns. These communities or local churches not only handed them on as oral traditions about the Lord's teaching and experiences of his public ministry, but also reflected upon them theologically to determine how they applied to their own lives as disciples of the Lord. The third and final stage was the work of the four evangelists who were special individuals called to become a part of the process of selection in the previous stage. But their involvement, under the special charism of the inspiration of the Holy Spirit, was to result in the four written Gospels. In the Church's Tradition, under the infallible guidance of the same Holy Spirit, these came to be identified as part of the canonical New Testament writings and so handed on in the Church ever since. As believers within the Catholic Tradition, our main responsibility, in preserving and nourishing our faith, is to find our sources about Mary or any other Christian mystery in these inspired Gospels. The particular theological purpose of each one of the four evangelists has made his Gospel quite distinctive.

And it will reflect somewhat his own selection of pre-Gospel traditions during the second stage of the origin and development of the final redaction or completed form of his written Gospel. Our treatment of the Gospel Madonnas will be informed in this matter by recent New Testament scholarship. This second-stage process of selection in accord with the special audience being addressed by the evangelist, his own theological purpose, etc., is the principal reason why there are four distinct Gospel Madonnas. Let us note here that "distinct" does not imply that they are incompatible or contradictory and that they cannot form a unified composite of the New Testament portrait about Mary. The most difficult questions to answer in New Testament studies about Our Lady are those which inquire about the "Mary of history." These inquiries seek to know the historical facts of stage one, e.g., whether or not Mary was one of those who followed Jesus during his public ministry, or did she remain at home? Indeed it is impossible to answer such questions on the basis of New Testament evidence, at least in accord with the requirements of the historical-critical method. If there has been so much difficulty in the quest for the historical Jesus, about whom there is an abundance of material in the Gospels, then we must recognize that it is that much more difficult to find in them a historical Mary, about whom very little is explicitly revealed. This fact ought not to discourage us in searching the Scriptures about her, but should make us realistic in our expectations by keeping stage one separate in our inquiries. Nor should it be interpreted to mean that, if there is no historical evidence in the Gospels that Mary was an active disciple of Christ during his public ministry, then she must have shared in the unbelief or lack of faith attributed to other members of Jesus' physical family. Likewise, such a caution does not imply that there is no basis at all in the Gospels for any historical conclusions, e.g., that Mary must have been a believer and disciple in the early Christian community (cf. Luke/Acts, John). And finally, the way the Gospels have unfolded in the Catholic Tradition under the guidance of the Magisterium can teach us truths about Mary *beyond, not against*, historical criticism.

References to the Synoptics in Vatican II's Mariology
     The following excerpts from LG 56, 57, 58, and 59 provide the

context for the New Testament references to Mark and Matthew, but especially to Luke/Acts, found in Chapter VIII, the Second Vatican Council's teaching about Mary in the *Dogmatic Constitution on the Church*:

> Enriched from the first instant of her conception with the splendor of an entirely unique holiness, the virgin of Nazareth is hailed by the heralding angel, by divine command, as "full of grace" (cf. Luke 1:28), and to the heavenly messenger she replies: "Behold the handmaid of the Lord, be it done unto me according to thy word" (Luke 1:38). Thus the daughter of Adam, Mary, consenting to the word of God, became the Mother of Jesus. (LG 56)

> This union of the mother with the Son in the work of salvation is made manifest from the time of Christ's virginal conception up to his death; first when Mary, arising in haste to go to visit Elizabeth, is greeted by her as blessed because of her belief in the promise of salvation and the precursor leaped with joy in the womb of his mother (cf. Luke 1:41-45); then also at the birth of Our Lord, who did not diminish his mother's virginal integrity but sanctified it, the Mother of God joyfully showed her firstborn son to the shepherds and the Magi; when she presented him to the Lord in the temple, making the offering of the poor, she heard Simeon foretelling at the same time that her Son would be a sign of contradiction and that a sword would pierce the mother's soul, that out of many hearts thoughts might be revealed (cf. Luke 2:34-35); when the child Jesus was lost and they had sought him sorrowing, his parents found him in the temple, engaged in the things that were his Father's, and they did not understand the words of their Son. His mother, however, kept all these things to be pondered in her heart (cf. Luke 2:41-51). (LG 57).

> In the course of her Son's preaching she received the words whereby, in extolling a kingdom beyond the concerns and ties of flesh and blood, he declared blessed those who heard and kept the word of God (cf. Mark 3:35; parallel Luke 11:27-28) as she was already doing (cf. Luke 2:19;51). Thus the Blessed Virgin advanced in her pilgrimage of faith, and faithfully persevered in her union with her Son unto the cross, . . . (LG 58).

> But since it had pleased God not to manifest solemnly the mystery of the salvation of the human race before he would pour fourth the Spirit promised by Christ, we see the Apostles before the day of Pentecost "persevering with one mind in prayer with

the women and Mary the Mother of Jesus, and with his brethren" (Acts 1:14), and we also see Mary by her prayers imploring
the gift of the Spirit, who had already overshadowed her in the
Annunciation. (LG 59)

It should prove helpful to have seen how Vatican II wove together and
commented upon these texts before we examine each of them.

Mary in Mark and Matthew

Mark's Gospel, it is generally accepted among New Testament
scholars, is the first of the four Gospels, and a common source for Matthew and Luke, the other two Synoptists. Because of the great similar-
ity of the first three Gospels, they can be placed in parallel columns for
the sake of comparison, and this arrangement is called a synopsis,
whence come the terms Synoptic Gospels and Synoptists.[3] At the same
time there are significant differences between them, as will be clearly
evident in their Marian material, which gives rise to the Synoptic problem. It is well beyond the scope of our study to analyze the various
solutions that have been proposed. Sufficient for our purposes is to
adapt what is considered the simplest and most widely accepted theory
that attempts to solve the problem. The similarities basically are accounted for by holding that both Matthew and Luke, while not knowing each other, used Mark as a common source along with another
document called Q (from the German word *Quelle* meaning "source').
Mark's Gospel, the same as we have it now, cannot explain all the similarities, since there are many others found in Matthew and Luke which
are not in Mark. And so Q has been postulated to account for these.
The differences arise from the diverse theological purposes, the distinct
audiences, etc., of each Synoptist. And so, when Matthew and Luke
were working through stage three of composing their Gospels, both
Mark's completed Gospel and Q constituted the stage two or common
sources of their pre-Gospel material. Of course, the different sources
used by Matthew and Luke for their Gospels, such as the various oral
traditions, further account for the differences between them.

Mark's Gospel was written apparently for Christians of pagan origin outside of Palestine. He shows little concern about explaining the
connection between the Christian Gospel and the Old Testament, but
does take the time to help his audience understand Jewish customs and

whatever might be necessary for non-Jewish Christians to grasp the real meaning of the Good News for them. Of course, all four Gospels are "confessional documents," as distinct from apologetical works; i.e., they were written by men of faith for people who were already believers, and not precisely to win converts to Christianity. Mark's special theological purpose is to proclaim the authentic meaning of Jesus' messiahship and to provide instruction on true discipleship in light of that proclamation. It is important to bear this in mind as we consider the significant reference to Mary in Mark's Gospel.

The single reference to the first of the evangelists that we saw in Vatican II's Mariology quoted above is Mark 3:35: "Whoever does the will of God is my brother, and sister, and mother." The wider Marcan context for this saying of Jesus begins with verse 20 of the passage. The immediate setting, however, starts with the thirty-first verse: "And his mother and his brethren came; and standing outside they sent to him and called him." This sets up the situation which Mark uses to draw a definite division between those "standing outside," namely, the physical family of his blood relatives, and those "sitting about him," his true family of believing disciples. The theological concern of the evangelist is to teach that not kinship but the faith of discipleship counts in the kingdom of God. The Mariological question is whether or not Mark intended to include Mary herself among his relatives who were hostile toward him and thought that he was out of his mind: ". . . they went out to seize him, for they said, 'He is beside himself'" (3:21). The members of his physical family, according to Mark's redactional theology or the way in which he interpreted and shaped the pre-Gospel material in keeping with his theological purpose, certainly misunderstood the messianic mission of Jesus. He seems to portray Jesus as replacing his natural family, "standing outside" waiting "to seize him" because "He is beside himself," with the "eschatological" family of disciples "sitting about him" inside, his real "brother, and sister, and mother" who are open to the word of God.

The difficulty about Mary's possible inclusion among those of Jesus' relatives who opposed him at this stage of his public ministry cannot be bypassed. Neither does it seem to be soluble on the basis of the historical-critical method alone. Nor is one forced to conclude that historically Mary must have misunderstood her Son and only became a member of the family of disciples sometime after the episode to which Mark refers in this passage. The parallel passages in the other two Synoptists do not present the same problem. Neither Matthew's Gospel (12:24-50) nor Luke's (8:19-21) take from Mark his harsh introduction about the relatives (3:20-21). Both, however, do follow his essential teaching that the "real" family of Jesus is to be found among his believing disciples, who hear the word of God and do the will of the Father. Matthew's account, which like Luke's omits any reference to the relatives' wishing to seize him because they think he's beside himself, seems neutral concerning the physical family and just uses them as the occasion for the saying of Jesus about the eschatological family. So there is not the same Mariological problem as there is with Mark. Luke's interpretation of the incident, on the other hand, is quite positive toward the physical family: "Then his mother and his brethren came to him, but they could not reach him for the crowd. And he was told, 'Your mother and your brethren are standing outside, desiring to see you.' But he said to them, 'My mother and my brethren are those who hear the word of God and do it' " (8:19-21). Luke removes any sense of hostility about his relatives being outside, explaining that it was the crowd which prevented their going inside. Unlike Mark and Matthew, in Luke Jesus does not ask the challenging question about their status as his true family once he has been informed that they are waiting to see him. Neither is there indicated in his Gospel that Jesus points to his family of disciples on the inside as a contrast to his relatives outside. Luke, therefore, is much clearer than Mark or Matthew that the mother and brethren of the Lord, his natural family, meet the requirements of belonging to his "eschatological" family. Concerning Mary, as we shall see, this is consistent with the Lucan portrait of her from the beginning of his Gospel.

It is interesting to note that Vatican II's reference to Mark 3:35 merely states that Mary heard this saying of her Son and seems to favor Luke's interpretation of the incident by teaching that she was already hearing and keeping the word of God. This is indeed the understanding that has prevailed in the Catholic Tradition. And certainly it is safe to assert that Luke is much clearer about Mary's inclusion among the members of the "eschatological" family during her Son's public ministry than Mark and Matthew are concerning her exclusion from them.

Let us now turn to the first two chapters of Matthew's Gospel, the infancy narrative. As an evangelist writing later than Mark, probably after A.D. 70, he was gathering together his material during a time in the early Church when Christians were growing more interested in the events of Christ's life before his passion, death, and resurrection. This eventually led back to the circumstances surrounding his origins, who were his parents, etc., and so the infancy narratives of Matthew and Luke became integral parts of their Gospels. Mary then would have a more prominent place in them, a place, however, that would always be Christocentric or a means of throwing greater light upon the mystery of her Son. Matthew's theological purpose reflected his community, which was composed of a base of Jewish Christians with an increasing number of Gentile converts. He wishes to reach both groups by showing, through the use of many Old Testament references, that Christ and Christianity are the fulfillment of true Judaism, and that God had planned from the beginning to include Gentiles in the messianic mission of salvation. Matthew's infancy narrative is consistent with the theological purpose of his Gospel as a whole; e.g., Joseph and the Magi representing the best in the Jewish and Gentile worlds, while the Jewish king, the scribes, chief priests and all Jerusalem stand for corrupt elements in Judaism that were menacing Matthew's community.

Mary is the last to be mentioned in the long line of the "book of the genealogy of Jesus Christ, the son of David, the son of Abraham" (Matthew 1:1). Among Christ's ancestors, Abraham is named first. The evangelist of the second Gospel states: "So all the generations from Abraham to David were fourteen generations, and from David to the deportation to Babylon fourteen generations, and from the deportation to Babylon to the Christ fourteen generations" (1:17). The problem of the historical accuracy of this statement need not concern us here, only the theological significance of the genealogy, particularly in relation to Mary, of whom he says: ". . . and Jacob the father of Joseph the husband of Mary, of whom Jesus was born, who is called the Christ" (1:16). Worthy of special note is his departure from the usual pattern throughout the genealogy by not saying that Joseph is the father of Jesus, and his unusual inclusion of four Old Testament women, namely, Tamar, Rahab, Ruth, and Uriah's wife. The first point is explained by his immediate revelation regarding the virginal conception (cf. 1:18-25), and the second requires further examination.

Of the theories advanced to explain the inclusion of these women with Mary in the genealogy, the most satisfying seems to be that all five of them were instruments of God's messianic plans, even though there was something out of the ordinary about their marital unions.[4] Only Bathsheba's union with David was sinful, since she was the wife of Uriah. Tamar was the vehicle of God's grace in getting Judah to propagate the messianic line. Israel entered the promised land through Rahab's bravery. Ruth took the initiative in becoming, with her husband Boaz, the great-grandparents of King David. Finally, the prophecy of Nathan about the Messiah descending from the house and family of David came to be fulfilled only because of Bathsheba's intervention that Solomon succeed David as king. Matthew's theological message seems to be that God chose to work out his messianic plans at significant moments during the history of Christ's forebears through marital unions that were extraordinary, including that between Mary and Joseph in the pneumatological conception (i.e., the virginal conception of Jesus through the power of the Holy Spirit).

It is important for our purposes to have before us the entire passage of Matthew 1:18-25 if we are to be able to discuss its Mariological meaning as well as its significance for her husband, St. Joseph, who will also be considered at some length later on in this book.

> Now the birth of Jesus Christ took place in this way. When his mother Mary had been betrothed to Joseph, before they came together she was found to be with child of the Holy Spirit; and her husband Joseph, being a just man and unwilling to put her to shame, resolved to send her away quietly. But as he considered this, behold, an angel of the Lord appeared to him in a dream, saying, "Joseph, son of David, do not fear to take Mary your wife, for that which is conceived in her is of the Holy Spirit; she will bear a son, and you shall call his name Jesus, for he will save his people from their sins." All this took place to fulfill what the Lord had spoken by the prophet: / "Behold, a virgin shall conceive and bear a son, / and his name shall be called Emmanuel" / (which means, God with us). When Joseph woke from sleep,

he did as the angel of the Lord commanded him; he took his
wife, but knew her not until she had borne a son; and he called
his name Jesus.

In this passage, Joseph comes to center-stage in the portrayal of the origins of Jesus according to Matthew's infancy narrative. He had been
included in the genealogy, not as the real but as the legal father of Jesus through whom the Child belongs to the house and family of David
in fulfillment of God's promise through the prophet Nathan.

According to Jewish marriage customs there was a formal ex-
change of consent before witnesses, called a "betrothal," usually about
one year before the wife went to live with her husband, who had legal
rights in her regard. And so any infidelity on her part was punishable
as adultery. This could mean the death penalty by stoning. During this
period of betrothal, when Joseph saw that Mary was pregnant, he was
perplexed, as one might readily understand. Even though Matthew is
careful to inform the reader or his audience that Mary is "with child of
the Holy Spirit" to avoid any scandalous suspicions, to Joseph, who did
not know this at the time, it could have been interpreted as adulterous
behavior. In terms of stage one of the Gospel's formation, it cannot be
said with historical certitude just what Joseph thought about the way
his betrothed Mary came to be pregnant. The text does seem to indicate that, as a pious and observant Jew, he had to respect the law on
one hand; on the other, he did not want to expose her indiscriminately
to the rigorous penalty imposed by the law. Possibly this resulted from
the fact that, although he did not know about the virginal conception
of the Holy Spirit, he did know his betrothed Mary well enough to be
confident that she was not deliberately unfaithful to her solemn marital
promise. And so the best solution for this "just man" seemed to be "to
send her away quietly" without insisting upon his legal rights or that
she be punished under the law. Apparently his justice was rewarded by
the message of the angel, revealing to him the virginal conception "of
the Holy Spirit."

Matthew, as we have already seen in the previous chapter of this
book, saw in this pneumatological conception of Jesus in the womb of
the virgin Mary a fulfillment of Isaiah 7:14, the Emmanuel prophecy.
Although more recent biblical scholars do not hold this to have been

the literal sense intended by the prophet Isaiah, the fact remains that Matthew so used it under inspiration. An explanation of how a New Testament author might appropriate an Old Testament text this way need not distract us here. We have already discussed that the Old Testament generally came to be interpreted by the early Christians as fulfilled in Christ and his Church. It will be considered further in another context when discussing the development of Marian dogmas in the Tradition.

By his phrase "of the Holy Spirit," revealing the way that Mary came to conceive Christ, Matthew carefully avoids any pagan connotations about the mystery of the pneumatological virginal conception. It is accomplished entirely by divine power, which transcends sexuality and miraculously achieves human conception apart from the ordinary means of the marital act. And so there is no pagan mythology connected with it, as though male semen were somehow infused into Mary's womb from above. The theological importance of noting this is to preclude any opinion or hypothesis that the evangelist borrowed the idea from paganism instead of being inspired to record the truth in his Gospel from divine revelation.

When Matthew says that Joseph ". . . took his wife, but knew her not until she had borne a son, and he called his name Jesus" (1:24-25), he is not concerned with the question of Mary's perpetual virginity. That becomes an issue only much later in the Tradition. What he wishes to communicate to his audience is that Mary was a virgin in conceiving Christ and remained a virgin even till he was born, since Isaiah 7:14, according to the evangelist's interpretation, prophesies that a "virgin" will both conceive and *bear* a son. Neither does the statement that Joseph had no marital relations with Mary "until" the birth of Christ imply that he did so afterward, since that implication, which is easily taken in the English language, is not found in the Greek particle that means "until."

In telling about the Magi, or "wise men from the East," Matthew narrates their seeing the Child's star in the East, and their apparently following it to Jerusalem, where they sought King Herod's help in finding the place of his birth. After this: "When they had heard the king they went their way; and lo, the star which they had seen in the East went before them, till it came to rest over the place where the child was. When they saw the star, they rejoiced exceedingly with great joy; and going into the house they saw the child with Mary his mother, and they fell down and worshiped him" (Matthew 2:9-11). Vatican II singles out this teaching: ". . . the mother of God joyfully showed her firstborn son to the shepherds and the Magi" (LG 57).

The story of the Magi seems to be most reasonably understood today as the rewriting of an Old Testament theme or story suited to bring out the theological message of the evangelist.[5] Matthew's story of the Magi appears to be a Christian retelling of the Old Testament story about Balaam, a "wise man" from the East who saw the star rise out of Jacob (cf. Numbers 22-24). To call this "midrash" is not quite accurate, because the purpose of midrash is to make the Old Testament account understandable, which is not what Matthew and Luke precisely had in mind when they used this method in their infancy narratives. They wished to make Jesus' origins intelligible by showing how Old Testament expectations were fulfilled in his coming into the world. In the case of Matthew's telling the story of the Magi, he wished to get across the message, especially to his own Christian community, that already in the Old Covenant God revealed his will to save the Gentiles, which has come to fulfillment in Christ even beginning with his birth. His mother, Mary, plays a role in bringing about the new presence of a saving God, and she was prophesied by Isaiah as the virgin who would bear Emmanuel. Unlike Luke's infancy narrative, however, Matthew's is not concerned with Mary's personal attitudes of loving faith and obedience, or that she is the "perfect disciple" of Christ from the beginning at his conception, but with the fact that she is truly the mother of God's Son. Joseph is the one in Matthew's infancy narrative who stands for the virtues of an authentic Judaism, which should inspire the Jewish Christians in the community of the evangelist in the early Church not to be corrupted by a spurious Judaism, represented by Herod, the chief priests, etc., through any negative attitudes toward the Gentile converts.

The Madonna of Luke/Acts

From the first moment of her entrance into salvation history, ac-

cording to the account of the third evangelist's Gospel, to his final reference to her in the Acts of the Apostles, Mary is portrayed by Luke as
the "perfect disciple" who hears the word of God most prayerfully and
keeps it most carefully. He is no less concerned with the fact of her
motherhood of God's own Son, but he combines this Christocentric
emphasis ever so harmoniously with what we have been calling the ecclesiotypical, which sees Mary as the prototype of all discipleship in her
Son's Church.

Luke was inspired to write primarily for Gentile converts to Christianity. "Theologically, Luke/Acts reflects a definite plan or program,
best described as a salvation-history approach."[6] Conscious of world
history, he wishes to communicate the conviction that the salvation of
all is centered upon Christ, seen in relationship to God's merciful love
for his people in the past and to what he continues to accomplish
through his Spirit in the Church. And Luke awards Mary a very special
place in God's loving plan of universal salvation. Other theological
themes that are characteristic of Luke/Acts are the special role of
women, the joy of those who hear the word of God and do it, the de-
mands of discipleship, the blessedness of the poor, the spirit of prayer
and Temple piety, and the Gospel of the Holy Spirit. And each one of
these themes adds color to his Madonna, a portrait of Mary that is both
inspired and inspiring to those who will contemplate her in faith.

Luke's infancy narrative is a good illustration of the profound continuity between the two books, the Gospel and Acts. The first two
chapters of each parallel the birth of Christ and the birth of the
Church. What the Holy Spirit accomplished definitively in Christ is
continued through his active presence in the Church for the salvation of
the world. In keeping with his own theological purpose and with the
nature of his audience, the third evangelist gives an account of the origins of Jesus quite different in its literary structure from that of Matthew. It may be divided into two parts: that covering the period prior
to the births of John the Baptizer and Jesus (Luke 1:5-56); and that
recounting the births of both and their early growth (Luke
1:57-2:52). There is a certain parallelism in the account between John
and Jesus, but always showing the superior significance on the side of
Jesus and Mary in the divine plan of universal salvation. Luke seems to

narrate the origins of Jesus upon earth to a considerable extent through the literary device of imaginatively retelling Old Testament stories and themes. We've already mentioned this in the case of the Magi in Matthew's infancy narrative. It is important to note that such a literary form is completely compatible with the basic historicity of facts that are essential to our faith in the Catholic Tradition. In fact, one should expect that an author who is narrating salvation history would have to employ images and symbols in order to convey the mysterious divine intention behind events. Any special difficulties that may arise in this matter will be dealt with as they come up in our consideration of the texts.

Annunciation, the First Joyful Mystery

Luke's Gospel portrayal of the Annunciation scene (1:26-38) has inspired more Marian meditation and literature than any other passage of the New Testament. Our American bishops' pastoral letter on Mary states: "The chapter on Mary in the Dogmatic Constitution on the Church may be regarded as an extended commentary on her consent at the Annunciation" (BYM 28). And the precise reference to the first joyful mystery in Vatican II's Marian teaching is: ". . . the virgin of Nazareth is hailed by the heralding angel, by divine command, as 'full of grace' (cf. Luke 1:28), and to the heavenly messenger she replies: 'Behold the handmaid of the Lord, be it done unto me according to thy word' (Luke 1:38). Thus the daughter of Adam, Mary, consenting to the word of God, became the Mother of Jesus" (LG 56). Before making our Marian meditation on the mystery, it would be helpful to have the whole text handy:

> In the sixth month the angel Gabriel was sent from God to a city of Galilee named Nazareth, to a virgin betrothed to a man whose name was Joseph, of the house of David; and the virgin's name was Mary. And he came to her and said, "Hail, full of grace, the Lord is with you!" But she was greatly troubled at the saying, and considered in her mind what sort of greeting this might be. And the angel said to her, "Do not be afraid, Mary, for you have found favor with God. And behold, you will conceive in your womb and bear a son, and you shall call his name Jesus. He will be great, and will be called the Son of the Most

High; and the Lord God will give to him the throne of his father
David, and he will reign over the house of Jacob for ever; and of
his kingdom there will be no end." And Mary said to the angel,
"How can this be, since I have no husband?" And the angel said
to her: "The Holy Spirit will come upon you, and the power of
the Most High will overshadow you; therefore the child to be
born will be called holy, the Son of God. And behold your
kinswoman Elizabeth in her old age has also conceived a son;
and this is the sixth month with her who was called barren. For
with God nothing will be impossible." And Mary said, "Behold,
I am the handmaid of the Lord; let it be to me according to your
word." And the angel departed from her. (Luke 1:26-38)

The literary structure of this dialogue between Gabriel and Mary
is based upon Annunciation patterns of the Old Testament. Indeed it is
a format comparable to that used by Luke himself in the angelic annunciation to Zechariah (Luke 1:11-20), as well as by Matthew in the
message of the angel of the Lord to Joseph in a dream (Matthew
1:20ff). Old Testament parallels are the heavenly messages delivered
to Hagar (Genesis 16:7-15), to the wife of Manaoh (Judges 13:3-20),
and to Gideon (Judges 6:11-24). The basic pattern is: 1) the appearance of an angel of the Lord or the Lord himself, since God always
takes the initiative in the dialogue; 2) a reaction of fear, which is some-
times met with "Do not be afraid"; 3) an announcement about the
birth of a son; 4) an objection or a difficulty raised by the recipient of
the announcement; and, 5) the giving of a sign to reassure the recipient, who accepts the message with sufficient understanding before the
episode ends. It was the regular way in which biblical authors prepared
the reader for one who was to play a prominent role in salvation history
which was already known to the author.

Gabriel's greeting to Mary, "Hail, full of grace. . ." may also be
rendered "Joy be to thee, highly favored one. . ." (Luke 1:28). This
translation brings out more clearly the great joy that would come to the
"Daughter of Sion" (cf. previous chapter) and also the fact that the
holiness of Mary is the fruit of God's special love freely bestowed upon
her. The angel invites her as the "exalted Daughter of Sion" to rejoice
with a messianic joy. Thanks to God's favor, she is filled with longing
for the Promised One, the Messiah. In the angelic salutation to Mary
we hear clearly echoed the prophecy of old: "Sing aloud, O daughter

of Zion; shout, O Israel! / Rejoice and exult with all ·your heart, / O daughter of Jerusalem! . . . The King of Israel, the LORD is in your midst. . . . / Do not fear O Zion. . . . / The LORD your God is in your midst . . ." (Zephaniah 3:14-17). This prophecy is being fulfilled in her who is the "exalted Daughter of Sion" in person, representing all the aspirations of ancient Israel for true liberation by the Lord, and embodying in her self the best in the spirit of the *Anawim* (cf. previous chapter) of the Old Covenant. Indeed ". . . the Lord is with you," O Mary! You alone, favorite daughter of the Father, and you alone among us redeemed members of the Church, are all-holy, fully free from any sin. In you we find fulfilled the holiness to which we are all called.

But how could Mary possibly be "greatly troubled" over such a greeting of joy and hope? "The best explanation is the obvious one: Mary is "troubled," perplexed, because she does not yet understand for what purpose and to what extent she has been favored by God."' At once the angel of the Lord reassures her and announces to her God's calling, her unique vocation in salvation history to be the mother of "the Son of the Most High." Luke's account of this first joyful mystery is careful to place on the lips of the heavenly messenger those titles for her Son which show that he will live up to all Jewish expectations of the Messiah as "the Son of the Most High" (cf. Isaiah 9:6; Daniel 7:14). In him also will come to pass the prophecy of Nathan (cf. previous chapter) that ". . . the Lord God will give to him the throne of his father David, and he will reign over the house of Jacob for ever; and of his kingdom there will be no end" (Luke 1:32-33). Thus through Mary, the "Daughter of David," God makes his own Son and hers the "Son of David," keeping his promise to the great king of old.

Now we come to that point in the annunciation pattern where the hearer of the heavenly message brings up a difficulty: "And Mary said to the angel, 'How can this be, since I have no husband?' " (Luke 1:34). In the dialogue between Gabriel and Mary, the apparent objection that Luke's literary form has her bring up is in no way to be interpreted as a negative reaction on her part. It is a valid difficulty of one whose faith and obedience is intelligent and not blind, which is unworthy of a true human response to God's word. From what the angel has told her thus far, Mary understandably infers that the conception in her womb is to take place immediately. Replying that she has no husband would then really mean that her betrothed, Joseph, has not yet taken her into his home. And so her question is necessary if she is to give her consent with meaning to whatever God's will may have in mind for her. Her question sets the stage for Gabriel's revelation of the virginal conception: "The Holy Spirit will come upon you, and the power of the Most High will overshadow you; therefore the child to be born will be called holy, the Son of God" (Luke 1:35).

The language in which Luke has the angel of the Lord reveal how the child is to be conceived and who he will be has come to be called a "conception" Christology in the New Testament (cf. Chapter VII for further details). It is an expression of the faith of the Church after the resurrection that Jesus Christ was truly divine as well as human from the first instant of his conception in Mary's virginal womb. We should take note that, as much as Luke is concerned with Mary's motherhood and personal qualities, she is always subordinated to Christ, the evangelist's primary interest in his telling of the Good News.

It is also important to note, in terms of what we Catholics are committed to believe about Mary's virginity, that he is not implying through her question to the angel of the Lord that her difficulty was based upon her already having absolutely vowed virginity. According to the interpretation of St. Thomas Aquinas, as we shall consider (cf. Chapter X), Mary at this point may well have been inclined toward a virginal union with Joseph, but she was still completely open to God's will in the matter. Her absolute vow of virginity did not come about until that will was manifested, through the revelation of the virginal conception and the complete devotion to her Son, for the sake of the kingdom of God that he came to establish. There is just no foundation either in the sacred Scriptures or any well-founded tradition for holding that Mary had vowed her virginity at a tender age prior to her spiritual experience at the Annunciation. It is certainly not a required belief of our divine Catholic faith, and to hold it as a pious belief causes undue difficulties because it is so contrary to the customs of the times.

The Annunciation drama draws toward a conclusion with the sign given by the angel of the Lord to Mary. Appropriately enough for the occasion of announcing a birth, that sign is the pregnancy of Mary's older relative Elizabeth, who was considered sterile. She is now with child, "For with God nothing will be impossible" (Luke 1:37). This announcement of another marvelous conception and birth to come is characteristic of the extraordinary origins recorded in the Bible of those called to have special roles as instruments of God in salvation history. It is all really God's work, and the sign must show that he alone can accomplish it from the very beginning. The concluding comment from Gabriel, that God can do all things, is another indication that his creative religious imagination is at work on Old Testament material. "When Abraham was told that Isaac was to be born, God strengthened him with the reminder that all things are possible to God (Genesis 18:14)" (BYM 32). Mary, the "Daughter of Abraham" (cf. previous chapter), our father in faith, is about to become our mother in faith.

Mary's response to the heavenly messenger is really a reply to God's calling: "Behold, I am the handmaid of the Lord; let it be to me according to your word" (Luke 1:38). Her *"Fiat"* or "Yes" to God's will is wholehearted. Never has another followed his/her vocation more faithfully and generously. This is precisely how St. Luke wished to present his Madonna to us. She is the first to hear the Good News, and the foremost disiciple in believing it and carrying out her ministry of sharing her Son with all who believe it too.

Visitation, the Second Joyful Mystery

Mary did not keep the Good News to herself. Under the inspiration of the same Holy Spirit who "came upon" her at the virginal conception, she was off to the "hill country" immediately to share with Elizabeth and the child within her womb the liberating and joyful presence of God within her own. About this charming and inspiring scene of the encounter between these two holy women, the Lucan narrative tells us:

> In those days Mary arose and went with haste into the hill country, to a city of Judah, and she entered the house of Zechariah and greeted Elizabeth. And when Elizabeth heard the greeting of Mary, the babe leaped in her womb; and Elizabeth was filled with the Holy Spirit and she exclaimed with a loud cry, "Blessed are you among women, and blessed is the fruit of your

womb! And why is this granted me, that the mother of my Lord
should come to me? For behold, when the voice of your greeting
came to my ears, the babe in my womb leaped for joy. And
blessed is she who believed that there would be a fulfillment of
what was spoken to her from the Lord" (Luke 1:39:45).

After teaching that the "union of the mother with the Son in the work
of salvation is made manifest from the time of Christ's virginal conception up to his death," Vatican II continues: ". . . . first when Mary,
arising in haste to go to visit Elizabeth, is greeted by her as blessed because of her belief in the promise of salvation and the precursor leaped
with joy in the womb of his mother (cf. Luke 1:41-45)" (LG 57).

Receiving the sign of Elizabeth's wondrous conception as one God
freely chose to give her, and not one that she had asked for, Mary
"went with haste into the hill country. . ." (Luke 1:39). According to
a tradition dating back to the sixth century, "the city of Judah" where
the "house of Zechariah" was situated is the village of Ain Karim, five
miles west of Jerusalem.[8] It would have taken Mary four days to make
the journey from Nazareth. The spiritual significance of Luke's mentioning that she did so "with haste" seems to be calling our attention to
the love and friendship that inspired her visit. And each woman had
such Good News to share with the other!

Before Elizabeth acknowledges Mary's greeting, Luke informs us
that "she was filled with the Holy Spirit" (Luke 1:41). The action of
the Spirit is one of the main theological themes in Luke/Acts. The
Spirit is the central figure both in the birth of our Savior in his Gospel
and in the birth of his Church, with her mission of universal salvation,
in Acts. Another theological theme — i.e., the joy given to those who
hear the word of God and keep it — also comes up again in this context. On Elizabeth's own testimony, the child in her womb "leaped for
joy" when she heard Mary's greeting (cf. Luke 1:44). The true
messianic joy that was shared by the faith of these two holy women,
that they were in the special presence of the saving God, is the fruit of
the Holy Spirit. And that Spirit works his wonders of grace through the
simplest and most ordinary occurrences in life, such as the movement of
an unborn child in the womb of a woman six months pregnant.

Inspired by the same prophetic Spirit, Elizabeth declares that Mary is "blessed among women," a Hebrew way of saying that she is the most blessed of all women. The mother of John the Baptizer, the forerunner of Mary's Son, is inspired to make this joyful exclamation because her younger kinswoman is the mother of her Lord and because Mary believed the promise of the Lord. And she manifests her own humble sense of unworthiness to be graced with such a visitation.

In this scene, Luke places on the lips of Elizabeth the words that join with the angelic salutation of Gabriel at the Annunciation to form the first half of the "Hail Mary," the Marian prayer so precious in our Catholic Tradition. It would not be until some centuries later, during the Middle Ages, that the second half ("Holy Mary, Mother of God. . .") would be added to complete the prayer that we say so often — e.g., in reciting the Rosary. We should realize that the first half is the inspired word of God, and be familiar with the setting of its origins in Luke's accounts of the first two joyful mysteries.

"And blessed is she who believed that there would be a fulfillment of what was spoken to her from the Lord" (Luke 1:45). How appropriate that the first "macarism" or beatitude (blessedness or true Christian joy) in the Gospel be attributed to Mary! She was the first to show by her loving faith and obedience the response of the Christian disciple (cf. Luke 1:38). It is also significant to point out here how nicely Luke combines Mary's motherhood of God's Son with her calling to be the perfect disciple. He has Elizabeth praise her for both. We shall want to recall this fact later when discussing the theological controversies that have arisen regarding what is Mary's greatest privilege, her divine maternity or her holiness (faith) or, more abstractly, which is the primary principle of Mariology. Such matters did not concern Luke!

Over the ages, private devotion to Mary in the Litany of Loretto has invoked her by the title "Ark of the Covenant." I call it to your attention in this context, since Luke's narrative of the Annunciation and Visitation would certainly suggest its profound appropriateness. However, because it is not clear that Luke intended to present his Madonna as a true ark of the new covenant. I do not propose it as a part of our meditative commentary on the sacred Scripture. Still it is worth pointing out how this parallelism between the Old Testament theme of the Ark of the Covenant and Mary would have been inspired in our Catholic Tradition by Luke's Gospel. First, in the Annunciation scene, he has Gabriel reveal the virginal conception through the image of the "overshadowing" of the Spirit which makes her the "living tabernacle of the divine presence" (BYM 27). One finds a parallel in Exodus (40:16-21; 34-35), where the ark of the old covenant is "overshadowed" by a cloud, ". . . and the glory of the Lord filled the Dwelling" (cf. BYM 26). Then, in the Visitation scene, the child in Elizabeth's womb leaped with joy; she protests her own unworthiness that the "Ark of the New Covenant" enter her house, and Mary remained there "about three months" (Luke 1:56). There seems to be a parallel of these three points with those found in II Samuel 6: David dances before the ark with joy; he professes his own sense of unworthiness, "How can the ark of the Lord come to me?"; and, the ark remained in the house of Obededom the Gittite for three months (cf. BYM 27).

The Magnificat, Mary's Song of True Liberation

Although Scripture scholars cannot say with certainty what influenced Luke's composition of Elizabeth's words to Mary (Luke 1: 42-45), the opinion that it may have been based upon a hymn that the early Christians sang in praise of Mary is not improbable.[9] If this is the case, then the words have the added significance of reflecting a Marian devotion during apostolic times. Now we turn to the way in which Luke has his Madonna respond to the praise of her older cousin, singing out clearly that all the glory is due to God. Let us listen to this canticle sung daily over the centuries in the Tradition during Evening Prayer of the Church's Liturgy of the Hours:

> And Mary said, "My soul magnifies the Lord,
> and my spirit rejoices in God my Savior,
> for he has regarded the low estate of his handmaiden.
> For behold, henceforth all generations will call me blessed;
> for he who is mighty has done great things for me,
> and holy is his name.
> And his mercy is on those who fear him
> from generation to generation.
> He has shown strength with his arm,
> he has scattered the proud in the imagination of their hearts

> he has put down the mighty from their thrones,
> and exalted those of low degree;
> he has filled the hungry with good things,
> and the rich he has sent empty away.
> He has helped his servant Israel,
> in remembrance of his mercy,
> as he spoke to our fathers,
> to Abraham and his posterity forever." (Luke 1:46-55)

Whatever might be the precise origins of the *Magnificat*, Luke has Mary sing forth its poetic phrases of joyful praise and thanksgiving because it so suits his portrait of her and the purposes of his Gospel and Acts. It is likely a Lucan adaptation of Old Testament texts that fitted the occasion, or even of Jewish Christian hymns sung in the early Church. The following comments are made mainly to emphasize why the *Magnificat* was so appropriate for Mary to sing.

Mary begins her song of true liberation by joyfully praising and thanking God for blessing her, and through her, all of Israel (vv. 46-50). Luke's Gospel theme of joy continues as a constant refrain, and here it seems to echo words of the Old Covenant: "I will rejoice in the LORD, / I will joy in the God of my salvation" (Habakkuk 3:18). She immediately refers all the glory to God, who alone has blessed her for the sake of all Israel. And the unending praise to be given her is because she has completely accepted his holy will. Here Luke appears to be adapting a verse from one of the psalms: "the steadfast love of the LORD is from everlasting to everlasting / upon those who fear him" (Psalm 103 [102]:17). And as God's highly favored one, chosen by him to be mother of the Messiah, she is the most perfect of the *Anawim*, "poor of Yahweh," who place all their hopes in him. He has truly "regarded the low estate of his handmaiden."

The emphasis now switches from what God has accomplished for Mary, the individual person, to his mighty deeds on behalf of all his people through her, the "Daughter of Sion" (vv. 51-55). Her song of liberation bursts forth into one of victory for the *Anawim*, the lowly and hungry who are exalted and filled, while the proud, mighty, and rich are scattered, put down, and sent empty away. Another favorite theme of Luke/Acts emerges, that of God's favoring the outcasts, the downtrodden, the rejected, or the marginated and the exploited, as they are called today. This dramatic reversal is not the result of a social revolution, but of the true liberation of a saving God. Mary proclaims this Good News that would be heard throughout Luke's Gospel — e.g., the parable of Lazarus and the rich man (16:19-31), and the Beatitudes in his Sermon on the Mount (6:20-26). Mary reflects that what would be accomplished by her Son has always been the way in which the saving God of Israel has fulfilled his promises to his people. And this goes back even to the very dawn of salvation history, when Yahweh promised her father Abraham that in him all the nations of the world would count themselves blessed (cf. Genesis 12:3; 22:18). That promise is being kept in Mary's Son. And by portraying her, the "Daughter of Abraham," as the most highly favored among the *Anawim*, Luke gives to Mary a role in salvation history which represents the greatest fulfillment of God's promises.

Mary's *Magnificat* places her on the boundary of the Old and the New Covenants. Summing up and surpassing the best of the Old, and anticipating the greatest of the New, she represents the spirit of the *Anawim* that would carry over into Christian discipleship, especially according to Luke/Acts. That spirit contrasts their complete reliance upon the saving power of God, not so much to the wealthy as such, as to the pride of self-sufficiency of those who only trust in their own power and have no need of God. This theme arises again and again throughout Luke's Gospel and Acts, and will be pointed out in our comments each time that it does. One final comment in conjunction with the Visitation concerns Luke 1:57, which speaks about Mary's remaining with Elizabeth about three months and then returning to her home. Because the evangelist mentions this before narrating the birth of the Baptizer, we should not infer it to mean that Mary left before the event. He just wishes to round off one episode before starting another. We may take for granted that Mary remained as long as there was need for her, which was most likely through the birth. Also the fact that she returned to "her home" indicates that she and Joseph had not yet come to live together.

The Third Joyful Mystery, the Birth of Christ

The beginning of the second chapter of Luke's infancy narrative takes us, at least momentarily, from the Jewish world to that of the Gentiles: "In those days a decree went out from Caesar Augustus that all the world should be enrolled" (Luke 2:1). This reference to world history is an expression of Luke's plan to tell his version of the Good News by continually reminding his audience that Christ came to save the whole world. And this divine design was present and operative from his very birth. "And Joseph also went up from Galilee, from the city of Nazareth, to Judea, to the city of David, which is called Bethlehem, because he was of the house and lineage of David, to be enrolled with Mary his betrothed, who was with child" (Luke 2:4-5). In obeying the decree, Joseph had to travel from his own home in Nazareth to the birthplace of his ancestor in Bethlehem. Luke still refers to Mary as his "betrothed," although there is every indication that Joseph had completed their marriage agreement by taking her into his home. Perhaps the evangelist preserves the term "betrothed" as a delicate way of reminding us about the virginal conception, and that Joseph is not really the natural father of the child about to be born. And the Lucan details, about Joseph's being "of the house and lineage of David" and Bethlehem's being the birthplace of David, are much more than mere data of historical and geographical interest. They indicate that the prophecies that the Christ would come from the line of David and be born in Bethlehem are being fulfilled (cf. Micah 5:2-5).

"And while they were there, the time came for her to be delivered. And she gave birth to her first-born son and wrapped him in swaddling cloths, and laid him in a manger, because there was no place for them in the inn" (Luke 2:6-7). We behold in this scene, as Luke intended, the fact that Mary's Son, the foster-child of Joseph, is born amidst lowliness and poverty. How fitting that is, especially in the setting of Luke's Gospel! Christ, who would bring special liberation to the poor and oppressed, is born into a family of the *Anawim*, and would be himself the Poor Man of Yahweh without parallel. How nicely all this fits into Mary's *Magnificat*! The fact that Christ is called "her first-born son" has no connotation that he was the first of many sons born to Mary, since it is a technical expression of Jewish law prescribing the consecration of the firstborn male to God, even in the case of an only son. The place where Jesus was born, on the testimonly of an early patristic tradition, was a cave. Possibly it was one used for a stable, as the traditional Christmas crib scene portrays. It seems that the couple chose such a place, instead of a crowded inn, for the sake of privacy. Such a reason would be secondary in the evangelist's view (and also in ours, I trust), because the whole event was in the special providential plan of God, who willed his Son to be a man of the poor.

Fittingly enough, Luke has poor shepherds nearby hear the Good News about the birth first through a heavenly messenger: "And the angel said to them, 'Be not afraid; for behold, I bring you good news of a great joy which will come to all the people; for to you is born this day in the city of David a Savior, who is Christ the Lord. And this will be a sign for you: you will find a babe wrapped in swaddling cloths and lying in a manger' " (Luke 2:9-12). What a mysterious revelation to poor, simple shepherds! The "sign" given them by the angel is the birth of a child in the poorest of circumstances. Yet he is called "Savior" and "Christ the Lord." He is truly the Messiah, the promised Savior of the ages in Israel. But for Luke to give him the title "Christ the Lord," the only time in the entire New Testament, is to reveal that this helpless Child is also clothed with lordship and dominion (cf. Isaiah 9:5). In fact he is claiming that this Child is divine. The evangelist is obviously using language of faith in Jesus as "Christ the Lord" that arose in the Christian community after the resurrection. But he believes that Christ was truly so from the beginning of his life on earth, his conception and birth. And Luke seems to be saying that the claim to the title of a divine savior, so often made by arrogant emperors and kings in the pagan world, truly belongs to this little Child born in such lowly conditions by this world's standards of greatness. Indeed Luke proposes a divine paradox!

According to the account, the shepherds immediately act upon the angelic message. "And they went with haste, and found Mary and Joseph, and the babe lying in a manger. And when they saw it they made known the saying which had been told them concerning this child; and all who heard it wondered at what the shepherds told them. But Mary kept all these things, pondering them in her heart" (Luke 2:16-19). Good news, especially glad tidings that bring such great joy, is meant to be shared with others. The shepherds, one might say, could still hear the hymn of the heavenly host, "Glory to God in the highest, / and on earth peace among men with whom he is pleased" (Luke 2:14), re-sounding in the sky that first Christmas night. They and all who heard from them about this Child were filled with wonder. But more than any other, the Child's mother wondered at the mysterious words and events surrounding his birth, preserving the memory of them in her heart, prayerfully letting them sink deeply into her contemplative spir-it, seeking to penetrate their real meaning. Here we catch another glimpse of the Lucan Madonna, the perfect disciple in her more con-templative nature, listening with complete openness to the word of God as it invites her to enter ever more deeply into the mystery of her Son and the salvation of the world.

The Presentation of Jesus in the Temple, the Fourth Joyful Mystery
As we meditate *with* Mary as well as *about* her in the next mystery of her Son's infancy, as she did in her own continual listening to the word of God, we receive a prophetic premonition of the sorrowful mys-teries that lie ahead. We realize that Mary and Joseph were piously obeying the Jewish law by bringing Jesus, their firstborn son, to con-secrate him to God in the Temple at Jerusalem. At the same time, in obedience to the law, Mary was being ritually purified forty days after the birth of her Son, and her offering was that of the poor. But the Child is, of course, the center of the scene. Simeon, "and the Holy Spir-it was upon him" (Luke 2:25), happened to be there and was inspired to proclaim his *Nunc Dimittis* prophecy about Jesus (Luke 2:29-32), which is sung daily in the Church's Liturgy of the Hours at Night Prayer. It speaks to the Lord of the Child as "thy salvation," "a light for revelation to the Gentiles, and for glory to thy people Israel."
At this point in the scene, Luke mentions: "And his father and his mother marveled at what was said about him; and Simeon blessed them and said to Mary his mother, 'Behold, this child is set for the fall and rising of many in Israel, and for a sign that is spoken against (and a sword will pierce through your own soul also), that thoughts out of many hearts may be revealed'" (Luke 2: 33-35). Many and varied have been the interpretations of these words, but the one that seems most acceptable in light of recent biblical scholarship may be sum-

marized in this way. The basic reason why Mary's Son "is set for the fall and rising of many in Israel . . ." is that his preaching and whole way of life will demand a decision. In his presence, there is no possibility of remaining neutral. One must either accept or reject him. This will mean suffering for all who are involved: for Jesus, the Suffering Servant of Yahweh; for Mary, both as an individual, who must pay the price of discipleship, and as the "Daughter of Sion," representing all of Israel which will be divided by the sword of God passing through the land (cf. Ezekiel 14:17). For Luke, it seems that the sword is the revealing word of God, which challenges all to make a decision for or against Mary's Son, and which separates the wicked from the faithful remnant. At the same time, this interpretation does not coldly dismiss the fact that Mary's heart, the heart of a mother who pondered her mysterious Son over and over again, would be so deeply touched by his future.

The Fifth Joyful Mystery, the Finding of Jesus in the Temple

In the setting of Luke's infancy narrative, this scene is a further revelation of the sacrifices that the mother would be called upon to make if she is to be his disciple as well as his natural mother. The evangelist informs us that it was the custom of the parents of Jesus to celebrate the Passover feast every year in Jerusalem. When Jesus was twelve, he accompanied them. Whether this was his first visit to the Temple in Jerusalem since his Presentation as an infant cannot be inferred from the text. The whole episode is what Scripture scholars call a "pronouncement story," since its climax is found in the pronouncement made by Jesus: "Did you not know that I must be in my Father's house?" (Luke 2:49). Let us now listen to enough of Luke's narration of the story to get the context for its special Mariological meaning. The details of his parents' leaving for home without knowing that he had stayed behind in the Temple are familiar to us all. The story picks up: "After three days they found him in the temple, sitting among the teachers, listening to them and asking them questions; and all who heard him were amazed at his understanding and his answers. And when they saw him they were astonished, and his mother said to him, "Son, why have you treated us so? Behold, your father and I have been looking for you anxiously.' And he said to them, 'How is it that you sought me? Did you not know that I must be in my Father's house?' And they did not understand the saying which he spoke to them. And he went down with them and came to Nazareth, and was obedient to them; and his mother kept all these things in her heart" (Luke 2:46-51). Does the evangelist of the third Gospel intend that the reply of Jesus to his mother's very understandable complaint, or his "pronouncement" in the story, "How is it that you sought me? Did you not know that I must be in my Father's house?" be understood by his audience as a rebuke to his parents? If so, it is not sharp, but a gentle and clear calling of their attention to his priorities. The will of his heavenly Father comes first. Perhaps he is somewhat disappointed that they have not yet come to realize this: After all, according to Luke, they witnessed the wondrous events surrounding his birth, heard the prophecy of Simeon in the same Temple twelve years before, and still had not come to this conclusion about him! And yet ". . . they did not understand. . ." (Luke 2:50). But Luke points out once again about Mary: ". . . his mother kept all these things in her heart" (Luke 2:51). There is no doubt that she had to walk by faith like the rest of us redeemed disciples. The fact that she was truly his mother and filled with grace did not exempt her or her husband from finding it difficult to understand the mystery unfolding before their very eyes. They had to learn how to "let go," so that their Child could carry out his messianic mission. At the same time, Luke definitely indicates that their Son was truly devoted to them. Indeed it was the very will of his Father in heaven that he be obedient to his mother and foster-father upon earth. This is all part of the astounding mystery of the Incarnation for the sake of our salvation. In light of these comments, we may well listen once more to the meditation of Vatican II on the last two joyful mysteries with a deeper appreciation of how beautifully it epitomizes them: ". . .when she presented him to the Lord in the temple, making the offering of the poor, she heard Simeon foretelling at the same time that the Son would be a sign of contradiction and that a sword would pierce the mother's soul, that out of many hearts thoughts might be revealed (cf. Luke 2:34-35); when the child Jesus was lost and they had sought him sorrowing, his parents found him in the temple, engaged in the things that were his Father's, and they did not understand the words of their Son. His mother, however, kept all these things to be pondered in her heart (cf. Luke 2:41-51)" (LG 51).

Mary in the Public Ministry of Her Son

Unlike Matthew, Luke places his genealogy outside the infancy narrative, after the baptism of Jesus in the Jordan at the beginning of his ministry (Luke 3:23-38). At the baptism, the Father said: "Thou art my beloved Son; with thee I am well pleased" (Luke 3:22). And so in the genealogy Luke traces Christ's ancestry back to God through Adam, which also seems to be another expression of his theological theme about the universality of salvation, embracing all of humanity. The genealogy is, however, of only indirect Marian significance in adding parenthetically "as was supposed" to Jesus' being the son of Joseph (Luke 3:23). This is to safeguard the revelation of the virginal conception in the infancy narrative. Because we have already discussed the Lucan version of the true meaning of the "eschatological" family in distinction from the natural or physical family (cf. Luke 8:19-21), we shall go at once to a little passage that is peculiar to his Gospel, namely, the beatitude on Jesus' mother: "As he said this, a woman in the crowd raised her voice and said to him, 'Blessed is the womb that bore you, and the breasts that you sucked!' But he said, 'Blessed rather are those who hear the word of God and keep it!' " (Luke 11:27-28). How much ink has been spilled over this tiny text! Much too much in contrast to its profound simplicity. It has been unduly complicated by the introduction of the debate over the relative superiority of Mary's maternity and holiness into the interpretation. To get right at the heart of the matter, in no way is Jesus refusing to accept the beatitude or blessedness in praise of his mother. But he is directing our attention to the fact that the primary reason for calling his mother blessed is not to be seen in her physical relationship to him, but in her faithful discipleship, which makes her a member of his "eschatological" family. It would help if the "Blessed rather. . ." of the Lord's reply to the woman were to be rendered, "Yes, and even more blessed are those who hear the word of God and keep it." And the Lucan Madonna is preeminent among her Son's disciples. Again, he seems to balance nicely both her motherhood of God's Son and her perfect discipleship, since it would be inconceivable to be one and not the other.

Mary in the Jerusalem Community Prayerfully Preparing for Pentecost
The final stroke of the brush that completes the Lucan Madonna is found in the Acts of the Apostles: "All these with one accord devoted themselves to prayer, together with the women and Mary the mother of Jesus, and with his brethren" (Acts 1:14). Luke's portrait of Mary as the perfect disciple is now finished. As a group of New Testament scholars have nicely put it: "Mary's first response to the good news was: 'Behold the handmaid of the Lord. Let it be to me according to your word.' The real import of Acts 1:14 is to remind the reader that she had not changed her mind."[10] Luke / Acts does not provide any further explicit information about Mary. Although he does not say so specifically, we may very reasonably assume that she was present for the outpouring of her Son's Pentecostal Spirit. And who could have been more open than she to receive the fullness of that Spirit's gifts, fruits, and charisms. On the basis of a certain parallelism between the birth of Christ in the infancy narrative of Luke's Gospel and the birth of the Church in Acts 1-2, the following special relationship between the Holy Spirit and Mary in both accounts has been proposed.[11] At the Annunciation the Holy Spirit came upon Mary, inspired her to go to visit Elizabeth, as well as to sing her *Magnificat* during the Visitation. What the Spirit did for Mary alone according to Luke's Gospel, that same Spirit did for her together with her Son's nascent Church on Pentecost. The Holy Spirit came upon Mary and all who had gathered together in the upper room in Jerusalem to pray, and that same Spirit inspired them to speak in other tongues (cf. Acts 2:1-4). They were moved by the Spirit to speak in other tongues to the devout Jews who had come to Jerusalem for the feast (cf. Acts 2:5-13). And Peter was inspired to preach the Good News in the power of the Pentecostal Spirit: "So those who received his word were baptized, and there were added that day about three thousand souls" (Acts 2:41). The Spirit, who made Mary the mother of God's own Son, was giving her a maternal role among God's people.

CHAPTER IV

The Woman of Faith —
Mother of God's People

NOW we turn to gaze upon the Madonna of the fourth evangelist. For him she is the "woman of faith" *par excellence*. And as mother of the "beloved disciple," she is the most excellent example of faithful discipleship in her Son's "eschatological" family, the Church. In the two main references to her in the fourth Gospel, the inspired author does call her "mother of Jesus" (John 2:1,3) in the scene at Cana, and "his mother" in the scene at the foot of the cross (John 19:26). But the fact of her motherhood of God's Son is one that he seems to pre-suppose from the tradition of the Synoptists. As already discussed in the last chapter, this fact is what Mark and Matthew were interested in af-firming about Mary for the sake of proclaiming the real humanity of Christ as well as his divinity. And Luke/Acts, although very much in-cluding it in his version of the Good News, was even more concerned with showing that Mary was much more than merely the physical mother of the Lord; namely, she was his first and foremost disciple from the Annunciation through Pentecost. John's Gospel seems to build upon this by revealing Mary as the outstanding exemplar of what he means by faith in Christ, and by providing the biblical basis for what developed in the Catholic Tradition to be the belief that she is the spiritual "mother of God's people."[1]

As in the case of the other three evangelists, a few general observa-tions about the fourth Gospel are necessary before we can appreciate the Mariological meaning of the "woman at Cana," and the "woman at the foot of the cross."[2] The Gospel in its final form, as we have it to-day, was probably composed sometime after A.D. 85. It is also generally agreed by scholars that this complete Gospel is the work of a redactor other than the evangelist, and that his editing resulted in the addition of Chapter 21. What counts for our living faith in the Tradition, however, is that the Gospel of John handed on to us is a divinely inspired testimony of the faith in the apostolic Church.

John's Gospel presupposes not only the Synoptic tradition, but also a Christian audience that has been able to reflect upon that tradition for a generation. And so he could select from the events in the life of Christ that would be familiar to his audience and interpret them in accord with his special theological purposes. He seems to have written primarily for a Christian community that was deeply rooted in the Jewish traditions of liturgical feasts, etc. His Gospel is profoundly ecclesiological in the sense that it seeks to show that the Kingdom of God inaugurated by Christ finds its realization upon earth in the Church. John wishes to convince the Christian hearer of his message that the spiritual realities experienced by the disciples of Christ during his earthly sojourn are to be found in the Church. His Gospel teaching, therefore, is also deeply sacramental, especially in reference to Baptism and the Eucharist, as our contemplation of the Cana scene will consider. Again, he wishes to reveal that the sacraments of the Church are efficacious by reason of the redemptive work of the risen Lord, who continuously gives his Holy Spirit to enliven the faithful. Lastly, it is of great importance to be mindful that the fourth evangelist is one who loves to use symbols that have more than a single significance. If we are to interpret him intelligently, then, we must bear in mind that they can have, in addition to their primary level of meaning, a second or third layer, as will be exemplified in our comments upon the Cana scene. This extensive and rich usage of symbols, however, should not be the grounds for thinking that John's Gospel lacks any historicity. His symbolism does not distort the historical events, but penetrates to the divine intention behind them. Before looking directly at the Johannine texts, let us listen once more to the Marian teaching of Vatican II as it uses such texts and comments upon them:

> In the public life of Jesus, Mary appears preeminently; at the very beginning when at the marriage feast of Cana, moved with pity, she brought about by her intercession the beginning of miracles of Jesus the Messiah (cf. John 2:1-11). . . . Thus the Blessed Virgin advanced in her pilgrimage of faith, and faith-

fully persevered in her union with her Son unto the cross, where she stood, in keeping with the divine plan, enduring with her only begotten Son the intensity of his suffering, associated herself with his sacrifice in her mother's heart, and lovingly consenting to the immolation of this victim which was born of her. Finally, she was given by the same Christ Jesus dying on the cross as a mother to his disciple, with these words: "Woman, behold thy son" (John 19:26-27)." (LG 58) The Madonna of the fourth Gospel is beautifully framed by the beginning and by the end of her Son's public ministry. Although these are the only two passages of clear Marian import, they are enhanced by this fact in the context of the Gospel as a whole. For it is divided into "The Book of Signs" (John 1:19-12:50) and "The Book of Exaltation" (John 13:1-20:31). The Prologue to the Gospel (1:1-18) identifies the principal Johannine themes, and its Epilogue, which is commonly held to be an addition by the final redactor or editor, narrates the appearances of the risen Lord to his disciples (21:1-25).

In the first book the evangelist develops his teaching about the meaning of faith in Christ as opposed to unbelief. It is called "The Book of Signs," since he uses that term instead of "miracles," the word of the three Synoptists for the wondrous works of Christ. For John these miraculous occurrences were much more than manifestations of the divine power present in Jesus. They were symbols of spiritual realities given through faith in him during his life on earth, and ever since Pentecost, through that same faith in him who sends his Holy Spirit into the Church. The second book of the Gospel is called that of "Exaltation" because, although it deals mainly with the events of the first Holy Week, the Passion and Death of Christ, these historical events are contemplated by John in the eternal light of his glorification, to which they providentially led. This has been called John's "theology of the cross," according to which he beholds the crucified Christ as already glorified. The special significance of these considerations for our purposes will be pointed out in the proper contexts of our Marian meditation on the scenes depicting Mary's role at Cana and on Calvary.

The Woman at Cana

Mary's part in the wedding feast of Cana is of such significance ac-

cording to John's Gospel that it is important to have the entire passage
at our fingertips before making any meditative comments:

> On the third day there was a marriage in Cana of Galilee, and
> the mother of Jesus was there; Jesus was also invited to the mar-
> riage with his disciples. When the wine failed, the mother of Je-
> sus said to him, "They have no wine." And Jesus said to her, "O
> woman, what do you have to do with me? My hour has not yet
> come." His mother said to the servants, "Do whatever he tells
> you." Now six stone jars were standing there, for the Jewish rites
> of purification, each holding twenty or thirty gallons. Jesus said
> to them, "Fill the jars with water." And they filled them up to
> the brim. He said to them, "Now draw some out, and take it to
> the steward of the feast." So they took it. When the steward of
> the feast tasted the water now become wine, and did not know
> where it came from (though the servants who had drawn the wa-
> ter knew), the steward of the feast called the bridegroom and
> said to him, "Every man serves the good wine first; and when
> men have drunk freely, then the poor wine; but you have kept
> the good wine until now." This, the first of his signs, Jesus did at
> Cana in Galilee, and manifested his glory; and his disciples be-
> lieved in him. (John 2:1-11)

In order to grasp precisely what John intends to symbolize through
Mary's part, it is necessary to exegete the symbolic meaning of the
scene as a whole.

The spiritual significance of John's beginning this story of the
wedding feast at Cana by stating that it took place "on the third day" is
that it really is the seventh day of the new creation account in the Gospel. The third day in the Scriptures means the day after tomorrow;
e.g., Christ's rising from the dead on the third day, i.e., the first Easter
Sunday morn after Good Friday. According to John, who is more interested in a symbolic chronology than an accurate historical one, this
would be the third day after the calling of Philip and Nathanael, which
would give Jesus and his disciples a day to travel from Bethany to
Cana. But his concern is to evoke a memory of the resurrection by the
reference as well as to get into the first sign worked by Christ, which
reveals the new creation that has come forth from his redemptive activity.

"... and the mother of Jesus was there." Mary is never mentioned by name in John's Gospel. But he is beginning to paint his Madonna here by situating her in a symbolic setting of her intimate relationship with her Son, a portrait that will be completed only on Calvary at the foot of the cross. At this point in the account only five disciples of Jesus have been mentioned, but it is not clear how many of them would have accompanied him to the wedding feast. That some were on hand is significant (cf. John 2:11: "his disciples believed in him").

"They have no wine." Although there are those exegetes who would interpret this as Mary's merely informing her Son about the situation, it does not seem from the symbolism of the scene that the evangelist would have her just saying that. Mary is definitely playing the part of one who is seeking a sign from her Son.

"O woman, what do you have to do with me? My hour has not yet come." For a son to address his mother as "woman" is without precedent in the world of the evangelist, and so he must intend some symbolic meaning by it. It is certainly not disrespectful, since John has Jesus use this form of address for the Samaritan woman (4:21) and Mary Magdalene (20:13). He appears here at least to be deemphasizing the fact of Mary's natural motherhood by not having Jesus call her "mother." Like the Synoptists, then, his main teaching would be that the family of the disciples takes priority over the natural family. But before we make up our minds about this interpretation, let us examine the passage further and in a fuller context of the Gospel as a whole. Now his having Jesus immediately reply to his mother, ". . .what do you have to do with me?" is a Semitism, or Hebrew manner of speaking, that could be understood harshly as a rebuke that Mary is unjustly bothering her Son. But much more likely, he is saying to her that their running out of wine is really not his business. And the added "My hour has not yet come" would seem to support this interpretation. Jesus' "hour" in the fourth Gospel really symbolizes the hour of his suffering and death upon the cross, the hour of his passing over from this world to the Father, the hour of his glorification according to John's "theology of the cross." That is also the "hour" when he will make Mary mother of the "beloved disciple": "Woman, behold your Son!" (19:26).

It seems that John intends to convey a certain distancing between

Jesus and his mother as he begins the work of his Father in the public ministry. She no longer possesses the claim of a natural mother upon her son. And so the words of his response to her ". . .were an invitation to deepen her faith, to look beyond the failing wine to his messianic career" (BYM 35). Does, however, the fourth evangelist intend a deeper symbolism in the "woman" at Cana? Recall the "woman" of Genesis: Eve is the mother of all the living in the old creation story. Possibly, on this seventh day of the new creation story according to John, Mary is being portrayed as the "New Eve," the mother of all those who would receive the new life of her Son's saving mission from the Father. It is difficult to determine whether or not he intended to include this in the rich symbolism of the scene, but in light of the "woman" at the foot of the cross, when his "hour" also became hers, such an interpretation is not without its foundation and followers among scholars. At least it does seem to become a biblical basis for Mary's spiritual motherhood of God's people in the Tradition.

"His mother said to the servants, 'Do whatever he tells you.' " The very fact that the Johannine account has Jesus actually granting his mother's request for a "sign" must support the more gentle interpretation of the reply, "O woman, what do you have to do with me?" She indeed has faith in him, that he can work miracles, but he is using the occasion to invite her and all his disciples to deepen their faith in his true messianic mission of accomplishing the Father's will for our redemption. There is no doubt that she came to that perfect faith along with the "beloved disciple" at the foot of the cross on Calvary. But at Cana her "pilgrimage of faith" in life (cf. LG 58) is in its early stages according to the fourth Gospel. And in the framework of its literary structure, which supports a treasury of symbols, her spiritual odyssey does not reach its destination till she stands on the hill of Golgatha at her Son's crucifixion.

Asking for a sign, according to John, can have several meanings in relationship to his concept of faith. At times it manifests the hostility of unbelief; e.g., when the "Jews" wanted Jesus to show them a sign of his authority to drive the money-changers out of the temple (cf. John 2:18). Note that the Johannine use of the word "Jews" as a pejorative is in no way anti-Semitic, since he clearly intends it to designate that element among them, such as the spirit of the scribes and Pharisees, who willfully blinded themselves in unbelief because of their hostility to Jesus. At other times in the fourth Gospel, the apparently positive response to the signs done by Jesus is really a superficial form of faith that is not trustworthy; e.g., the many who believed in him during the Passover feast in Jerusalem (cf. John 2:23-25). In other instances, however the request for a sign can reveal a sincere but incomplete faith that has not yet matured to the right understanding of the Lord's Messiahship, but which leads to complete faith in Christ; e.g., the official from Capernaum who went to Cana when Jesus was there on another occasion and begged him to "come down and heal his son," but came to believe Jesus *on his word* that his son would live (cf. John: 4:47,48,53).

Mary's faith in requesting a sign from her Son at Cana seems to place her in this third category, *at least*. Granting that her faith was still not yet fully developed at the time, still we should consider the fact that it was the *first* of the signs worked by Jesus in the fourth Gospel. Here let us listen again to the pastoral letter of the American bishops: "For St. John, the signs (or miracles) of Jesus always have to do with the awakening or strengthening of the faith of his followers. It is striking that no sign is done to help Mary believe. The Mother of Jesus requires no miracle to strengthen her faith. At her Son's word, before "this first of his signs," she shows her faith" (BYM 35). If we accept this interpretation, then there was something special about her faith even when it was still somewhat naïve and misinformed. Her faith, which was further enlightened by the "sign" at Cana, was well disposed to be more fully formed and informed about her Son's messianic mission.

The symbolism of the Cana scene seems to be centered upon the Christological truth that in Christ the "water" of the Jewish purification rites was replaced by the "wine" of the new creation, the Church. This was the first of many ways the Gospel shows in which Christ replaced the institutions of Judaism. John also seems to intend a Eucharistic symbolism in the changing of water into wine, which would be a part of the sacramental teaching in his Gospel. It is a good instance of the richness of his symbolism, which can be interpreted on more than one level. This makes the sign at Cana a "sacramental sign," teaching Christians to behold through faith, the presence of Christ in the Church, especially her sacraments — the same Christ who was visibly present in the flesh to his first disciples. On the basis of this, perhaps we can perceive in the Marian symbolism of the scene another level of meaning whereby her significance is also richly ecclesial. Her involvement, particularly when she says to the servants, "Do whatever he tells you," might also be portraying her as changing from a type of the synagogue, the daughter of ancient Sion, into a figure of the Church, the new People of God (BYM 36). Such possible further interpretations, especially of John's polyvalent symbols, have proved to be enriching for our faith in the Catholic Tradition. They have contributed in a special way to Mariological developments, the criteria for which we shall be examining in future chapters.

Woman at the Foot of the Cross

This scene is so intimately related with the Cana episode that it has been impossible to interpret the Marian symbolism of the wedding feast without glancing ahead at Calvary. The text is so brief that it is easy to miss its profound meaning: "When Jesus saw his mother, and the disciple whom he loved standing near, he said to his mother, 'Woman, behold your son!' Then he said to the disciple, 'Behold your mother!' And from that hour the disciple took her to his own home" (John 19:26-27).

Who is this mysterious figure in the fourth Gospel called "the disciple whom he loved" or the "beloved disciple" of Jesus? Even though he is no longer identifiable, it is thought that he ". . . was a real person . . . who was thought to have been a companion of Jesus."[3] He had a special significance for the Johannine community in the apostolic Church. He is portrayed as the ideal disciple of Jesus who never deserted the Lord and who understood him most fully. The "beloved disciple" is the one who first came to believe in the risen Lord and became the greatest witness to the right understanding of Jesus in the community (cf. John 20:8; 19:35).

In light of this, when Jesus says to his mother, "Woman, behold your son!" he is apparently bestowing upon her a role in relationship to the "beloved disciple" that goes beyond one of physical motherhood. Neither Mary nor this ideal disciple is ever mentioned by name in the fourth Gospel, which indicates that John intends both to symbolize roles within the Christian community of faith. Also the fact that he again has Jesus address her as "Woman" instead of "Mother" would support the interpretation of a new mother-son relationship in the "eschatological" family of disciples. We are inspired by the evangelist to behold this as the "hour" to which Jesus referred when apparently refusing his mother's request for a sign at Cana. Now is the "hour" of his true and full glorification, when he has accomplished the work of redemption for which the Father has sent him into the world. "It is finished" (19:30) is the final one of his last words from the cross according to John. This is the mother's "hour" too. The sign at Cana just anticipated it, when the glory of her Son was inchoately revealed for the sake of her faith and that of his first disciples. Now, at the foot of the cross, it is her "hour" to enter fully into her role of spiritual motherhood in the Church.

"Then he said to the disciple, 'Behold your mother!' And from that hour the disciple took her to his own home." It is important that we be reminded once again that for John the whole Paschal mystery is being accomplished during the "hour" of Jesus. Included in his vision of the "theology of the cross" are the return to his Father and glorification, as well as the sending of the Pentecostal Spirit for the birth of the Church. ". . . and he bowed his head and gave up his spirit" (19:30) apparently means more for John than that Jesus died upon the cross, but that in the glorification at his death he was empowered to send forth the Spirit to enliven his community of disciples. And another remark, ". . . But one of the soldiers pierced his side with a spear, and at once there came out blood and water" (19:34), has been interpreted in the Tradition to symbolize the sacraments of the Eucharist and Baptism as constituting his Body the Church.

The "beloved disciple," who is a witness to all that took place on Calvary (cf. John 19:35), also has a representative role in relationship to Mary, his "mother" in the family of the faithful. For the fourth evangelist, this community of faith is being called into being by Christ and his Holy Spirit as he hangs upon the cross, having fulfilled the Father's

salvific will. John's remark that the beloved disciple "from that hour
. . . took her to his own home" signifies that he watched over Mary
and took good care of her. But the spiritual significance of the scene
goes well beyond this as interpreted in the Tradition. Mary and we,
represented by the beloved disciple, are related as mother and children
in the Church (cf. BYM 37).

Secondary or supplementary symbolism of this scene has also been
suggested by scholars. It is mentioned briefly because the spiritual
depth of Johannine symbols seems to have had a such a profound influence upon doctrinal developments in the Catholic Tradition, particularly in Marian doctrine and devotion. While the literal sense intended by
the fourth evangelist seems to be the birth of the Christian community
at the foot of the cross, with a mother-son relationship between Mary
and the beloved disciple who looks after her in the eschatological family, this meaning has been expanded within the Tradition. The emphasis is shifted from the disciple-son's care of the disciple-mother to
Mary's care of him and all the faithful disciples in the Church. This is
Mary's spiritual motherhood of God's People, her motherhood "in the
order of grace," as Vatican II teaches (cf. LG 61, 62). Can it be held
that this doctrine about Mary's spiritual maternity, which has been so
clearly taught and believed in the Tradition, is in any sense contained
in John 19:26-27? And also, is the Mary/Eve comparison, which will
emerge in the early patristic tradition as the "New Eve" image of
Mary, in any sense being insinuated in the scene as a biblical basis for
later developments? This Mary/Eve symbolism was also suggested for
the Cana scene. And we shall be considering it soon in our brief meditation upon the scriptural significance of the "woman" in Revelation
12, when its possibility will be further explored.

A concluding question about the scene at the foot of the cross:
Were Mary and the beloved disciple really there? Does John intend to
report a historical fact from stage one in the formation of his Gospel?
Or is it a literary creation to communicate his theological teaching
about the birth of the Christian community at the foot of the cross,
with the special roles of Mary and the beloved disciple in that community, including his care of her after the death of her Son? As we have
discussed before, such a question cannot be answered with certitude on

the basis of the historical-critical method. The New Testament scholars who use this method are keenly aware of the difficulties with affirming the historicity of their presence on Calvary, e.g, the variance with the Synoptic Gospels. The fact that certainty in the matter has not come to us from any authoritative source need not disturb us. It is not necessary for our faith. What is essential is the spiritual significance of the scene upon which we have meditated. And this is true whether or not Mary and the beloved disciple were actually present at the foot of the cross. In fact, "Paradoxically, if the scene is not historical and the presence of the mother of Jesus and the beloved disciple reflects Johannine theological inventiveness, that may enhance the importance of Mary for the Johannine community — the evangelist would scarcely have created a central crucifixion scene if it did not have significance."[4]

Woman Clothed with the Sun

Traditionally, the book of Revelation (The Apocalypse), along with the fourth Gospel and the three Letters of John, have been attributed to the apostle John. That is certainly not the common opinion of Scripture scholars today. The authorship of what has come to be called the "Johannine corpus" or writings is significant for the interpretation of Revelation 12, which seems to have some links with the fourth Gospel. On the basis of intrinsic evidence, comparing the two New Testament writings themselves, the differences demand that they were composed by different authors. This does not preclude the possibility, however, that their similarities can be accounted for by the authority that the Apostle John had in Asia till the end of the first century; and that he might have inspired all the Johannine writings, perhaps through a catechetical school at Ephesus, although their final redaction or editing would have been done by different disciples.[5]

Whatever might be the solution to the problem of authorship, Revelation definitely belongs to the apocalyptic literature of the Bible, along with the book of Daniel and parts of Isaiah in the Old Testament. This literary genre has some general characteristics: the prophet, who receives the revelation in a dream or vision, sees what is happening in heaven along with what will happen in the future and the end of the world. But he often beholds events, in heaven and upon earth, that are both present and future, and goes back and forth in a way that is bewildering to the reader. There is almost a wild use of symbols to describe the same set of events and persons with a multiplicity of images. Obviously, the interpretation of apocalyptic literature is usually very varied, as we shall see in our inquiry about the possible Marian symbolism of the "woman clothed with the sun" in Revelation 12. (Note that Apocalypse is a transliteration of the Greek word for revelation).

Apocalyptic writings often appear during times of persecution and promise a final deliverance by God. One common analysis is that the first part of the book (chapters 1-11) deals with God's past judgment upon the Jews for their rejection of Jesus and persecution of the early Christians. This happened during the Jewish Revolt that culminated in the destruction of the Temple in A.D. 70. Since Revelation was probably composed during the persecution of the Church that erupted toward the end of the reign of Domitian (81-96), the second part of the book (chapters 12-22) portrays God's contemporary and future judgment upon Rome and emperor worship, which will reach its culmination in the end of the world.[6] If this interpretation is accurate, then chapter 12 would begin the second part of Revelation.

Let us now glance at the symbolic images of the text that are most pertinent to our purpose of determining whether or not it may contain any Marian meaning: "And a great portent appeared in heaven, a woman clothed with the sun, with the moon under her feet, and on her head a crown of twelve stars; she was with child and she cried out in her pangs of birth, in anguish for delivery" (12:1-2). Then, according to the account, another portent appeared in heaven, "a great red dragon," who stood before the woman, waiting to devour her child once he was born. ". . . she brought forth a male child, one who is to rule all the nations with a rod of iron, but her child was caught up to God and to his throne, and the woman fled into the wilderness. . ." (12:5-6). God has prepared a place there so that she will be nourished for 1,260 days. Then the war arises in heaven when Michael and his angels defeat the dragon and his angels, throwing them down to earth. Finding himself upon earth, the dragon pursues the woman, who was given the two wings of the great eagle that she might fly from the serpent into the wilderness where she is to be nourished. Unable to overtake her, the dragon is angry with the woman, and goes off to make war on her offspring, ". . . on those who keep the commandments of God and bear testimony to Jesus" (Revelation 12:17).

This story of how the dragon was unable to destroy the child of the woman, and of the ways in which God protects the woman and her offspring, clearly fits into the general purpose of the inspired author of Revelation, namely, ". . . to assure his readers of ultimate victory in times of persecution."[7] But precisely what does he mean by the symbol of the "woman" in the passage. Most likely, the "woman" personifies Israel, God's people of the Old Covenant, and, in the Christian appropriation of the symbolism, the "woman," after the birth of the Messianic child, becomes the Church, God's people of the New Covenant.

But does this leave any room for the possibility of a secondary symbolism in reference to Mary? Although there is no known Mariological interpretation before the fourth century in the Tradition, it does seem that the "woman" of Revelation 12 may have an extended meaning in relation to Mary. If the "woman clothed with the sun" can be brought into the context of the "woman" at Cana and at the foot of the cross in the Johannine writings, then the biblical basis of Mary as the "New Eve" might be further established. Then the ecclesial symbolism of the primary meaning of "woman" might be extended to include the mother of the messianic child, who is a corporate personality representing holy mother the Church.

CHAPTER V

New Eve

AFTER the New Testament Madonnas, the earliest image of Mary in the Tradition is the one which is firmly founded upon the biblical revelation, and has come to be called "New Eve" or "Second Eve." Basically it is a portrait of Mary that draws a comparison between her and Eve, Adam's "helpmate" (cf. Genesis 2:18) and "the mother of all living" (Genesis 3:20). In our treatment of Mary's scriptural portraits, this image emerged as possibly being implied in the "woman" at Cana, on Calvary, and "clothed with the sun" in the Johannine writings. The biblical texts that actually inspired the early Fathers of the Church to meditate upon Mary's role in our redemption and the restoration of the whole human race will be discussed in this chapter. It is important to note from the outset that this comparison between Mary and the first Eve is really more a contrast or antithetical parallelism. The similarities between them, e.g., both being virgins at the time of the temptation and Annunication, are far outweighed by the profound differences, principally the disobedience of Eve in succumbing to the fallen angel's (serpent's) suggestion, and the obedience of Mary in her *fiat* (yes) to God's will, as communicated through the good angel.

Although the precise phrases, "New Eve" or "Second Eve," were not used by the first Fathers to develop this reflection on the Eve-Mary analogy, what they actually taught about it is well expressed thereby. And among Mariologists during recent years, there has been a renewed interest in its precise meaning, especially as the symbol or typology that can shed further light upon the Mary-Church analogy. We have seen that the ecclesiotypical emphasis, in which Mary is contemplated as the prototype of the Church, has characterized Mariology since Vatican II. In this context the Council teaches:

For in the mystery of the Church, which is itself rightly called mother and virgin, the Blessed Virgin stands out in eminent and singular fashion as exemplar both of virgin and mother. Through her faith and obedience she gave birth on earth to the very Son of the Father, not through the knowledge of man but by the over-shadowing of the Holy Spirit, in the manner of a new Eve who placed her faith, not in the serpent of old but in God's messenger without wavering in doubt. (LG 63)

In the same context of connecting the "New Eve" image with the Mary-Church typology, the American bishops' pastoral letter teaches:

The understanding of Mary in Christian history unfolded along the lines of the Scriptures. The Church saw herself symbol-ized in the Virgin Mary. The story of Mary, as the Church has come to see her, is at the same time the record of the Church's own self-discovery. (BYM 38)

Even more anciently, the Church was regarded as the "new Eve." The Church is the bride of Christ, formed from his side in the sleep of death on the cross, as the first Eve was formed by God from the side of the sleeping Adam. As the first Eve was the "mother of the living," the Church becomes the "new mother of the living." In time, some of the maternal characteristics of the Church were seen in Mary. . . . (BYM 41)

In light of all this, we see that the "New Eve" symbol, although the most ancient about Mary by Christian writers after the Scriptures, is still current in the Catholic Tradition.

Patristic Witness to Mary as the "New Eve"

The three ancient Christian writers who give the earliest testimony in the Tradition to the Eve-Mary analogy are St. Justin Martyr (d. c. 165; cf. TH 211), St. Irenaeus (d. after 193; cf. TH 189-191), and, Tertullian (d. after 220; cf. TH 337-338). Our consideration will con-centrate upon the work of St. Irenaeus, because he developed the typology most fully. But the writings of all three are significant, since they are together a witness to the faith of the universal Church dur-ing the latter half of the second century concerning Mary.[1] St. Justin, native of Palestine who was converted to Christianity in 133, came into touch with the religious belief of Ephesus and Rome. St. Irenaeus, a native of Asia Minor, was a priest in the Church of Lyons (modern

France) from at least 177 and became bishop there. Tertullian, a convert from paganism and the first of the Latin Fathers, represents the faith of the African Churches of the time. The fact that these three men used the Eve-Mary parallelism as a proof of their testimony to basic Christian truths, without trying to prove its own validity, is an indication that this Marian theme had already been a part of the Tradition. Let us now examine in some detail how Irenaeus put it to good use in his theology, and also determine what its apostolic inspiration may have been.

Irenaeus was the disciple of St. Polycarp, the bishop of Smyrna in Asia Minor, who was martyred in 155 or 156. Through Polycarp (b. 69 or 70), Irenaeus was brought into a living contact with the apostolic Church.[2] He was possessed with a great spirit of preserving and handing on the authentic faith of the Apostles. He was the first to use the New Testament as we do, and has been called the "Father of Christian Theology." With him, Mariology was given birth. Irenaeus brought toward its perfect expression the principle of *recircumlatio*, which Justin applied in his pioneer attempts at theological reflection on the data of sacred Scripture. This term, defying translation into English, simply means that, in salvation history, God provides that the original evil is undone by the counterparts of those who had been involved in the first place, Adam by Christ, the tree of Eden by the wood of the cross, and Eve by Mary. The parallelism is, therefore, antithetical, because the work or function of one undoes that of his / her / its counterpart.

Irenaeus developed his Mariological doctrine about the Eve-Mary antithesis in two of his works: *Adversus Haereses (Against Heresies)*, where he treats it twice; and *Demonstratio Apostolicae Praedicationis (Proof of the Apostolic Preaching)* in which he uses the theme once. His use of the Eve-Mary contrast must be viewed against the backdrop of his pastoral concerns to defend the apostolic faith about Christ and redemption in opposition to the heretical Gnostics, who destroyed the unity of God's plan in salvation history by holding that the Old Testament is the work of the devil. Also he utilizes the Eve-Mary theme in a completely Christocentric context.

Irenaeus applies the principle of *recircumlatio* primarily to the Adam-Christ (the "New Adam" or the "Second Adam") antithesis.

His Christology is within the Pauline perspective of Romans 5, where the disobedience of the first Adam is set in contrast to the obedience of Christ, according to which the gift of our justification through the grace of the "New Adam" abounds much more than did the condemnation through the sin of the "Old Adam." And on the basis also of Ephesians 1:10, "to reestablish all things in him [Christ]," he constructed his "theory of recapitulation" or the "re-heading, the re-commencing," of the human race in Christ. It is in this theological setting of our being a new creation in Mary's Son, which in effect has begun the human race anew, that we are to understand the following passage that pursues the Old Eve/New Eve antithesis:

> But in accordance with this special design we also find the Virgin Mary, obedient and saying: "Behold the handmaid of the Lord; be it done unto me according to thy word!"
>
> If Eve was disobedient and became, both for herself and all the human race, the cause of death, Mary, betrothed to a man yet still a virgin, through her obedience became, both for herself and all the human race, the cause of salvation.
>
> It is on account of this parallelism that the Old Law calls a woman who has been joined to a man, even though she may still be a virgin, the spouse of him who has betrothed her, manifesting through these similitudes that the meaning of the life which comes through Mary has its back-reference in Eve; for what has been joined can be put asunder only when the bonds of union are undone by an inversion of the process by which they were knotted, so that the former bonds are loosed in the fastening of the second; or in other terms, the second loose the first.
>
> It is for the same reason that Luke begins his genealogy with the Lord while carrying it back to Adam, to indicate clearly that it was not our fathers who gave the Savior life, but on the contrary he who caused them to be born again in the Gospel of life.
>
> Likewise also the knot that Eve's disobedience had tied was untied by Mary's obedience; for what the virgin Eve had bound by her unbelief, the Virgin Mary unbound by her faith. (*Against Heresies*, 3, 22, 3-4; MG 7, 958-959A)

The biblical basis for this antithetical parallelism between Eve and Mary is found in the account of the temptation and fall of our first parents in Genesis 3, and in the Annunciation to Mary in Luke 1:26-38.

The details of the counterparts in the contrast that are contained in the above passage may be shown in this schema:[3]

1) Eve	1) Mary
2) still a virgin	2) the virgin
3) the spouse of Adam	3) already betrothed
4) was disobedient	4) through her obedience
5) became both for herself	5) became both for herself
6) and all the human race	6) and all the human race
7) the cause of death	7) the cause of salvation
8) what the virgin Eve	8) the virgin Mary
9) had bound	9) unbound
10) by her unbelief	10) by her faith

For such an ancient Mariology, these statements attribute to Mary an intimate association with her Son in the accomplishment of our salvation. The Christocentric context of the above passage from his polemical work *Against Heresies* leaves no doubt in our minds that Irenaeus teaches the apostolic faith that only Christ is our redeemer. Still he does make great claims for her role: through her obedience, she became for herself and the entire human race the cause of salvation; and by her faith, she counterbalances what Eve's disobedience and unbelief had brought about, by liberating us from the bondage of sin and death. It is all the more marvelous that he says such astounding things in a work that is defending orthodoxy when he would want to be as careful as possible to reflect only what was certain in the Tradition. And so such beliefs about Mary must have been already universally recognized. At the same time, we are not suggesting that answers to contemporary questions — e.g., the precise causal role Mary may have played in our redemption — can be derived from the text. But this basic content is there: Mary restores Eve, and is the cause of human salvation, only because she is the mother of Jesus, and was favored with the grace of obedience by God at the Annunciation, unlike her sister and counterpart in salvation history, the first woman, Eve, who was disobedient in the Garden of Eden. Vatican II sums it all up very nicely:

> Thus the daughter of Adam, Mary, consenting to the word of God, became the Mother of Jesus. Committing herself whole-

heartedly and impeded by no sin to God's saving will, she devoted herself totally, as a handmaid of the Lord, to the person
and work of her Son, under and with him, serving the mystery of
redemption, by the grace of Almighty God. Rightly, therefore,
the Fathers see Mary not merely as passively engaged by God,
but as freely cooperating in the work of man's salvation through
faith and obedience. For, as St. Irenaeus says, she, "being obedient, became the cause of salvation for herself and for the whole
human race." Hence not a few of the early Fathers gladly assert
with him in their preaching: "the knot of Eve's disobedience was
untied by Mary's obedience: what the Virgin Eve bound through
her disbelief, Mary loosened by her faith." Comparing Mary
with Eve, they call her "Mother of the living," and frequently
claim: "death through Eve, life through Mary." (LG 56)

There is no doubt that the Council Fathers found this teaching of St.
Irenaeus most pertinent to their Christocentric and ecclesiotypical
Mariology. The only other Father mentioned by name in the text of
chapter eight in LG is St. Ambrose, and it is significant that immediately after their reference to his teaching about the Mary-Church
typology, the Council Fathers refer once again to the "new Eve" (cf.
LG 63, which was quoted earlier in this chapter). Both the Mary-
Church and the Eve-Mary analogies seem to be closely connected in the
conciliar teaching. This most ancient Marian theme still enjoys considerable relevance in contemporary Mariology.

St. Irenaeus had developed the "New Eve" symbol for Mary to
such perfection in his theological reflections upon the sacred Scriptures
that the future Fathers had but to appropriate it in their own writings.[4]
They do, however, extend its application to their meditations upon other parts of the Bible besides the temptation scene in Genesis and the
Annunciation scene in Luke. In a homily on the birth of Christ, St.
John Chrysostom extends the analogy from the Annunciation to the
cross on Calvary:

Of old the devil deceived Eve, who was a virgin; for this reason
Gabriel brought good tidings to Mary, who was a virgin. But
when Eve was deceived, she brought forth a word that was the
cause of death; when the glad tidings were brought to Mary, she
gave birth in flesh to the Word, the author for us of life eternal.
Eve's word made known the wood, through which it cast Adam

from paradise; but the Word from the Virgin made known the cross, through which he brought the robber into paradise in place of Adam. (MG 56, 392-393)

Note that the same principle of *recircumlatio* is at work in which the evil from Eve's word and the tree of paradise, which made an outcast of Adam, is being undone by the good from Mary's Word incarnate on the cross, paradoxically leading one who was a thief (the "good thief" crucified with Jesus) into paradise (cf. Luke 23:43). For St. John Chrysostom (354-407, cf. TH 198-199), the symbols of our defeat — a virgin (Eve), the wood (tree of paradise), and death (loss of immortality) — became the symbols of our victory in the Virgin Mary: the wood of the cross, and the redeeming death of Christ that restored our life.

St. Germanus of Constantinople (c. 635-733; cf. TH 156-157), who was a devoted supporter of devotion to Mary there, preached in a homily on the Dormition of the Virgin:

> Indeed you are the Mother of true life, the leaven of Adam's re-creation, Eve's freedom from reproach. She was the mother of dust, and you of light; hers the womb of death, yours of immortality; she, the dwelling place of death, you the transition from death. (MG 98, 349)

With St. Germanus, the age of the Fathers was coming toward a conclusion, and so the "New Eve" image of Mary had spanned the patristic tradition. As we shall see in our consideration of other aspects of Marian doctrine and devotion, it was a period of great development. And this is because the sacred Scriptures were the source not only of theological reflection but also of liturgical celebration in which the fuller meaning of God's revealing Word became audible to the faithful.

Surely out of the Church of the Fathers came the conviction of faith: "death through Eve, life through Mary," as witnessed by St. Jerome (c. 347-420; cf. TH 195-197, ML 22, 408), St. Augustine (354-430; cf. TH 63-66, ML 38, 335), St. Cyril of Jerusalem (d. 387; cf. TH 114-115, MG 33, 741 AB), and St. John Damascene (c. 675-750; cf. TH 199-201, MG 96, 728).

Later Usage of the "New Eve" Image in the Tradition

Between the fifth and early thirteenth centuries, two hundred texts have been identified containing the Eve-Mary contrast (cf. TH 139-141). One contribution made to its development by the Latin Church was the adaptation of Genesis 2:18, "a helper like unto himself," to Mary. Hermann of Tournai (d. c. 1147; cf. TH 383) seems to have been the pioneer in this insight, and an entire doctrine about the auxiliary role of Mary in our redemption followed from it. St. Bernard (1090-1153; cf. TH 75-76) preached in a sermon on Revelation 12:1, *In signum magnum (On the great portent)*, in which he shows Mary's role in the plan of salvation starting with the antithesis between Adam-Eve and Christ-Mary: "We need a mediator to the Mediator and there is none more beneficial to us than Mary. Eve was cruel, and through her the ancient serpent gave baneful poison to the man; but Mary is faithful who provided the remedy of salvation to men and women" (*in St. B. Omnia Opera*, ed. by J. Leclercq & H. Rochais, V, 263). Although Bernard admits that the "woman" of Revelation 12 is the Church, he believes that the vision can also be applied to Mary "with no inconvenience." He adjusts the biblical imagery a bit, and says that "the woman placed between the sun and moon is Mary set between Christ and his Church" (*op. cit.*, V, 265).

During the last century the Eve-Mary typology was used by the outstanding German theologian Matthias J. Scheeben (1835-1888; cf. TH 318-320). He draws upon the medieval adaptation of Genesis 2:18, "a helper like unto himself" to Mary to establish his theory that she is the bridal mother of Christ. The fundamental principle of his Mariology is that Christ gave himself to Mary not only as her Son but also as her Bridegroom (*Mariology* I, 162-163).

Also in the last century, John Henry Cardinal Newman (1801-1890; cf. TH 262-266) made extensive use of the New Eve image. His Mariology will be applied in several other parts of this book. For him, as an outstanding patristics scholar, he appealed to the Eve-Mary typology as the great "rudimental teaching" of the Fathers about the role of the Lord's mother in our restoration (cf. his *Letter to Dr. Pusey* in defense of Catholic belief and practice). Newman believed that the Immaculate Conception and Assumption are doctrines that follow directly from Mary's position as the New Eve," which is part of the tradition handed down from the Apostles.'

In the papal teaching of the past century, Pius IX referred to the Eve-Mary comparison when defining the dogma of the Immaculate Conception on December 8, 1854. It is Pope Pius XII who contributed to the typology in a special way prior to Vatican II. He made considerable use of the "New Eve" image in his Marian teaching in *Mystici Corporis Christi* (Encyclical on the Mystical Body of Christ, June 29, 1943), in *Munificentissimus Deus* (bull defining the dogma of the Assumption, November 1, 1950), and in *Ad caeli Reginam* (Encyclical on Mary's Queenship, October 11, 1954). Mary offered her Son on Golgotha, "like a new Eve, for all the children of Adam, contaminated through his unhappy fall" (Encyclical on Mystical Body). His teaching brought together both the New Eve and Woman of Genesis 3:15 traditions, and set the Eve-Mary analogy on Calvary instead of the Annunciation because he saw her compassion there as the basis for her role in our redemption.

CHAPTER VI

Ever-Virgin

IN THE Catholic Tradition, the mystery of Mary's virginity has been contemplated according to its three principal parts: her virginal conception of Christ *(virginitas ante partum)*; her virginity in parturition or giving birth to Christ *(virginitas in* or *durante partu)*; and her remaining a virgin after the birth of Christ for the rest of her life upon earth *(virginitas post partum)*. The usage of this triple formula became standard with St. Augustine (354-430; cf. TH 63-66, ML 38, 1008), St. Peter Chrysologus (c. 400-c. 450; cf. TH 284-285, ML 52, 521), and Pope St. Leo the Great (Pope, 440-461; cf. TH 217-218, ML 54, 195). And the expression that Mary is "ever-virgin" or always a virgin *(semper virgo)* became very popular after the middle of the fourth century.[1] As we shall consider in some detail during this chapter, Catholic faith and teaching about Mary as "ever-virgin" has been constant in the Tradition from the latter part of the fourth century on. And the Mariology of Vatican II clearly reaffirms that teaching: "This union of the mother with the Son in the work of salvation is made manifest from the time of Christ's virginal conception up to his death" (LG 57). ". . . then also at the birth of Our Lord, who did not diminish his mother's virginal integrity but sanctified it, the Mother of God joyfully showed her firstborn Son to the shepherds and the Magi" (LG 57). "Joined to Christ the head and in communion with all his saints, the faithful must in the first place reverence the memory 'of the glorious ever Virgin Mary, Mother of God and of our Lord Jesus Christ' " (LG 52).

It is significant for us to take note that the quotation within the last reference, "of the glorious ever Virgin Mary, Mother of God and of our Lord Jesus Christ," is found in the Roman Canon of the Mass or

Eucharistic Prayer I. This is especially noteworthy here because we wish to call to your attention that the mystery of Mary's virginity is a dogma of our Catholic faith by reason of the Ordinary Universal Magisterium, and not as a result of being solemnly defined as are the dogmas of her motherhood of God incarnate, her Immaculate Conception, and her Assumption. And the sacred liturgy, particularly the Eucharistic sacrifice, is the great organ of communicating the truths of the Ordinary Universal Magisterium in the Catholic Tradition.

A question that has been the special topic of theological discussion in recent years is whether or not Mary's virginity must be interpreted literally, i.e., as a historical fact; or does it do justice to our traditional faith to understand it as a special symbol, e.g., the virginal conception as symbolizing that Christ, because of his divine origins, has only one Father in heaven? Related to this issue is the scriptural exegesis of Matthew and Luke regarding the historicity of the virginal conception. Likewise, the proper interpretation of the "brothers of the Lord" in the New Testament poses a problem about Mary's perpetual virginity. And the real meaning of Mary's virginal parturition has also been the subject of theological debate during recent years. These problems will be addressed as they arise in various parts of the chapter.

Mary's Virginal Conception of Christ

Although this aspect of the mystery has often been called the "virgin birth," the term "virginal conception" will be used to avoid any possible confusion with Mary's virginity while giving birth to her Son. We recall to your minds the New Testament evidence for the virginal conception already considered in our comments upon Matthew 1:18-25 and Luke 1:26-38 in Chapter III. There is no doubt that these evangelists in the context of their infancy narratives understood it literally, i.e., as a historical reality, and not exclusively as a Christological symbol of the Child's transcendent origins from his one Father in heaven. We want to point out at once that such symbolism is present in the intentions of Matthew and Luke, but that they saw it based upon a virginal conception of Christ that was factual. As was clearly indicated in our comments on their texts, both evangelists revealed the mystery in a way that would avoid any pagan misinterpretations. It is the divine power of the Holy Spirit who comes upon Mary and over-shadows her that causes this "pneumatological" conception, and not through any preternatural transferences of male semen as found in pagan myths. Mary's coming to be with child is completely the mirac-ulous work of the Spirit of God in her virginal womb, and the Child, truly divine and human from the first instant of his conception, is the new creation *par excellence*. Patristic testimony to the virginal concep-tion as a fact came very early in the Tradition. St. Ignatius of Antioch (d. c. 110; cf. TH 177) was the third bishop of that ancient Church where St. Peter first established his chair before going to Rome. St. Ig-natius was his second successor and is called an "apostolic Father" be-cause his witness is during the lifetime of some of the Apostles. He died a martyr's death about the year 110. After the Gospels, he is the first to give written testimony about Mary. In writing his *Letter to the Ephesians*, one of the several that he sent while a prisoner on the way to his martyrdom in Rome, St. Ignatius asserts: "And the Prince of this world was in ignorance of the virginity of Mary and her childbearing and also the death of the Lord — three mysteries loudly proclaimed to the world, though accomplished in the stillness of God" (MG 5, 659). He refers to Mary's virginity as a distinct mystery, but his principal concern is Christocentric, in defending the mystery of the Incarnation against the Gnostic Docetists who denied that Christ had become truly human by assuming real flesh and blood from his mother's virginal womb.

St. Justin Martyr (d. c. 165), one of the apologists among the early Fathers and a pioneer in using the "New Eve" image of Mary, also gives witness to the virginal conception of Christ, seeing in it a fulfill-ment of Isaiah 7:14: "We find it proclaimed beforehand in the books of the prophets that Jesus our Christ would come to earth, be born through the Virgin and be made man . . . would be crucified and die, and be raised again, and ascend into heaven" (*First Apology* 1, 31; MG 6, 377-378). His testimony sounds like an early credal formula.[2] It is indeed significant to see how early the virginal conception becomes a part of the rule of faith.

The testimony of St. Irenaeus (d. after 193) to belief in the virgin-al conception is obvious from his witness to Mary as the "New Eve," which was treated at some length in the previous chapter. In his polemical work defending the apostolic faith against the Gnostic heresies, he describes barbarian tribes who do not have any written scriptures but only the Christian traditions that are inscribed in their hearts as believing ". . . in one God, the maker of heaven and earth and all things that are in them, through Christ Jesus the Son of God, who because of his outstanding love toward his creation endured the birth of the Virgin, uniting in himself man to God. . ." (*Against Heresies* 3, 4, 2; MG 7, 855f). Like Justin Martyr, he was familiar with the brief baptismal creeds of his day, used in questioning the catechumens. He believed that Mary's virginal conception of Christ was a doctrine of the Church handed on from the Apostles and so considered it to be a part of what he called the "canon of truth" (*Against Heresies*, 1, 10, 1; MG 7, 549-552).

Tertullian included it in what he named the "rule of faith" i.e., a body of truth handed down in the Church by sacred Scripture and Tradition. He taught that ". . . this Word . . . entered into the Virgin Mary by the spirit and power of God his Father, was made flesh in her womb and was born from her as Jesus Christ. . ." (*De Praescriptione Haereticorum* 13, ML 2, 26). His "rule of faith" seems to be based upon a baptismal creed of Tertullian's time (d. after 220).

St. Hippolytus of Rome (d. 235; cf. TH 172), in his work, *Apostolic Tradition*, provides the first document that shows what appears to be a fixed creed in its integrity. In this creed there is another early witness to the faith of the universal Church in Mary's virginal conception of Christ: "Do you believe in Jesus Christ, the Son of God, who was born of the Holy Spirit and the Virgin Mary. . . ?"[3] And Origen (c. 185-254; cf. TH 274), writing a little later in the 230s, seems to be referring to a creed from his native Alexandria. He maintains, commenting upon John 13:19, that there are certain articles of faith which are absolutely essential, and the Church cannot pick and choose from among them, but must believe all of them. He includes the virginal conception among these articles of faith.[4]

The doctrine was made part of the creed promulgated by the First Council of Constantinople in 381. This creed has come to have a universal recognition that no other creed enjoys.[5] Its authority has been accepted both in the East and the West from 451 to the present day. The virginal conception of Christ by Mary was presupposed in the solemn definition of the *Theotokos* at the Council of Ephesus in 431, and was explicitly taught in the authoritative letter of Pope St. Leo the Great to the Council of Chalcedon in 451 (cf. DS 150, 252, 291-292).

The witnesses to the virginal conception in sacred Tradition, as Matthew and Luke in the sacred Scriptures, testify to the mystery as a physical fact, a biological reality that was miraculously accomplished by the power of the divine Spirit. The writings of the Fathers, the teachings of the councils, and the faith of the Church formulated in her creeds have been traditionally interpreted this way, and no authoritative judgment has been made to the contrary. The American bishops taught:

> The Virgin birth is not merely a symbolical way of describing God's intervention in human history, not just a literary device to convey the divine preexistence of the Word. Nor is the Virgin birth a human construct, as if Christians feared that the divinity of Jesus would be compromised by his having a human father. What really matters here is the matter in which God in fact chose to "send his Son in the fullness of time." We know what God has done, not only from the text of the Bible, taken in isolation, but from the Bible as read, interpreted, and understood by the living Church, guided by the Holy Spirit. Catholic belief in the Virgin birth rests not on the Scriptures alone, but on the constant and consistent faith of the Church. (BYM 44)

The proposal that the virginal conception may be interpreted only as a *theologoumenon* or *Christologoumenon* — i.e., purely as a symbol for the truth of our Christian faith that Christ was really divine as well as human from the first instant of his conception — is contrary to the way in which Matthew and Luke have been understood in the Catholic Tradition. On the other hand, once we have granted its historicity, then its symbolic value and spiritual significance are especially rich. The theological tradition from Augustine through Aquinas offers many reasons of fittingness for the virginal conception; e.g., Christ has one Father in heaven, and the members of his Body are born of a virginal mother Church through the spiritual regeneration of Baptism. As we have already discussed, such a Christocentric and ecclesiotypical em-

phasis is characteristic of contemporary Mariology. The factuality of
the virginal conception also is a safeguard of the spiritual understanding of the Incarnation as the completely gratuitous work of God, a reason why Karl Barth, the great Reformed theologian of our century,
held fast to it.[6] Finally, the use of such theological reasons of appropriateness for why God chose that his Son be conceived and born of a virgin should help remove any suspicion that the mystery implies a negative attitude toward the marital act. After all, Christ has inspired his
Church to celebrate marriage as a true sacrament that sanctifies the
conjugal union (cf. NCE 17, 691-692).

Virginity of Mary in Giving Birth to Christ

Matthew's infancy narrative (1:25) is careful to convey that Mary
remained a virgin through the birth of Jesus. This is important to the
evangelist, who perceives in her the fulfillment of Isaiah 7:14, which
has the "virgin" both conceiving and *bearing* the child. In the patristic
tradition Mary's virginity in parturition came to mean that she gave
birth to Jesus without losing her bodily integrity and without experien-
cing the ordinary pangs of childbirth. The teaching of the Fathers in
both East and West, however, did not reach any universal agreement
on the doctrine until the period between 375-425. The earlier Christian writers, particularly Tertullian, were concerned with the Gnostic
Docetists, who denied that Christ really assumed human flesh and
blood from our Lady and feared that the doctrine would play into their
hands.

In the year 390, the doctrine of Mary's virginity in parturition is
clearly formulated in a letter that was sent to Pope Siricius from the
Synod of Milan, signed by St. Ambrose (339-397; cf. TH 17-22) and
his suffragan bishops. The letter was to make public the true teaching
in the matter, since it was rejected by Jovinian and his followers, whom
Ambrose had expelled from Milan after he had fled there for support
following his condemnation in Rome. The following excerpts show
how the signers of the letter appealed to sacred Scripture and the faith
of the Roman Church as expressed in her creed, which they considered
the Apostles' Creed:

> Let them believe the Apostles' Creed, which the Church of Rome

ever guards and preserves inviolate. . . . This is the virgin who conceived in her womb and as a virgin bore a son. For thus it is written: "Behold a virgin shall conceive in the womb and bear a son" (Isaiah 7:14). He has said not only that a virgin shall conceive but also that a virgin shall give birth. Now who is that gate of the temple, that outer gate toward the east, which remains closed "and no one," he says, "shall pass through it, except the God of Israel alone" (Ezekiel 44:2)? . . . The portal is the Blessed Mary of whom it is written that "the Lord shall pass through it and it shall be closed" after birth, because a virgin did conceive and give birth. (*Epist.* 42, 4; ML 16:1125-1126)

The "closed gate" of Ezekiel became an important text for the biblical basis of Mary's virginity throughout the Middle Ages.

St. Augustine expresses his witness to the doctrine of the virginal parturition by saying very succinctly and clearly: "She conceives and is a virgin; she gives birth and is a virgin" (ML 38, 1319). Besides the frequent repetition of the teaching by Augustine, several Eastern Fathers of the fourth century assert it repeatedly, especially St. Basil the Great (c. 330-379; cf. TH 71), St. Gregory of Nazianzus (c. 329-c. 390; cf. TH 160), St. Gregory of Nyssa (c. 335-394; cf. TH 160-162), and St. Epiphanius (c. 315-403; cf. TH 134-136).

In 449 Pope St. Leo the Great wrote a letter to Flavian, the Archbishop of Constantinople, to prepare for the Council of Chalcedon two years later. In it he stated: ". . . she [Mary] brought him forth without the loss of virginity, even as she conceived him without its loss . . . [Jesus Christ was] born from the Virgin's womb because it was a miraculous birth. . ." (DS 291, 294). This teaching was wholeheartedly accepted by the ecumenical council, which would be an indication of the general acceptance of the *virginitas in partu* in the East and the West at the time.

Generally speaking, the Western Fathers emphasized the preservation of Mary's bodily integrity, while the Eastern Fathers stressed the aspect of her joy and freedom from pain in giving birth to Jesus (NCE 14: 693). Mary's bodily integrity in the virginal parturition was illustrated in the patristic tradition by comparing it with Christ's miraculous rising from the enclosed sepulcher, and with his appearance to the Apostles in the upper room when he entered into their midst through closed doors (NCE 14: 694). Is it a matter of faith that we interpret the sayings of the Fathers about Mary's bodily integrity literally?

This kind of question has received special attention in recent years, ever since a book by Albert Mitterer appeared about ten years before Vatican II which raised doubts about the manner of Christ's birth associated with the traditional teaching.[7] Mitterer was of the opinion that to deny the opening of Mary's womb and its ordinary consequences is to compromise the realism of her motherhood. His interpretation seems to empty the doctrine of any content in its traditional understanding.

Karl Rahner did attempt to confront the problem posed by Mitterer and preserve the truth of Mary's virginal parturition as a mystery of our faith.[8] Whereas Mitterer's theory would attribute birth pangs to Mary's bringing forth of Jesus, simply seeing it as an application of her perpetual virginity to the act of her delivery, Rahner avoids the concrete genetic details. He was convinced that divine revelation did not address such matters, but did try to explain the virginal character of her birthing Christ in a way that does give some conceptual content to the teaching. The virginity *in partu*, Rahner proposes, was the act of child-bearing by a woman who is the immaculate mother of the Word incarnate and so free from all sin and concupiscence. Each aspect of her experience of having a child must have been essentially different from those who are subject to sin and concupiscence. Rahner's theological theory, and it is nothing more than that, does seem to be in the tradition of the Eastern Fathers, who spoke of Mary's virginal parturition more in terms of the joy that she experienced.

To what extent we are bound to believe the genetic details of the traditional teaching of the Fathers about the virginity *in partu*, i.e., that Mary's womb remained closed in giving birth to Jesus, has not yet been authoritatively determined. One must be careful not to desert the theological level in favor of the biological in understanding the mystery. The Holy Office (now called the Congregation for the Doctrine of the Faith) on July 27, 1960, issued an instruction that cautioned against the unbecoming manner of discussing the problem ". . . clearly opposed to the traditional doctrine of the Church and to the devotional sense of the faithful" (NCE 14:695). In light of all this, it seems to me

that Rahner's approach is the most acceptable, since it both avoids any
unbecoming way of addressing the delicate question, and also proposes
content for the doctrine that is spiritually significant (cf. NCE
17:691).

Mary's Perpetual Virginity

Although the truth that Mary remained a virgin throughout her
life did not really come into prominence till the latter part of the fourth
century, there was considerable testimony to it for some time before
that. During the first part of the third century, Origen upheld the doctrine after his predecessor, Clement of Alexandria (d. before 215; cf.
TH 103), had also affirmed it. Although he does not consider a denial
of Mary's perpetual virginity to be heretical, Origen did regard it as
senseless and contrary to true Christian sentiment. A century later, St.
Hilary of Poitiers (c. 315-367; cf. TH 171) referred to those who reject it as "irreligious and very far removed from spiritual teaching"
(ML 9, 921-922). And in the East during the same period, St. Basil
the Great, though considering only the virginal conception to be a
dogma of faith, was teaching: "The friends of Christ refuse to admit
that the Mother of God ever ceased to be a virgin" (MG 31, 1468).

As has so often happened in the development of Marian doctrines
throughout the history of the Catholic Tradition, faith and devotion
were intimately joined in the growth of belief about Mary's perpetual
virginity. St. Athanasius of Alexandria (c. 295-373; cf. TH 61-62),
the great champion of the true apostolic faith about divinity of the Son
in the Blessed Trinity during the Arian crisis in the fourth century,
gave great importance to Mariology in his development of Christology.
In his *Letter to the Virgins*, Athanasius portrays Mary as their model.
This would greatly influence St. Ambrose, in the West, who is an excellent example of the debt owed by the Western Church to the East in
the theology of Mary (cf. TH 17). Athanasius was probably the first
among the Fathers to use the scene of Mary at the foot of the cross
(John 19:25-27) as an argument in favor of her perpetual virginity:
". . . because she was a virgin after having been his mother, he gave
her to the disciple as mother" (cf. TH 61). St. Epiphanius, also an
Eastern Father, defended Mary's perpetual virginity in his *Panarion*,

and condemned its rejection as "unheard-of insanity and preposterous novelty" (MG 42, 705). He is also the one responsible for introducing "ever-virgin" into the Eastern form of the Nicene Creed, and frequently uses the expression in his own writings. "Ever-virgin" became a very popular title for our Blessed Mother after the middle of the fourth century, and the period 383-392 provided an abundance of testimony in favor of her perpetual virginity.

Soon after the controversy with Jovinian, who had denied Mary's virginity *in partu*, Ambrose was confronted by the error of Bonosus, from a diocese in Illyricum, who was teaching that she had children after the birth of Jesus. This great Father and Doctor of the Church, particularly in Marian doctrine and devotion, met this challenge of the denial of Mary's virginity *post partum* by composing a letter for the bishops of Illyricum that was approved by his own suffragan bishops around Milan. In this letter, following Athanasius, he appeals to the argument based upon John 19:25-27, when Christ entrusted Mary to the beloved disciple, which would not have made sense were there other children to look after her. In his other writings, such as the *De Institutione Virginis*, he deals with other difficulties that arise in the New Testament regarding Mary's perpetual virginity, such as the "brothers of the Lord" (cf. TH 18).

Our consideration of such objections based upon the Gospels, however, will be mainly through the teaching of St. Jerome (c. 347-420; cf. TH 195-197). The Church singles him out as an outstanding Scripture scholar among the Fathers and Doctors of antiquity. His Marian teaching dealt mainly with the topic of our Lady's virginity. It was in the context of a debate about the superiority of virginity over marriage that was going on in his day, particularly around Rome. Jerome's part in the controversy, however, came to extend far beyond fourth-century Rome. It was a reply to Helvidius, who came out with a work that defended the equality of marriage and virginity. Helvidius held Mary's virginal conception of Christ as a model for virgins in the Church, while her normal married life with Joseph after the birth of Christ would make them a model for those called to marriage. This was his interpretation of the Lord's "brothers" and "sisters" mentioned in the Gospels and other New Testament books. Jerome's response is found in his *Book One against Helvidius on the Perpetual Virginity of the Blessed Mary* (ML 23, 183-206B). He argues, with even more than his usual polemical passion, that all the phrases selected in support of Helvidius's thesis are able to be interpreted in keeping with Mary's perpetual virginity. We read from his *Book vs. Helvidius*:

> But just as we do not deny what is written, we reject what is not written. That God was born of a virgin, we believe because we read it. That Mary consummated marriage after her childbirth, we do not believe because we do not read it. Nor do we say this in order to condemn marriage, for virginity is itself a fruit of marriage, but because there is no license to draw rash conclusions about holy men. . . . You say that Mary did not remain a virgin: even more do I claim that Joseph was also virginal through Mary, in order that from a virginal marriage a virginal son might be born . . . he who merited to be called father of the Lord remained virginal with her. (ML 23, 203AB)

Jerome interpreted the "closed gate" of Ezekiel 44:2 as a basis for his belief in the mystery of Mary's perpetual virginity, although the Fathers generally used it in reference to her virginity *in partu*.

With St. Paula and her daughter Eustochium, he founded monasteries in Bethlehem, and he was a pioneer in appealing to Mary as the special model for virginity in the Church. As time passed, this notion of the imitation of Mary would become more and more important. He had an interesting commentary upon Matthew 12:46-50: "They are my mother who each day beget me in the souls of believers; they are my brothers who do the deeds of my Father" (CCSL, 77, 100). He told Eustochium that she too "can be a mother of the Lord" (ML 22, 422). We shall see more about the calling in the Church to become spiritual virginal mothers of Christ in imitation of Mary when we discuss her spiritual maternity.

St. Jerome's theory that the "brothers of the Lord" in the New Testament really refers to his cousins, while it was the predominant explanation for a long time, can no longer stand the test of textual criticism.[9] If the inspired authors wanted to speak of the cousins of Jesus, they did have a Greek word for it and did not have to use "brothers" in order to do so. The explanation that seems to take this into account and still not run contrary to the traditional teaching about Mary's perpetual virginity is that "brothers" does really refer to those who were cousins of Jesus. They were cousins, however, on Joseph's side who came to live with the Holy Family when their own father died and so came to be called the "brothers" of Jesus by the people of Nazareth. According to this hypothesis, and it is nothing more than that, the mother of these "brothers" was Joseph's sister.[10] In this context, a theory that had gained some currency during the time of Sts. Jerome and Augustine attempted to explain the "brothers" as children of Joseph by a previous marriage. Both men clearly rejected this opinion because they were convinced of Joseph's virginity as spouse of Our Lady and foster-father of the Lord.

From the end of the fourth century, there is general unanimity among the Fathers that the doctrine of Mary's perpetual virginity is binding in faith. In the fifth century it was presumed at the Council of Ephesus, which defined Mary to be the *Theotokos* (Birth-Giver of God), and was explicitly taught in Pope St. Leo the Great's dogmatic letter to Flavian, which was accepted at the Council of Chalcedon. The regional Lateran Synod (649), whose acts were received by the ecumenical Council at Constantinople III (681), also witnessed to the teaching. Finally, in 1555, during the ecumenical Council of Trent, but not as one of its conciliar decrees, Pope Paul IV reaffirmed the Church's traditional faith in Mary's virginity "before birth, during birth, and forever after birth" (DS 1880). Vatican II's teaching was cited earlier in this chapter.

The doctrine about Mary's perpetual virginity in the Catholic Tradition clearly illustrates a development in the Church's understanding of her faith not explicitly found in her Scriptures. The fact that it spread during the same period as the spread of consecrated virginity in the Church, for the sake of God's kingdom on earth and in heaven, shows its deep spiritual significance (cf. BYM 50).

CHAPTER VII

Theotokos: the Birth-Giver of God

To CALL Mary "Theotokos," the Birth-Giver of God, is to give her the most glorious name that she has received in the Catholic Tradition. To call upon her by this name is to invoke her as Christians have been doing in their prayers for about seventeen hundred years. As Vatican II teaches: "From the earliest times the Blessed Virgin is honored under the title of 'Mother of God' (Theotokos), under whose protection the faithful take refuge together in prayer in all their perils and needs" (LG 66). In the footnote to this text, our attention is called to the ancient prayer "We fly to thy protection" (*Sub tuum praesidium confugimus*), which probably dates as far back as the third century (cf. TH 336). In this prayer, she is addressed as "Theotokos."

This Greek word is very difficult to translate into English. Most frequently it has been rendered into our vernacular as "Mother of God," which is accurate but fails to capture the richness of the original. "Birth-Giver of God," or "God-Bearer," or "Bringer-forth-of-God" have all been attempts to convey its meaning more fully. The first literary use of the term, as far as can be said with certainty, appears in Alexander of Alexandria (d. 328; cf. TH 13-14): "In these things we know the resurrection of the dead; of this the first fruits was our Lord Jesus Christ, who truly and not merely in appearance bore flesh taken from Mary Theotokos" (MG 18, 568C). He wrote this in 325 (cf. TH 342), and that same year took part with his deacon Athanasius as a champion of the true faith about Christ's divinity in the Council of Nicea. Athanasius, who succeeded him as Patriarch of Alexandria, shows some dependence upon his teaching in his own *Letter to the Virgins*, proposing Mary as "the example and the image of the heavenly life [virginity]" (CSCO 151, 72-76). After this time (325), "Theotokos" is found frequently in St. Athanasius and the Alexandrians, in Palestine with Eusebius of Caesarea (c. 260—c. 340; cf. TH 138-139) and St. Cyril of Jerusalem (d. 387; cf. TH 114-115), as well as the three Cappadocians in Asia Minor (Sts. Basil the Great, Gregory Nazianzus, and Gregory of Nyssa).

A similar problem to ours is found in trying to translate Theotokos into Latin. *Mater Dei* (Mother of God), *Dei Genetrix* (She who has borne God), and *Deipara* (Birth-Giver of God) have been the most customary in the tradition of the Latin Church. Etymologically, *Deipara* is the closest to Theotokos and is found in the Latin text of the title of Chapter VIII in LG as well as the reference in LG 66 quoted earlier. Ordinarily the original "Theotokos" is used in this book, with its occasional translation as Birth-Giver of God or God-Bearer.

The value of trying to determine the meaning of Theotokos as clearly as possible is that it helps us understand better the controversy which led to its formal definition at the Council of Ephesus (431). The controversy, which was essentially Christological, centered around Nestorius, who became the Patriarch of Constantinople in 428. The title of Theotokos had been in use for at least a century by then, but apparently he was asked to make a pronouncement on its suitability soon after he became the head of the Church in Constantinople. His ruling was that the title was less than appropriate and that "Christotokos" was proper and preferable.[1] He argued that to call Mary "Christ-bearer" would avoid the danger of "God-bearer," which makes her appear to be a goddess who has begotten divinity. Or it runs the risk of reducing the Son of God to a mere creature, as Arius did in his heresy, condemned in the previous century. Another fear entertained by Nestorious concerning the title "Theotokos" was that it could make Christ's humanity seem incomplete, which was the heresy of Apollinarius that had been also condemned the previous century at Constantinople I. His main problem was with the "communication of idioms," according to which whatever Christ did and suffered in his human nature could be attributed to the divine Person. And so it can be said that God was conceived, was born, suffered, and died. Of course, this was more than twenty years before the Council of Chalcedon (451), which brought much clearer precision to the formulations about the mystery of Christ's hypostatic unity and duality.

Those in Constantinople who favored the use of Theotokos as a title for Mary appealed to St. Cyril of Alexandria for help. He had been
the Patriarch there since 412. He did intervene in 429, but the details
of his controversy with Nestorius are well beyond the scope of this
book (cf. TH 111-113). Cyril sent a large dossier on the case to Pope
Celestine, and Nestorius had already given Rome a report of the debate
from his side. To support his own teaching, Cyril cites the authority of
numerous texts from the Fathers of the Church. He is the first to use
the "patristic argument."

When the bishops convened for the fourth ecumenical council in
the history of the Church, at Ephesus, June 22, 431, they made the following passage from Cyril's dogmatic letter to Nestorious their official
teaching:

> For we do not say that the nature of the Word became man by
> undergoing change; nor that it was transformed into a complete
> man consisting of soul and body. What we say, rather, is that by
> uniting to himself in his own person a body animated by a ration-
> al soul, the Word has become man in an inexpressible and in-
> comprehensible way and has been called the Son of Man; not
> merely according to will or conplacency, but not by merely as-
> suming a person either. And we say that the natures that are
> brought together into true unity are different; still from both
> there is one Christ and Son; not as though the difference between
> the natures were taken away by their union, but rather both
> divinity and humanity produce the perfection of our one Lord,
> Christ and Son, by their inexpressible and mysterious joining into
> unity. . . . It was not that first an ordinary human being was born
> of the holy Virgin, and then the Word descended upon that
> man; but in virtue of the union he is said to have undergone birth
> according to the flesh from his mother's womb, since he claims as
> his own birth, the generation of his own flesh. . . . Thus [the
> Holy Fathers of the Church] have not hesitated to call the holy
> Virgin Theotokos. (TCT 399, DS 250-251)

And so the glorious title that had been bestowed upon Mary by the Fathers and the faithful of the Church for at least a century, and probably
longer, was solemnly declared to be a dogma of Catholic teaching or a
truth revealed by God for our salvation in Christ. The entire passage

was quoted above in order to impress us with the fact that this dogmatic doctrine which proclaims "the holy Virgin Theotokos" is essentially and primarily a Christological dogma of our Christian faith. Obviously this does not mean that "Theotokos" attributes nothing to Mary, since it truly is her most glorious title to call her the "Birth-Giver of God." Rightly understood in the context of her holiness, it is really the main Marian idea or the central mystery about Mary. Rather, it means that both historically and theologically the Theotokos dogma is Christocentric. Cardinal Newman, after his very careful and prayerful meditation upon the witness of the Fathers, summed it all up very eloquently when he preached: "Her glories are not only for the sake of her Son; they are for our sakes too."[2] Indeed the meaning of "Theotokos" is for our sakes also, since to know the truth about Christ is for the sake of our salvation.

The principal concern of the Council Fathers at Ephesus, therefore, was that Christ was true God as well as true man from the first instant of his human conception in the virginal womb of Mary. To deny that she should be called "Theotokos" is to reject the mystery of the Incarnation, that the Word was really made flesh and dwelt among us from the beginning of his human nature, the start of our salvation in Christ. In Mary, the holy Virgin, he became one of us without ceasing to be himself divine, the Son of God as well as truly her Son. If this were not so, then the human explanation of the union of his divine nature with his human nature leads to a heretical misunderstanding of that intimate union between God and man in Christ. And so the teaching of Ephesus rejects any idea that Mary is merely "Christotokos," as though she bore a man who was somehow united with divinity later on by becoming inhabited by the Word of God: "It was not that first an ordinary man was born of the holy Virgin, and then the Word descended upon that man. . . ."

As has already been pointed out, the problem of Nestorius was with the "communication of idioms," whereby what is properly attributed to Christ's manhood can be predicated of God, e.g., that God is born of the Virgin Mary, etc. Because of the hypostatic union, or the mysterious unity of the divine nature and the human nature of Christ in the one Person who he is — the Son of God, the Word, the second

Person of the Blessed Trinity — even what could never be said about the nature of God becomes the deed or experience of God the Son, who assumed a human nature in the Theotokos. This marvelous mystery of Christ would become further clarified in the ecumenical councils that followed Ephesus, namely Chalcedon (451), II Constantinople (553), and III Constantinople (680-681).[3] And the dogma of the Theotokos continued to be a safeguard of the divine revelation regarding Mary's Son. The theological reflections upon this great mystery of the Redemptive Incarnation have contributed significantly to its meaningfulness in the Catholic Tradition. These further elaborations about the intelligibility of Mary as the Theotokos, in light of Chalcedonian Christology which clearly teaches that her Son's two natures are united in the Person of the Word, God's own Son, will be discussed in Chapter X.

The divine paradox proclaimed in Mary's *Magnificat*, that God has exalted the lowly and put down the mighty, and preached by her Son that the one who "exalts himself shall be humbled, and he who humbles himself shall be exalted" (Luke 14:11), has been verified of her both upon earth and in heaven. The solemn definition of her most glorious title, "Theotokos," although completely for His sake and ours, led immediately to a magnificent spread of Marian devotion throughout Christendom. St. Cyril preached at Ephesus what has been called "the most famous Marian sermon of antiquity," a few phrases from which are: "Through thee the Trinity is glorified; through thee the Cross is venerated in the whole world . . . through thee, the fallen creature is raised to heaven. . ." (MG 77, 992BC). This is indeed a clear manifestation of faith concerning the salutary power of Mary's mediation in God's plan of redemption. And so God raised the lowly Virgin of Nazareth to be the Theotokos, lovingly revered by all the faithful for the sake of Christ's glory and their salvation. Vatican II teaches concerning this spread of Marian devotion early in the Catholic Tradition: ". . . following the Council of Ephesus, there was a remarkable growth in the cult of the People of God toward Mary, in veneration and love, in invocation and imitation, according to her own prophetic words: "all generations shall call me blessed, because he that is mighty hath done great things to me (Luke 1:48)" (LG 66)

Roots of the "Theotokos" Dogma in the New Testament revelation

The Anglican priest and New Testament scholar Reginald Fuller has explained why "roots" is the proper word to use in this context: "We should look then, not to 'prove' the legitimacy of 'Theotokos' from Scripture, but rather to see whether there is any continuity between the Christological affirmations of the NT, especially in connection with Jesus' birth, and the later Christological doctrine of the *Theotokos.*"[4] In his excellent paper on this topic, delivered to us members of the Mariological Society of America at our annual convention in 1978, Dr. Fuller treated what the New Testament says about the origin of Jesus (represented by the *tokos* of *Theotokos*) and about the divinity of Jesus (represented by the *Theo* of *Theotokos*). He also briefly indicated how the New Testament revelation started a trajectory or line of development in the Tradition that paved the way to Ephesus.

There are a number of portraits of Christ or Christologies revealed in the New Testament. One may be called a "Son of David — Son of God" Christology which can be found in Paul; e.g., "[Jesus] who was descended from David according to the flesh, and appointed Son of God in power..." (Romans 1:3). Another pattern, also found in Paul, but in Hebrews and John as well, is the "sending-of-the-Son" Christology, e.g., "... God sent forth his Son, born of a woman ... so that we might receive adoption as sons" (Galatians 4:4-5). Paul combines both Christological traditions, so that it is God's Son who is being sent into the world, although his birth to a woman is primarily portrayed as a necessary prelude to his future role in our redemption. The virginal conception in the infancy narratives of Matthew and Luke also combines the "Son of David — Son of God" and the "sending-of-the-Son" Christologies, but in a way that more clearly identifies the origin of Jesus as the Christ or the anointed One, the Messiah. This may be called a "conception Christology," bringing us a step closer toward Ephesus in the New Testament developments. Finally, there is a "preexistence Christology," found in Paul, Hebrews, and John. Paul speaks of "the Lord Jesus Christ, through whom are all things and through whom we exist" (I Corinthians 8:6). Implied in the context of this verse is that there became flesh in Christ a preexistent reality which had acted at creation. Jesus is the incarnation of divine wisdom. Hebrews 1:2 combines this with the sending-of-the Son Christology by identifying the preexistent wisdom with the Son of God. In the prologue, John's Gospel takes us a step further along the road to Ephesus by explicitly affirming the divinity of the preexistent One: "The Word was God" (John 1:1). For the first time, *Theos* is predicated of the preexistent One.

Now what happened in the Tradition following the New Testament period is that the "preexistence Christology" was actually combined with the "conception Christology" of the infancy narratives. Although this had not been done by the inspired writers themselves, they did make possible their eventual convergence and so provided the "roots" of Theotokos. This is a good example of how dogmas may develop from the sacred Scriptures in the sacred Tradition under the guidance of the Magisterium. The Christological dogma defined at Ephesus in Mary's title "Theotokos" is in complete continuity with the inspired teaching of the Scriptures.

But a true development has taken place in the Tradition. The New Testament authors never found it necessary to predicate *Theos* of the *tokos*, or the One conceived and born of the Virgin Mary. But, after the expression had already been in use for at least a century, and probably longer, both in prayers and theological writings and regional formularies of the faith, St. Cyril and the others at the Council of Ephesus were called upon to give it a canonical status in the universal Church. They found it necessary to do so in order to confront the Nestorian crisis, which had raised questions and difficulties about the divinity of Christ from the beginning of his human conception in Mary. And not only did they have to respond to a question that had not been addressed to the New Testament authors, but they also had to answer it on the level where it was raised. This required what might be called an ontological Christology, in contrast to the functional Christologies characteristic of the New Testament. For the biblical revelation about Christ is primarily concerned with his messianic function, with what he did to accomplish our redemption. Later on, in order to meet the challenge of heresies and to safeguard the real basis for Christ's redemptive activity as true God and true man united in one Person, the teaching Church had to find a way that would express the nature of Christ. This ontological mode of speaking, characteristic of the early councils of the Church, became necessary when questions arose about the Trinity and Christ that could not be satisfactorily answered by who the saving God is *for us*. The human intelligence of the believer wished to know who this God is *in himself*, the mystery of his own inner life, the internal relationships of the divine Persons, and the meaning of the mystery that One of those Persons was made One of us in the womb of the Virgin Theotokos. Although such questions led to heresies, they are nonetheless questions which our minds inevitably and legitimately raise, and the teaching of the Church must be ready to respond to them.[5]

Special Significance of Theotokos Today

"In my opinion, we have yet to come up with a better title for Mary [than "Theotokos"] which would express more aptly and with such succinctness the revealing word of God about Mary's predestined place in salvation history."[6] I made that statement in a paper delivered at an international ecumenical conference on Mary in the Fall of 1981 at Canterbury, England, and still stand by it today. This is my conviction, for reasons that are not only ecumenical, but theological and spiritual. Because the three sets of reasons are intimately related, they shall be treated together.

It is no secret that the Eastern Churches, both Orthodox and Catholic, have a deep devotion to the "Theotokos" which they express especially in their liturgical celebrations. In the *Decree on Ecumenism* (*Unitatis Redintegratio*, UR), issued November 21, 1964, the very same day as LG, Vatican II states:

> In this liturgical worship, the Eastern Churches pay high tribute, in beautiful hymns of praise, to Mary ever Virgin, whom the ecumenical synod of Ephesus solemnly proclaimed to be the holy mother of God (*Deipara, Theotokos*) in order that Christ might be truly and properly acknowledged as Son of God and Son of Man, according to the Scriptures. (UR 15)

A glance at the ancient liturgical texts of the great Churches in the East reveals how frequently "Theotokos" appears. To take part in a liturgical celebration of one of the Oriental Rites means to hear this title of Mary as a constant refrain. And it is much more inspiring to do the latter, since liturgical texts can be fully appreciated only in the setting of actual worship for which they are composed.

The mere repetition of "Theotokos" in the Eastern liturgies is not what matters the most. Were there not a rich spirituality and theology behind the practice, it would mean very little. Let us listen for a moment to the reflections of Father René Laurentin, one of the Church's foremost Mariologists, concerning this custom:

> This is intuitively and fundamentally the position of the Eastern Churches. For them *Theotokos* is enough. Sometimes, even, they seem to think that the additions made to this by the Latins have done nothing but diminish Mary's true stature. It would be a mistake to imagine that they reduce her to her simplest expression. What they are doing is seeing her at her highest; there they pitch their tent. The best representatives of this tradition never seem to lose sight of the fact that Mary's virginity, conception in holiness, and assumption, as well as her present relationship with mankind, are precisely the virginity, sanctity, conception, and assumption of the *Theotokos*, or in other words, a particularly privileged illustration of the mystery of the redemptive Incarnation. However, let us not exaggerate. I am not arguing here for a mistrust of formulae, or for an impoverishment of concepts. There is no need for us to be ashamed of our Latin passion for explicit analyses. Nevertheless, do let us see these formulae, always, in their most essential, most theological, most Christological light, the light that shines in the word *Theotokos*.[7]

Such a serious testimony from an outstanding contemporary theologian of Mary merits our careful consideration. Greater emphasis upon the Christological dogma "Theotokos," particularly upon its true meaning in our living Tradition about Jesus and Mary, does not mean the elimination of other theological insights and devotional titles. But it does provide for them all a spiritual center of gravity about which they can cluster so as not to lose their real meaning and value for our Christian faith as a whole.

Ecumenically our Catholic belief about Mary as the Virgin Theotokos not only unites us more closely in Christ with our separated brothers and sisters in the Orthodox Churches of the East, but with those in the Anglican and Protestant Churches as well. When its Christocentric emphasis is properly portrayed, many of the difficulties concerning Mary in the Catholic Tradition are clarified, if not cleared up completely. One of the basic objections, namely, that we Catholics tend to attribute to her prerogatives which can belong only to her Son or the Holy Spirit, is more readily responded to by our renewed emphasis upon the centrality of Theotokos. The significance of this title is entirely so that we may live and worship out of the one true faith in Christ. Further ecumenical implications of Theotokos will be elaborated in the chapter devoted to Mary and the quest for Christian unity today.

One special theological quality of Theotokos is its concrete character, which helps us avoid making an artificial abstraction out of Mary's motherhood of the incarnate Son of God. As we know from tracing its historical origins, the term, along with the idea behind it, concretizes or coalesces nicely the aspects of the mystery of Christ and Mary that appear to contradict human reason. The temptation here is for the human mind to resolve that apparent contradiction by rejecting one or another aspect of the mystery, in this case, either Christ's divinity or his humanity. Theotokos has proven a most practical way for all the faithful, not only theologians, to preserve the truth of the mystery that Christ, the one subject Christ, is truly "Son of God" and "Son of Mary" as we say together in one of the penitential rites of the Eucharistic liturgy. The special spiritual significance of Theotokos, an immediate consequence of its doctrinal richness, is that we can never intelligently invoke Mary by this title without letting her inspire in us a deep desire for a more intimate union with God through her Son.

CHAPTER VIII

Chosen by God to Be the Holy Virgin Theotokos — the Immaculate Conception

IN MARY, God has chosen his own mother. How fitting that she be filled with grace from the first instant of her conception! From all eternity the Father predestined her to be the Theotokos, the mother of his own Son. Mary was an intimate part of the divine plan that the human race would be redeemed by the Word made flesh. To fashion her into the woman who would be worthy of the calling to be the Birth-Giver of God, the Father willed that she be most highly favored with gifts of the Holy Spirit. The third Person of the Blessed Trinity, the Sanctifier, filled Mary with his holy presence from the very beginning of her human existence in the womb of St. Anne. She is the master-piece of the new creation in Christ, the first fruits of his redeeming love. She is the Immaculate Conception. Although conceived by her parents, traditionally Sts. Joachim and Anne, in the ordinary manner, Mary was preserved free from original sin. No other human person in salvation history has ever been so graced by God. No other has been chosen and called to be the Theotokos.

The Apostolic Constitution *Ineffabilis Deus*, issued by Pope Pius IX on December 8, 1854, solemnly defined as a dogma of our faith that Mary is the Immaculate Conception. It offered many reasons behind the final papal decision that this is a truth contained in divine revelation for the sake of our salvation. The primary reason given was that Mary was chosen to be the Theotokos by the triune God.

> And indeed it was wholly fitting that so wonderful a mother should be ever resplendent with the glory of most sublime holiness and so completely free from all taint of original sin that she would triumph utterly over the ancient serpent. To her did the Father will to give His only-begotten Son — the Son whom,

> equal to the Father and begotten by Him, the Father loves from
> His heart — and to give this Son in such a way that he would be
> the one and the same common Son of God the Father and of the
> Blessed Virgin Mary. It was she whom the Son Himself chose to
> make His Mother and it was from her that the Holy Spirit willed
> and brought it about that he should be conceived and born from
> whom He Himself proceeds.[1]

This passage, although not a part of the actual definition of the dogma
but a prelude to it, links up nicely the mystery of the Holy Trinity with
that of the Theotokos. It places Mary in a very special relationship with
each one of the divine Persons. We might say that she is the most highly favored daughter of the Father, the virgin mother of the Son, and
the all-holy temple of the Holy Spirit. The final sentence of the statement makes clear that the Son himself, as the one true God with the
Father and the Holy Spirit, chose his own mother, and was conceived
and born of the Blessed Virgin Mary as a result of the action of the
Holy Spirit, who proceeds from the Son in the bosom of the Trinity. It
is always important for us to let our beliefs about Mary shed light upon
and deepen our faith in the central mysteries of our Christian faith.[2]

As we reflect upon the ways in which the dogma of Mary's Immaculate Conception seems to have developed in the Catholic Tradition, the other reasons behind its solemn definition given in *Ineffabilis
Deus* will be considered in the context of contemporary scholarship.
Let us look now, however, at the precise words of the definition to
know just what we are called to believe by our divine Catholic faith:

> We declare, pronounce, and define that the doctrine which holds
> that the most Blessed Virgin Mary, in the first instant of her
> Conception, by a singular grace and privilege granted by
> Almighty God, in view of the merits of Jesus Christ, the Savior of
> the human race, was preserved free from all stain of original sin,
> is a doctrine revealed by God and therefore to be believed firmly
> and constantly by all the faithful. (PTOL 80-81)

A number of truths are expressed in this definition (cf. TH 179-184).
First, the person of the Blessed Virgin Mary — i.e., her body and soul
united, and not the soul alone — is the subject of her preservation from
original sin; ". . . in the first instant of her Conception" signifies,
therefore, the very beginning of her existence as a human person, an
embodied soul, within her own mother's womb, and does not attempt

to define precisely when that takes place in the development of an embryo; ". . . by a singular grace and privilege . . ." indicates that this divine favor is unique in Mary and has not been bestowed upon another human person conceived in the course of salvation history. Then we come to that phrase in the definition which is of the greatest Christological and soteriological (theology of redemption) significance: this unique grace and privilege has been granted by Almighty God "in view of the merits of Jesus Christ, the Savior of the human race. . . ." Mary is truly redeemed by her Son, and, as we shall see in some detail, the problem that prevented many great saints and scholars over the centuries from accepting this doctrine was finally definitively resolved. The basic Christian belief that every single descendant of Adam (member of the human race) can be saved only through the redemptive work of Christ seemed to be at stake until it was seen that Mary's Immaculate Conception would not make her an exception. It was the notion of "anticipatory" ("in view of the merits of Jesus Christ") or "preservative" redemption in the Tradition that helped pave the way for the dogmatic definition. Finally, "was preserved free from all stain of original sin" means that Mary, through her Son's redemption of her by anticipation, was in no way contaminated by any effect that Adam's sin could have upon a human person.

In subsequent teaching, this doctrine has been reaffirmed on a number of occasions. On the 50th anniversary of *Ineffabilis Deus*, Pope St. Pius X issued an encyclical, *Ad Diem Illum* (Feb. 2, 1904, cf. TH 5), in which he recalled the dogma. Pope Pius XII in his encyclical *Fulgens Corona* (Sept. 8, 1953, cf. TH 151) repeated the entire dogmatic formula on the occasion of its centenary. He also spoke about the apparitions at Lourdes that occurred only a few years afterwards (1858), in which Mary introduced herself to Bernadette with the words: "I am the Immaculate Conception." Of course, this is a private revelation, and Pius XII was not using it as a source for the dogma as he did the scriptural, patristic, theological sources along with the devotion of the faithful to confirm the definition. Having himself defined the dogma of the Assumption just a few years before (1950), he showed the relationship between the two dogmas of our faith. Pius XII also took the occasion to share his thoughts about the appropriate ways to celebrate the Marian year that he had declared for 1954. Finally, Vatican II adopted the dogmatic formula of the definition: ". . . the Immaculate Virgin preserved free from all stain of original sin. . ." (LG 59). The most recent ecumenical council makes an earlier reference to the mystery of Mary's Immaculate Conception in the context of painting its New Testament Madonna: "Enriched from the first instant of her conception with the splendor of an entirely unique holiness, the virgin of Nazareth is hailed by the heralding angel, by divine command, as 'full of grace' (cf. Luke 1:28) . . . and to the heavenly messenger she replies: 'Behold the handmaid of the Lord, be it done unto me according to thy word' (Luke 1:38). Thus the daughter of Adam, Mary, consenting to the word of God, became the Mother of Jesus" (LG 56).

Insinuation of the Immaculate Conception in Scripture and Tradition

Is there really any basis for this dogma in the Bible? If not there, can we discover it among any of the Fathers of the Church? These are difficult questions, but we Catholics must be ready to offer some response to them, especially in this period of our history. Otherwise, it will appear that we lack a firm foundation for our faith in God's revealing word about Mary's Immaculate Conception.

From our own searching of the sacred Scriptures in Chapters II-IV of this book, we can readily reply that there is no explicit biblical revelation of the dogma as it came to be defined in the Church. Is the consequence of such a conclusion that we look for it in Tradition alone, apart from any reference to Scripture? There does not seem to be any such thing as "Tradition alone," any more than there is a "Scripture alone" without any reference to a living community of faith, worship, and mission in which those sacred writings reveal their real meaning. If we appeal to the traditional testimony of the Fathers in the early Church, we find that their teaching about the apostolic faith is grounded in the Scriptures. If we turn to the magisterial teaching of the Church, we soon discover that the dogmas defined are proposed with a biblical foundation. And so, even though we know that what we read in the Scriptures does not reveal the explicit content of the dogma of the Immaculate Conception, still we look there first to find what might have inspired the development of the dogma in the Catholic Tradition. As a contemporary systematic theologian asserts:

.. since the Church receives no new revelations, one must be able to show one way or another that the later dogmas really come from the deposit of faith, which was closed long ago, and that they have not been merely added to it. There is no need to demonstrate an explicit continuity. But human psychology contains much more than merely "explicit knowledge." Thus God let the sacred writers view Mary, for instance, under the unheard of traits of the ideal "Daughter of Sion," which had never been realized by Israel. Thereby he formally *suggested*, precisely by means of these traits of which the apostolic times were conscious, the later Marian dogmas. These are therefore formally and not just virtually *revealed*.[5]

The Marian dogmas are not "just virtually revealed" because they are not logically deduced from the revealed premises of what is explicitly and formally revealed in the Scriptures, as though they were the conclusions of a theological proof. They are formally revealed, but implicitly; i.e., what God has "suggested" or insinuated in what has been explicitly revealed. Such a distinction is necessary if we are to show in any real sense that they are doctrines revealed by God as the Magisterium declares them to be.

Let us now set about our task of examining what might be the biblical themes and texts that were the divine suggestions or insinuations which launched the development of the dogma of the Immaculate Conception in the Catholic Tradition. Again, we must bear in mind that this Tradition is not only one of purely intellectual reflection upon the archives of our faith in the Scriptures, but an atmosphere in which our faith grows through the experience of God in worship and mission.

The principal biblical references that have been invoked in support of the dogma are: Genesis 3:15, "I will put enmity between you and the woman, and between your seed and her seed; he shall bruise your head, and you shall bruise his heel"; Luke 1:28, "And he [Gabriel] came to her and said, 'Hail, full of grace, the Lord is with you' "; and Luke 1:42, ". . . and she [Elizabeth] exclaimed with a loud cry, 'Blessed are you among women, and blessed is the fruit of your womb!' " The Papal Bull or apostolic constitution *Ineffabilis Deus* itself made use of these references in its prelude of reasons for defining the Immaculate Conception as "a doctrine revealed by God." And Vatican II refers to Luke 1:28, the angelic salutation at the Annunciation, when teaching that Mary was "enriched from the first instant of her conception with the splendor of an entirely unique holiness. . ." (LG 56).

In Chapters III and IV we discussed the various New Testament Madonnas, particularly those of Luke and John, in light of the influences that such Old Testament themes as the "Daughter of Sion" (cf. Chapter II) might have had upon them. The question kept coming up as to whether or not the "woman" of Genesis 3:15 may have had any conscious connection in the intention of the fourth evangelist with his "woman" at Cana and the foot of the cross. Then the "woman clothed with the sun" appeared in Revelation 12, and we wondered about the possible Marian significance that she might have. And then there is the related question of whether or not Luke had the "Daughter of Sion" motif in mind when portraying his Madonna in the third Gospel and Acts. Although it is not possible for us to answer such questions with certitude regarding the strict literal sense intended by the inspired authors, we do believe that such texts and themes have come to bear a Marian meaning in the Catholic Tradition, and so in some sense a biblical basis for such a dogma as the Immaculate Conception. This seems to be at least implicit in Vatican II's teaching about the woman in Genesis 3:15:

> The earliest documents, as they are read in the Church and are understood in the light of a further and full revelation, bring the figure of a woman, Mother of the Redeemer, into a gradually clearer light. Considered in this light, she is already prophetically foreshadowed in the promise of victory over the serpent which was given to our first parents after their fall into sin (cf. Genesis 3:15). (LG 55)

The key phrase for our purposes is ". . . as they are read in the Church and are understood in the light of a further and full revelation. . . ." Certainly this is what Pope Pius IX had in mind when appealing to the Scriptures generally, and in particular to Genesis 3:15, since he refers to it in the sense that it came to have in the living Catholic Tradition. This includes very much, if not principally, the liturgical sense of the Scriptures, or the new meanings that they can receive in the context of worship. Being more sensitive to the critical methods of contemporary scholarship in biblical studies, the Fathers at Vatican II were more cautious in their reference to Genesis 3:15 than Pius IX and his collaborators could have been well over a century ago. The above quotation carefully phrases it by saying that Mary "is already prophetically foreshadowed in the promise of victory over the serpent . . . ," and does not speak as though it was in the explicit consciousness of the sacred scribe.

Without attempting to trace it precisely, the impact of the "woman" in Genesis 3:15, of the woman who is clearly Mary in Luke/Acts and John's Gospel, and of the "woman" who might have a Marian symbolism in Revelation 12 upon the faith-understanding about Mary in the Catholic Tradition has been considerable. She has come to be seen as the "exalted Daughter of Sion" (cf. LG 55) and the "New Eve" (cf. Chapter V) who was perfectly associated with Christ in his complete conquest of sin and death symbolized by the "serpent." For her to have been tainted by original sin, even for an instant, would have marred the perfection of her Son's redemptive act, since his own mother would have actually come under the dominion of Satan. As we shall soon see in greater detail, this seems to have been the way, very generally speaking, that the relevant biblical themes and texts gradually yielded their fuller meaning in the Tradition of faith and worship until the dogma became clarified in the explicit faith-consciousness of the Church teaching and the Church believing. The "sensus fidelium," or the testimony of the beliefs and devotion of the faithful, was most influential in the matter.

There are, as always, a number of theological ways to explain this process of dogmatic development in the Tradition. One way is the following theory.[4] The same Holy Spirit who inspired the sacred Scriptures is still active in the Church today. If he were not, the Church would cease to exist as the living Body of Christ in the world. And although the Spirit's guidance and inspiration is operative in a special way in the charisms of those called to be "shepherds" in their ministry of the Magisterium for the good of all the faithful, the whole Church is enlivened by his Pentecostal presence. Every one of us graced with faith in Christ is called to take an active part in handing on the Tradition. So, when there is adequate testimony, it seems reasonable to conclude that the same Spirit who inspired the Scriptures can also inspire us to make explicit truths of revelation that were originally only implicit, or divinely suggested and insinuated. We Roman Catholics believe that precisely what the Magisterium judges to have developed authentically from the Scriptures in the living Tradition of the whole Church is truly a dogma of our faith, a doctrine somehow formally revealed by God, even though only implicitly. It is not as though we were reading something into (*eis-egesis*) the sacred Scriptures, but it is truly inspired there, even though not in the actual intention of the original author. It seems that the Spirit, the eternal God who sees all things at once, put into the text or theme of the Bible a "prophetic expansibility" that has become explicit and clear in the course of the Church's salvation history. It is a genuine exegesis or reading *from* the text and not *into* it, because the Spirit, according to this theological theory, inspired an "objective dynamism" that would eventually move toward emergence into an explicit doctrine of our faith in light of the Tradition.

Now let us glance at the testimony of the Fathers that, at least implicitly, seems to support the development of the dogma. The New Eve image (cf. Chapter V) must have certainly contributed toward a Madonna of the early post-apostolic Church who was considered to have an intimate share in the total victory of her Son over Satan, the ancient "serpent." Since her contrast with the first Eve has already been discussed at length, especially in the patristic witness of St. Irenaeus, suffice it to call to your attention that the "New Eve" theme continued to have considerable influence in the early Tradition of the Church. It developed into the proverbial saying "death through Eve, life through Mary," used by St. Jerome (cf. LG 56). The holiness of the "New Eve" is unique.

Cardinal Newman believed that the Immaculate Conception, like the Assumption, is a doctrine that follows directly from this "New Eve" image of Mary. More than that, he considered it to be a part of the tradition handed down from the Apostles themselves. Although few others might go that far (cf. TH 180), still it is worth listening to this great theologian of the last century:

> St. Justin, St. Irenaeus, Tertullian, are witnesses of an Apostolical
> tradition, because in three distinct parts of the world they enun-

ciate one and the same definite doctrine. And it is remarkable that they witness just for those three seats of Catholic teaching, where the truth in this matter was likely to be especially lodged. St. Justin speaks for Jerusalem, the See of St. James; St. Irenaeus for Ephesus, the dwelling-place, the place of burial, of St. John; and Tertullian, who made a long residence at Rome, for the city of St. Peter and St. Paul.'

One does not have to go all the way with Newman's opinion about an explicit apostolic tradition for the "New Eve" image in order to attribute to it considerable influence upon the developments that eventually led to the dogma of the Immaculate Conception.

St. Ephraem of Syria (c. 306-373; cf. TH 132-134) appears to give some basis for Mary's Immaculate Conception when he writes in one of the *Nisibene Hymns*: "Thou alone and thy mother are in all things fair; for there is no flaw in thee and no stain in thy mother. Of these two fair ones, to whom are my children similar?" (Hymn 27, v. 8, in CSCO 219, 76). Ephraem, who deserves the title "Marian Doctor," uses the "New Eve" image abundantly, basically as the life-death antithesis. He clearly applies the "woman" in Genesis 3:15 to Mary in this context. He is probably the first to call Mary the "Bride" of Christ, ". . . along with the chaste [virgins]" (cf. Nativity Hymns, 11, 2 in CSCO 187, 61).

St. Ambrose, another Marian Doctor, says as a witness of the Western Church to belief in Mary's sinlessness (not explicitly freedom from original sin): "Adopt me, however, not from Sarah but from Mary, so that it might be an incorrupt virgin, virgin by grace free from all stain of sin" (ML 15, 1521). Seeing Mary in the "woman" of Genesis 3:15, he attributes to her a share in the victory over Satan won by her Son on the cross (cf. ML 16, 1400).

We find in the dispute between St. Augustine and Pelagius (cf. NCE, 11, 58-60) about the necessity of grace for salvation a significant reference to Mary's sinlessness that comes closer to our interest concerning her freedom from original sin. St. Augustine held that Mary was indeed free from personal sin because of God's special grace. But one of Pelagius's disciples, Julian by name, charged that Augustine was placing Mary in the power of Satan by not exempting her from original sin. The great Father and Doctor of Grace was convinced that all hu-

man beings conceived and born in the ordinary manner of the marital
act must inherit original sin. In his reply to Julian's taunt, he asserted:
"We do not deliver Mary to the devil by the condition of her birth;
but for this reason, because this very condition is resolved by the grace
of rebirth" (cf. TH 180). Because of Augustine's incomparable authority in the Western Church's Tradition, this text had a very negative influence on the development of the dogma of the Immaculate
Conception. For him, Christ was immune from original sin by the virginal conception, but Mary apparently was not, because she was conceived through conjugal intercourse. His belief is what we would call
today a theologoumenon, or theological speculation, about the way in
which original sin is transmitted. Augustine, however, evidently considered it an indispensible component of the doctrine of original sin and
the necessity of the grace of rebirth for all except Christ. In an earlier
response to the heresy of Pelagius, he had affirmed: "except the holy
Virgin Mary, about whom, for the honor of the Lord, I want there to
be no question where sin is mentioned" (*On Nature and Grace* 36, 42
in ML 44, 267). The later episode with Julian, however, would seem
to indicate that he held only for Mary's freedom from all personal sin
and not original sin.

In the East there was a development from the teaching that Mary
was graced with a special holiness to her complete holiness. Theoteknos
of Livias, a writer of the sixth century whose works have been found
only in the recent past, spoke of Mary in a homily on the Assumption
as "all fair," "pure and without stain," and "from pure and immaculate clay" (cf. TH 180). St. Andrew of Crete (c. 660-740; cf. TH
24-25) wrote more about Mary than any of the other Fathers of the
Church. Preaching a homily on Mary's Nativity, he said:

> Today the pure nobility of men receives the grace of the first
> creation by God and thus returns to itself: and the [human] na-
> ture that clings to the [newly] born Mother of the Beautiful One
> receives back the glorious beauty which had been dimmed by the
> degradation of evil, and the best and most marvelous new for-
> mation. And this new formation is truly a re-formation, and the
> re-formation a deification, and this restoration to the first state.
> (Homily I on the Nativity, 812A)

Andrew did not have the idea of original sin which prevailed in the

West at that time, and does not identify the conception of Mary as the time of her original holiness. On another occasion, however, he does preach that she was "deified in Christ, the image completely resembling the original beauty" (Homily I on the Dormition, 1068C). He is probably the first witness to the feast of Mary's Conception celebrated in the East on December 9, and he composed a Canon for the Mass. More will be said of this feast in our consideration of the development in Tradition. St. Germanus of Constantinople (c. 635-733; cf. TH 156-157), along with St. Andrew and St. John Damascene, completes the list of great Marian theologians of eighth-century Byzantium, the end of the patristic age. In a sermon on the Presentation, Germanus calls Mary "most pure," "surrounded by untouched and immaculate virginity," "wholly without stain," "holier than the saints," and "more glorious than the Cherubim" (MG 98, 292-309). It seems he saw no sin in Mary, not even original.

Looking briefly at the liturgical witness to the early development of the doctrine about Mary's complete sinlessness or holiness, we find that the feast of her Nativity was celebrated in the East at least by the latter half of the sixth century. Since, in the Tradition, only the birthdays of those considered sanctified at birth were recognized as liturgical feasts, this is certainly a testimony to the general belief that Mary was sinless at birth. Ordinarily it is the day of the holy person's death, the saint's "birthday" in the fullness of eternal life, that is celebrated as his/her feast day in the liturgical calendar, which continues to be the custom. The birthday of John the Baptizer is also celebrated in the Catholic Church (June 24), because of the popular belief that he was sanctified in Elizabeth's womb during Mary's Visitation. Now a feast of Mary's Conception did emerge toward the end of the seventh century. It probably originated in the monasteries of Syria and spread throughout the Byzantine world (cf. NCE 7, 380). The feast of Mary's Conception reached England about 1050, but was suppressed for a time after the Norman conquest under William the Conqueror, who reigned 1066-1087 following the famous Battle of Hastings. When the feast was revived, about 1125, an argument arose in which, for the first time, there was critical discussion about the theological meaning of the feast. This discussion gradually brought the doctrine of the Immaculate Conception to general attention. Before this the discussion had been whether or not it was right to celebrate the new feast, which did not represent Mary's conception as immaculate, but honored the event and came to signify that she was sanctified sometime before her birth. The feast did spread, after its revival in England, into Normandy, France, Belgium, Spain, and Germany, and provided the foundation for the development of the doctrine which is always indispensible, namely, the *sensus fidelium*, the belief and devotion of the faithful.

Later Medieval and Modern Developments up to the Dogma of 1854

The earliest extant defense of the feast and of the doctrine is found in a treatise *On the Conception of the Blessed Mary* (ML 159, 301-318) by Eadmer (c. 1060/640; cf. TH 125-126), an English monk and close associate of St. Anselm of Canterbury (1033-1109; cf. TH 33-34). For a long time this treatise was erroneously attributed to Anselm. In it Eadmer considers that the devotion of the faithful is a better guide than the learned who were opposing the feast. After all, he argued, if Jeremiah and John the Baptizer were sanctified in the womb, "who would dare say that the unique propitiation of the whole world and the unique and sweetest resting-place of the only Son of almighty God was in the beginning of her conception deprived of the grace and illumination of the Holy Spirit." He had to combat the Augustinian idea that original sin is transmitted by the concupiscence that is inherent in the marital act. God could certainly will that Mary be conceived amidst the thorns of sinful concupiscence without being harmed, and the holiness of Jesus requires that his mother have a holy beginning. And he argued further that God, who kept the good angels sinless, must be capable of preserving from all sin his own mother. In his other work, *On the Excellence of the Virgin Mary*, Eadmer teaches that Mary was redeemed by Christ: "But God who assumed a man from your most chaste flesh did this for your and our common salvation" (ML 159, 580A). Even though it was to take several more centuries before the doctrinal difficulties could be resolved concerning the mystery, Eadmer's insights made a significant contribution to the development of the Immaculate Conception in the Church, especially through his contact with the belief and devotion of the faithful in promoting the feast of Mary's Immaculate Conception.

A very influential man of the time, and deservedly so, who opposed both the feast and the doctrine, was St. Bernard of Clairvaux (1090-1153; cf. TH 75-76). In 1138 he wrote a letter to the canons of Lyons calling them to task for celebrating the feast of Mary's Conception. Although he held that Mary was sanctified before her birth, he could not see how it was possible for her to have been immaculately conceived because of the Augustinian idea that original sin is inescapably transmitted by the concupiscence of the marital act. He considered the feast contrary to Tradition.

Doubtless St. Bernard exercised great influence upon the outstanding scholastics of the thirteenth century who could not reconcile the Immaculate Conception with their theologies of Christ as the Redeemer of everyone, including his own mother. These great saints and scholars are Bonaventure, Albert the Great, and his Dominican disciple Thomas Aquinas, who taught: "Now it is simply not fitting that Christ should not be the savior of the whole human race (cf. I Timothy 4:10). Hence it follows that the sanctification of the Blessed Virgin was after her animation" (III, q.27, a.2). The theologians of the time were effusive in their praise of Our Lady's holiness and believed that her sanctification took place as soon as possible after animation (conception), but were unable to see how she could have been redeemed by Christ unless Mary actually incurred original sin, at least for an instant. Indirectly this did contribute to the development of the doctrine which would always have to be understood in such a way that Mary was really redeemed by her Son, and is no exception to his universal salvation.

Then there appeared on the scene the theologian who was able to untie the Gordian knot, John Duns Scotus (1266-1308; cf. TH 320-322). He was a Franciscan, born in Scotland, a teacher at Oxford and Paris. He came up with the formula that was able to reconcile Mary's Immaculate Conception with the universality of her Son's redemptive work. Although historical research reveals that others made their contributions, especially William of Ware (d. c. 1305; cf. TH 367), it is still generally agreed that the real breakthrough came with Scotus. The essence of his position seems to rest upon the perfection of Christ. As the most perfect mediator, Christ could perform the most perfect act of mediation. But this would not have taken place unless he merited to preserve his mother from original sin. The Blessed Trinity, he argued, is not perfectly appeased unless the offense of all sin is prevented in at least one case. And, unless it is contrary to the authority of the Church or Scripture, it is fitting to attribute to Mary what is more excellent. This actually makes her need for the redemption of Christ even greater, since she needed him to prevent her from contracting any sin. The concept of preservative redemption had clearly come into the consciousness of the Church. Once the formidable objection against the Immaculate Conception had been resolved, then the obstacle to the natural inclination of the faithful to believe it was removed. This did not mean the immediate cessation of all theological controversy, but the way was definitely open to the eventual definition of the dogma. At first the popes left the matter open for free discussion among the theologians. The controversy at times, however, became so acrimonious that the popes had to intervene for the sake of peace in the Church. In 1482 and 1483 Sixtus IV prohibited either side in the debate from accusing the other of heresy. This pope had given permission for a new Mass and liturgical office of the Conception, which was reassuring to those who favored the belief and devotion. It also inspired a great number of artistic representations of the Immaculate Conception, especially in Spain. There, Murillo (1617-1682) did his famous painting during the seventeenth century, when many requests were sent to Rome for a dogmatic definition of the mystery. The Fathers at the Council of Trent (cf. TH 345-346), when discussing the doctrine of original sin during 1546, made an exception of the Blessed Virgin Mary, although the majority of them did not deem the time opportune for a full definition of Mary's privilege. They said: "This holy Synod declares, nevertheless, that it is not its intention to include in this decree, where original sin is treated of, the blessed and immaculate Virgin Mary, Mother of God. . ." (DS 1515). The Council did teach in its Canons on Justification that Mary, "by a special privilege of God," was free from all sins, even venial sins, throughout her entire life (DS 1573).

During the next century, Pope Alexander VII (1599-1670) made an important contribution to the development of the doctrine of the Immaculate Conception by issuing a Bull on December 8, 1661, which clearly specified the precise object of the feast. The words that he used were essentially written into the actual definition of the dogma in 1854 (cf. TH 13). The feast was extended to the universal Church in 1708. The eighteenth century, however, was a quiet period. Then in the nineteenth, requests began to pour into Rome once again as the devotion to the belief continued to increase. The apparition of Our Lady to St. Catherine Labouré at Paris in 1830 helped considerably to further this devotion through the "Miraculous Medal," and so the final stage of development was accompanied by the widespread use of the prayer: "O Mary conceived without sin, pray for us who have recourse to thee."

Our American Catholic Church played an important role during the final decade before the definition. In 1846, at the sixth provincial council of Baltimore, the bishops decided to request the Holy See that Mary, under the title of her Immaculate Conception, be named Patroness of the United States. Pope Pius IX granted this request the following year (cf. BYM, p. 54).

In response to the worldwide movement in the Church to define the dogma, Pius IX issued the encyclical *Ubi Primum* on February 2, 1849, in which he asked his brother bishops two questions: first, he wanted to hear what they, their clergy, and their people believed about the Immaculate Conception; and secondly, whether these three groups in the Church desired the Holy See to define it. Of the 603 bishops who were contacted with the encyclical letter, 546 responded favorably; 56 or 57 were opposed, but only four or five held that the doctrine could not be defined; 24 were undecided whether or not a definition was opportune at the time; and ten proposed an indirect definition, which would not condemn the opposite view as heretical. Between this overwhelmingly favorable response, reflecting the *sensus fidelium*, the belief and devotion of the faithful, as well as that of bishops and clergy, and the actual definition on December 8, 1854, Pius IX proceeded very carefully in his preparations by collaborating with theologians, etc. As we reflect for a moment upon the main dynamism throughout the development of the dogma of Mary's Immaculate Conception, it might be called the "people's dogma" more than the "papal dogma." That dynamism, under the inspiration of the Holy Spirit, always active in the whole Body of Christ, was the devotion of the faithful. In his definition, Pius IX was actually using the charism of his office and ministry in the Magisterium to endorse the faith and practice of God's people in the Church.

Further Reflections upon the Significance of the Dogma

In an address delivered at a consistory held on the day following the definition, Pius IX expressed his prayerful hope that this great privilege of Mary would be a powerful means of helping the Church to overcome the errors of the time. These were essentially the denial of sin, both original and actual, as well as the secularistic rejection of the need for redemption. No dogma should ever be viewed in isolation from the Church's faith and morals as a whole, particularly those truths and practices that are central to the Christian message for the sake of our salvation. And so, as Pius IX did in his day, let us meditate for a few moments upon the relevance of the dogma to the spiritual needs of our own era.

Karl Rahner was inspired to share his theological reflections upon the mystery of the Immaculate Conception in response to Pius XII's encyclical *Fulgens Corona* of December 8, 1953, in which the Pope announced the Marian Year in 1954. He especially called for sermons and lectures on the dogma in each diocese ". . . so that this Christian doctrine might be made clearer to men's minds." Rahner clearly affirmed: "Mary is intelligible only in terms of Christ. . . . It may indeed be said that a sense of Marian dogma is an indication of whether Christological dogma is being taken really seriously. . . ."[6] It is only in the context of truly believing that she is the Theotokos that one can accept the other Marian dogmas. Rahner, in anticipation of Vatican II's "hierarchy of truths in Catholic doctrine" (cf. UR 11), proceeded to show the connection of the Immaculate Conception with the primary truths in that hierarchy, namely, the Redemptive Incarnation predestined by the triune God. Of all the redeemed, Mary, the immaculately conceived, alone was included in that predestination with Christ, since only she was so intimately involved in the saving mystery of the Word made flesh. The consent that she was called upon to give freely at the Annunciation (Luke 1:38) engaged her cooperation in the work of universal salvation through her Son. The fact that she was "full of grace" made that freedom possible, but in no way diminished the voluntary responsibility of her consent. In Mary's preservative redemption, we behold the fullest revelation of God's redeeming love in Christ. In her, the graces of the Holy Spirit were totally uninhibited by the consequences of original sin such as concupiscence, which can spiritually split even the holiest among us (cf. St. Paul's "I do not do the good I want, but the evil I do not want is what I do," Romans 7:19). Mary, because she is the first fruits of redemption, sharing in her Son's total victory over Satan, is a completely undivided person who is able to give herself entirely to love of God and neighbor. In her, everything is grace, *sola gratia*. There is no guilt to impede her freedom to hear God's word and faithfully follow his will (cf. Luke 11:28).

Because of our faith in the mystery of Mary revealed in the dogma of her Immaculate Conception, we should be convinced that, thanks to the redemptive act of her Son, even in our sinful world grace has an absolute priority over guilt.[7] Even we who are conceived and born in original sin come into a world where the power of the triune God's redeeming love, totally victorious in her who was predestined to be the Theotokos, makes good concretely predominate over evil. The mystery of light is much greater than the mystery of darkness or iniquity in our world. Even before our baptism, our own being conceived immaculately and born again in Christ, we enter a history immersed in salvation in which "the light shines in the darkness, and the darkness has not overcome it" (John 1:5). Although we realize that redemption in the case of us sinners is a gradual process, and the complete sinlessness and holiness of Mary will not be ours until we are all united with her and her risen Son in heaven, still our belief in the Immaculate Conception fills us with great hope and expectation here and now. The grace of Christ that was entirely victorious in her from the beginning inspires us to be completely confident in and cooperative with the gracious God who makes all things possible (cf. Luke 1:37), even the Immaculate Conception and our sanctification. Now we turn to meditate upon the mystery of Mary's glorious Assumption, the final fulfillment of the grace of her Immaculate Conception.

CHAPTER IX

Mother and Son Reunited — Mary's Glorious Assumption

THE FULL blossoming of Mary's holiness, the first seeds of which were divinely sown in the grace of her Immaculate Conception, is revealed in her Assumption into heaven, where she has been most joyously and intimately reunited with her risen Son in glory. How fitting that the New Eve, who was so closely associated with the New Adam upon earth, be his face-to-face companion in their eternal home! Like the rest of us who are redeemed by Christ, Mary's grace was the seed of glory, which reaches its complete growth only with the light of glory and the direct vision of the triune God. She alone, however, insofar as we know with the certitude of our divine Catholic faith, has been taken up or gloriously assumed "body and soul," or in her total human personhood, into companionship with Christ in his risen humanity. What an appropriate reunion between mother and Son! Jesus, who took his human body from her at the virginal conception in Nazareth, now in the home of his heavenly Father welcomes her with the glorified body that she has received through his resurrection. His redemption of her is complete. Her glorious Assumption is the first fruits of his own glorification. As she had been immaculately conceived through her Son's foreseen merits, Mary is assumed into heaven after he has accomplished his Father's mission. And the Holy Spirit has finished his masterpiece in the Madonna of glory.

Let us immediately look at the precise words of the dogma of the Assumption as defined by Pius XII in the Papal Bull or apostolic constitution *Munificentissimus Deus*, November 1, 1950:

We pronounce, declare, and define it to be a divinely revealed dogma: that the Immaculate Mother of God, the ever Virgin Mary, having

completed the course of her earthly life, was assumed body and
soul into heavenly glory. (PTOL 524)

As in the previous chapter on Mary's Immaculate Conception, let us
first understand as clearly as possible just what our divine Catholic
faith summons us to believe regarding the dogma of the Assumption.
Then we shall survey the way in which it seems to have developed in
the Tradition and reflect upon its special relevance for our time.

We note that the Pope sums up all the traditional dogmas about
Mary as the subject of the definition: her Immaculate Conception,
motherhood of God, and perpetual virginity. ". . . having completed
the course of her earthly life. . ." is significant because Pius XII ad-
visedly left open to further discussion the question whether or not Mary
died, a question that we shall address in some detail shortly.[1] The definition of the dogma does not settle it. We are free to accept either
opinion — namely, that she experienced death, or that she did not die
before being taken up into heavenly glory.

". . . was assumed . . ." indicates that Mary, a creature redeemed
by her divine Son incarnate, was taken up into heaven by the power of
God. She did not ascend into heaven as he did through his own divine
power. The Assumption is different from the Ascension.

". . . body and soul . . ." means Mary's complete human personhood. As was said in relationship to her Immaculate Conception, the
subject of her holiness or freedom from original sin was in her person,
the substantial union of body and soul, and not the soul alone; so too,
in this mystery, she is glorified in her complete humanness, and not just
in her spirit or a separated soul. The dogma also seems to leave open
the question whether or not this privilege is unique to Mary, as is her
Immaculate Conception. Pius XII did refer to her glorious Assumption
as "the brilliant diadem that crowns her singular prerogatives" in his
address to the faithful who assembled in St. Peter's Square on the occasion of the solemn definition November 1, 1950 (PTOL 526). Theologians, however, are still free to discuss whether or not it is a singular
privilege in the sense that no other redeemed person, e.g., St. Joseph,
has been completely glorified by this anticipated resurrection of the
body. Of course, we have the certainty of faith only concerning Mary.
And even if others have been so favored by God, Mary's unique role as

the Immaculate Mother of God would give a certain singularity to her glorious Assumption.

".... into heavenly glory" refers to the mystery of a completely new way of life beyond the limits of space and time. The various aspects of this mystery are found in other dogmas and doctrines of the Church. What is important to realize here is that any attempt to interpret the dogma as a pure myth is contrary to its real meaning. It speaks of the historical person, Mary, who was truly glorified in the fullness of her human personhood ("body and soul") after her life upon earth was completed. It is a mystery that can be accepted only by the gift of faith, and so cannot be verified by empirical means. As one author has forthrightly put it: ".... the Assumption is outside the domain of the historian and of natural scientists. Television cameras at the time of Mary's passage from this world would have been useless."[2] Her Assumption is a reality for those with faith, those who do not restrict their notion of the real to that which is perceptible to the senses or exists in space and time.

Questions deliberately unanswered by the definition are: Did Mary die? If she did, where was she buried? And if she died and was buried, did her body corrupt; i.e., was it reduced to ashes? We shall address these questions as they arise in the course of our considering the testimony to Mary's Assumption in Tradition. But first let us see whether there is any biblical basis for it.

Insinuations of Mary's Glorious Assumption in the Sacred Scriptures

As with the dogma of Mary's Immaculate Conception, there is no explicit reference to her glorious Assumption in the Bible. But that does not mean that there is no biblical basis for it. We remind you of our considerations in Chapter VIII of the way in which a dogma of our faith might develop out of texts and themes of the sacred Scriptures, the fuller meaning of which comes to light only in sacred Tradition. Thus the suggestions or insinuations in the biblical revelation become explicit under the guidance of the same Spirit in the Church who inspired them originally. As Catholics, we do believe that the authority of the Magisterium is required to determine what takes place as authentic development in matters of faith and morals. But all the faithful have a hand in this process of helping make the divine suggestions or insinuations of the Scriptures clear and explicit. And so the beliefs and devotion of the faithful are an important witness to what is contained in the deposit of faith, especially in the Marian dogmas of the Immaculate Conception and Assumption which are there implicitly. It is in this sense that we are to understand Pope Pius XII when he teaches that the Sacred Writings are the "ultimate foundation" for any proofs and considerations of the Fathers and theologians regarding the Assumption (cf. PTOL 518).

In the apostolic constitution *Munificentissimus Deus* (MD), when discoursing about the reasons for holding the Assumption to be a "divinely revealed dogma," Pius XII appeals to the intimate association between the New Eve and the New Adam in that struggle "which, as foretold in the *protevangelium*, would finally result in that most complete victory over the sin and death which are always mentioned together in the writings of the Apostle of the Gentiles" (cf. PTOL 519). Once again we see the "woman" of Genesis 3:15 is brought into the picture.

The Pope pursues his argument on the basis of St. Paul's teaching: "When the perishable puts on the imperishable, and the mortal puts on immortality, then shall come to pass the saying that is written: 'Death is swallowed up in victory' " (1 Corinthians 15:54). Just as the glorious resurrection of Christ was an essential part and the final sign of this victory, so too Mary, who as the New Eve had such an important role in the struggle, should share in the victory over sin and death by the glorification of her virginal body.

When invoking the authority of the scholastic theologians in the Tradition, e.g., Sts. Albert the Great, Thomas Aquinas, and Bonaventure, Pius XII points out that they have always considered it noteworthy that "this privilege of the Virgin Mary's Assumption is in wonderful accord with those divine truths given us in Holy Scripture" (PTOL 505). He said that they recognized the truth as signified in Revelation 12:1, "the woman clothed with the sun" (cf. PTOL 507). In the same context he singles out "Hail, full of grace, the Lord is with you! Blessed are you among women" (Luke 1:28, 42). According to the Holy Father, the scholastic Doctors saw the Assumption as "the fulfillment of that most perfect grace granted to the Blessed Virgin and the special blessing that countered the curse of Eve" (PTOL 507).

As with the development of the dogma of the Immaculate Conception in the Tradition, once again we recognize that those biblical texts and themes that seemed to be most influential in the inspiration of the New Eve image have also provided the scriptural seedlings for the development of the Assumption dogma. In the last century Cardinal Newman, following upon his very careful examination of the Fathers of the Church, concluded that both Marian dogmas were implicit in the image of Mary as the New Eve.[3] Let us keep this in mind as we glance at the testimony of post-apostolic Tradition regarding Mary's glorification.

Survey of the Tradition Leading to the Dogmatic Definition of 1950

"Historically, the Assumption ran a smoother course than the Immaculate Conception."[4] This observation, made by Father Eamon Carroll, the outstanding Carmelite Mariologist, still does not mean that its historical course can be traced without considerable difficulty. We must bear in mind that the process from implicit to explicit teaching is a very gradual one and does not follow the laws of logic. Also, we must try to view the testimony of the Fathers and Doctors of the Church as much as possible in the context of their own historical concerns. Often enough, we shall be able to get at the substance of the dogma only through questions that they were explicitly raising, but which did not come to be defined in 1950, such questions as her death, burial place, and bodily corruption. And we must be especially mindful of the *sensus fidelium*, or beliefs of the faithful, which are reflected most significantly in the liturgy.

The earliest testimonies to the Assumption are liturgical. During the fifth century, Christians were already celebrating a feast called the "Memorial of Mary," which was patterned on the "birthday into heaven" of the anniversaries of the martyrs (cf. BYM 58). This feast was observed in the East on August 15, and eventually came to be called the *koimesis* (Greek) or *dormitio* (Latin) — i.e., the "falling asleep" — of the Virgin Mary. This expressed the deep faith of the early Christians in life after death and the resurrection when the body and soul would be reunited. For them, at death the body fell asleep and rested until awakened in the glory of eternal life. And so they looked upon the death of the saints and martyrs as the day of their "falling asleep" in the Lord, and joyfully celebrated it as their "birthday" into a new life (cf. NCE 4, 1017). It is interesting to note that our English word "cemetery" is derived from the Greek *koimeterion* which means sleeping chamber or burial place.

During the reign of Emperor Mauricius Flavius (582-602), it was decreed that the liturgical feast of Mary's Dormition, or "falling asleep," be celebrated on August 15 throughout the Byzantine Empire. And so the feast had evolved from the early fifth century "Memorial of Mary," which celebrated all her privileges as Mother of God, through the early sixth century, with the emphasis put on her dormition, or death, at a basilica at Gethsemane, Jerusalem, where popular belief placed her tomb. When the Emperor decreed that Mary's Dormition would be an annual feast throughout the empire, then preachers began speaking more clearly about not only her death but her glorious Assumption. In the Eastern liturgies of today, the feast is more commonly called the "Assumption" or "Journey of the Blessed Mother of God into Heaven," which celebrates belief in her bodily Assumption. Rome adopted the feast in the seventh century, and Pope Sergius I (687-701) called for the celebration of a procession on the feast. Under Pope St. Adrian I (772-795) its title became "Assumption" in place of Dormition. From its inception in the West, the feast centered on Mary's bodily Assumption.

Although the question of whether or not Mary died is still unresolved, the tradition appears to favor the fact that she did experience death. Besides the liturgical feast of her Dormition, the majority of the Fathers believe that Mary did die. All of the great scholastic theologians taught it. After the Council of Ephesus (431), apocryphal literature about the end of Mary's life upon earth began to circulate (cf. TH 58-61). Although this group of writings is historically and theologically unreliable, they have influenced the development of doctrine by providing valuable evidence of popular piety. They have had a special influence upon the dogmatic development of the Assumption, and we briefly call such legends to your attention insofar as they testify to the *sensus fidelium*, or beliefs and devotion of the faithful. One of these is the Pseudo-Melito document, which is often referred to as the *Transitus Mariae* ("Passage of Mary"). The author is unknown, but it was attributed to Melito, a bishop of Sardis during the late second century. In this literature there is general agreement that Mary died, but that her body did not corrupt. In some of these *Transitus* stories, as they are called, Mary is assumed into heaven while the Apostles are still staying in Jerusalem, while in others they are miraculously reunited at her deathbed after having dispersed. Mary's body just disappears, according to some accounts, while in others it is buried. In some the Assumption takes place soon after her death, and in others only after a period of time. Amidst this diversity, however, the *Transitus* stories all agree that Mary died a natural death and was neither martyred nor immortal. This seems to reflect the faith of the whole Church at the time.

Theoteknos, Bishop of Livias on the left bank of the Jordan between 550 and 650, speaks of the feast as the Assumption (*Analepsis*) and not Dormition (*Koimesis*). In a homily he said: "It was fitting that the most holy body of Mary, God-bearing body, receptacle of God, divinized, incorruptible, illuminated by divine grace and full of glory . . . should be entrusted to the earth for a little while and raised up to heaven in glory, with her soul pleasing to God" (TH 57). This is a clear patristic testimony to Mary's bodily Assumption (the dogma) as well as to her death and burial (not included in the dogma). By the eighth century, the doctrine of the Assumption was completely accepted in the East, taught by St. Germanus of Constantinople and St. John Damascene, the great Doctor of the Assumption, as clearly shown by his three homilies on the feast (cf. TH 200). Pius XII in MD (PTOL 502) quotes from his second homily: "It was fitting that she, who in childbirth kept her virginity undamaged, should also after death keep her body free from all corruption" (MG 96, 741B). Of her body, he says in the first homily that "it will not remain in the power of death and is not subject to decay" (MG 96, 716B).

In the West, St. Gregory of Tours (d. 593), borrowing the imagery of the apocryphal *Transitus* legends, said that Mary's body was "taken up and borne on a cloud into Paradise, where now, reunited with her soul and rejoicing with the elect, it enjoys the good things of eternity which shall never come to an end" (ML 71, 70B). In the so-called Gregorian Sacramentary sent to Charlemagne by Pope St. Adrian I (772-795), the entrance prayer spoke of the Mother of God, who "suffered temporal death, but nevertheless could not be held back by the bonds of death, she who brought forth your Son, Our Lord, incarnate from herself" (TH 57). But after such a promising beginning in the doctrinal development of the Western Church, progress became irregular. Pope Leo IV (847-855) decreed that a vigil and an octave be added to the celebration of the feast, but it received a setback when the Abbot of Corbie, Paschase Radbert (d. 865), published a letter that he falsely attributed to St. Jerome. In it, the Assumption was not denied but called into doubt. Unfortunately, part of this spurious letter, carrying with it the alleged authority of St. Jerome, became one of the readings in the Divine Office. Then a monk named Usuard (d. c. 875) furthered the doubts about the doctrine by publishing a Martyrology saying that the Church preferred pious ignorance to frivolous and apocryphal stories. It was not until the sixteenth century that Usuard's doubt was removed from the Martyrology, and Pope St. Pius V had the Pseudo-Jerome reading of Radbert taken out of the Breviary. But meanwhile both had had their negative effect.

On the other hand, another letter appeared in the early eleventh century, falsely attributed to St. Augustine, but by an unknown author, which favored the belief in the Assumption. Its reasons were based, not on fables or legends, but on doctrine. By the middle of the thirteenth century, devotion to Our Lady of the Assumption regained its strength. It was supported in the liturgy and by the teaching of the great Doctors, especially Sts. Albert the Great, Thomas Aquinas, and Bonaventure. During the sixteenth century, the feast became the greatest among the Marian celebrations, and one of the most prominent of the liturgical year.

In the apostolic constitution MD, Pope Pius XII mentions the names of many Doctors of the Church who followed the great thirteenth-century scholastics and promoted the doctrine. They are: St. Bernadine of Siena (1380-1444; cf. TH 77-79); St. Robert Bellarmine (1542-1621; NCE 2, 250-252); St. Francis de Sales

(1567-1622; TH 149-150); St. Alphonsus Liguori (1696-1787; TH 14-15); and St. Peter Canisius (1521-1597; TH 282-283). And Pius XII says that Francis Suárez (1548-1617, TH 334-336) held in the sixteenth century that the Immaculate Conception and the Assumption could be defined as dogmas of our faith (cf. PTOL 513-517 for these references). As he reflects upon the many and varied witnesses to the Assumption in the Catholic Tradition, the Pope apparently finds the strongest reason for defining it as a dogma in the "outstanding agreement of the Catholic prelates and the faithful" (PTOL 492). This, of course, resulted from the Ordinary Magisterium, or the constant teaching and preaching of the Church, which had nourished the faithful in their belief and devotion for centuries, especially through the liturgy.

The faith of the whole Church clearly revealed itself between 1849 and 1950, when an astonishing number of petitions for the definition of the dogma came to Rome from the various members of the Body of Christ: 113 cardinals, 18 patriarchs, 2,505 archbishops and bishops, 32,000 priests and men religious, 50,000 religious women, and 8,000,000 lay people. On May 1, 1946, just as Pius IX had done a century earlier, Pius XII issued an encyclical, *Deiperae Virginis*, to the bishops of the world asking them whether they thought that the bodily Assumption of the Immaculate Blessed Virgin could be defined and whether their priests and people also desired it. In response, only 22 ordinaries out of 1,181 dissented, but just six of these thought it was not a revealed truth, while the others questioned the timeliness of the definition. In the other categories there were among those dissenting: two out of 59 abbots and prelates *nullius*; three out of 206 vicars apostolic; and five out of 381 titular bishops. These statistics are indeed significant! It is no wonder that Pope Pius XII concluded that this universal agreement in the Church was a "certain and firm proof" that Mary's bodily Assumption is a truth divinely revealed and made the requisite preparations for its solemn definition on November 1, 1950.

Reflections upon the Defined Dogma of Mary's Glorious Assumption

Pius XII expressed his high hopes for the salutary results that the dogmatic definition, coming as it did toward the end of the Holy Year 1950, might have in promoting virtue in individuals and peace, justice, and freedom among nations as well as overcoming error and evil, especially for the many who still sit in darkness (cf. PTOL 473-477). Above all, he shared his prayerful aspiration that Mary defend the Catholic Church, falsely accused and unjustly persecuted in many parts of the world (cf. PTOL 478). And finally he hoped "that belief in Mary's bodily Assumption into heaven will make our belief in our own resurrection stronger and render it more effective" (PTOL 522).

Vatican II's teaching on the Assumption supports this hope:

> In the meantime the Mother of Jesus in the glory which she possesses in body and soul in heaven is the image and beginning of the Church as it is to be perfected in the world to come. Likewise, she shines forth on earth, until the day of the Lord shall come (cf. II Peter 3:10), a sign of certain hope and comfort to the pilgrim People of God. (LG 68)

The Council, in contemplating the dogma of Mary's glorious Assumption, continues its ecclesiotypical Mariology. It beholds in her glorification "a sign of certain hope and comfort" for the Church as a whole, as well as for her individual members. Perfect redemption in Christ, after all, is to be seen as primarily the bringing of the pilgrim Church toward its final completion as the heavenly Church. And Mary, glorified in her total human person, is already "the image and beginning of the Church as it is to be perfected in the world to come."

Karl Rahner, as he had done with the Immaculate Conception, reflected upon this defined dogma as "only really intelligible in the totality of the one saving Truth."[5] He related it "essentially and immediately" with two articles of the Apostles' Creed: the virgin birth and the resurrection. Mary, as the holy Virgin Theotokos, freely entered into the event of human salvation that initiated the divine work completed only in Jesus' resurrection and ours. It is fitting that she who, as the New Eve, took such an intimate part in that great event, also be perfectly redeemed by her Son. For us in the pilgrim Church upon earth who believe in the mystery behind the dogma, the conviction that the promise of perfect redemption has been fulfilled in at least one member of our Church is a powerful motive for our hoping to share in the resurrection of the Lord also. And again, as Cardinal Newman preached, "The glories of the Mother are for the sake of her Son, and for our sake too." Her glorious Assumption is a constant safeguard of our faith in the reality of his resurrection, and a sign of hope that we too shall rise again as he has already accomplished for his mother. Then, and only then, will the whole pilgrim Church be reunited in the Lord with Mary and all the saints and come to the final fulfillment of the redemption begun in her womb. In the meantime, living in the loving anticipation of our faith and hope in the resurrection, Our Lord's, Our Lady's, and our own, we can proclaim with Vatican II: "... in the most Blessed Virgin the Church has already reached that perfection whereby she exists without spot or wrinkle" (LG 65).

Vatican II, like the solemn definition itself, left open to further theological inquiry and discussion such questions as the fact of her death, the place of her burial, and the corruption of her body. The Council clearly declared that it did not intend to provide a "complete doctrine on Mary," nor to decide upon questions that theologians have not yet "fully clarified," and so the faithful are free to follow those opinions "which are pronounced in Catholic schools concerning her" (cf. LG 54).

Regarding whether or not she actually died, the "immortalists," those who hold that she did not taste death before being taken up unto heaven, argue that Mary's Immaculate Conception exempted her from the consequence of original sin that is death. Unlike her Son, whose death was willed by the Father for our atonement, there was no reason for her to die. Besides, it was most fitting that her most pure and virginal body, which bore the Author of all life and the Conqueror of death, not be subject to this penalty of sin. After all, she did have an important role in her Son's victory over the "ancient serpent," as prophetically foreshadowed in the "woman" of Genesis 3:15. She is the New Eve.

Respectfully recognizing the force of such argumentation, we so-called "mortalists," who hold that Mary died, still have the great testimony of tradition on our side. As has already been shown, the witness of most of the Fathers and Doctors, along with the relatively ancient feast of Mary's Dormition, or "falling asleep" (i.e., dying in the Lord), favor this theological opinion. In reply to the truth that Mary was not bound to death as a consequence of sin, contemporary theologians make a distinction between death experienced by the sinner and by the saint.[6] Accounts of the way in which very holy people faced death certainly indicate that they looked upon it serenely and not with terror as a penalty for sin. Their life of faith, hope, and love transformed the experience into a necessary condition for a human person to be born into a new life in the Lord. This was the deep conviction of the early Christians, who celebrated the death of the saints as their "birthdays," their "falling asleep" in the Lord. And so Mary would have indeed welcomed death as the way to be fully reunited with her Son. She, the sinless one, the Immaculate Conception, the all-holy Virgin Theotokos, was certainly not subject to death as part of the dominion that the power of Satan still holds over a sinful world. Pope Paul VI, in a homily that he preached only a year before his own death, declared his own belief that Mary died: "She died, in fact, but immediately crossed that abyss which led her to ascend to the fullness of life in the glory of God. Mary is in paradise. There she still preserves and multiplies her contacts with us. With the Lord she becomes the Mother of the Church, the mother of humanity."[7] It is especially significant that he preached this in a parish church on the feast of the Assumption. The faithful themselves believe that she also shared death itself with her Son, as a contemporary theologian asserts.[8]

Although today two places claim Mary's burial site, Jerusalem and Ephesus, excavations in 1972 strongly favor the Holy City as the location of her tomb. It is found near the Garden of Gethsemane, where Jesus prayed and suffered his agony, and, in fact, where a basilica was erected in the early Church and the feast of Mary's Dormition was celebrated. The recent excavations seem to corroborate the ancient tradition that Mary's tomb is in the Valley of Cedron (Kidron) very close to Gethsemane, and even make credible the *Transitus Mariae* account of her burial in the apocryphal Pseudo-Melito mentioned earlier. Even to this day the Greek Orthodox faithful celebrate the death of Mary with a procession from the Benedictine Abbey Church of the Dormition, located near the Cenacle in Jerusalem, to Gethsemane. Muslims, who honor the mother of Jesus, also take part in this procession.

Another question left open to further theological inquiry and dialogue is whether or not Mary's body underwent physical corruption. For the "immortalists," of course, this and the previous question about the tomb are no questions at all. Some theologians today would not exempt Mary's body from the general law that all human cadavers decompose in the grave. They argue that this in no way opposes the substance of the defined dogma since the glorified body does not require the material of one's body in this world, which itself changes periodically. "The corpse in the grave is not the body in heaven," as one recent author put it.[9] Mary's glorified body, as will be the case with the rest of us redeemed people of God, is a transformed human enfleshment of her soul, which really gives personal identity to the body whether in heaven or upon earth.

Other theologians, however, look upon Mary's Assumption as in the likeness of Christ's resurrection: her body did not decompose after her death and burial, they say, but was taken up to heaven intact. As we have seen from our survey of Tradition and from the constitution MD of Pius XII where he refers to its testimony, the theological opinion that Mary's body was not reduced to ashes has this authority on its side. The theological debate about the connection between an earthly body and its existence in glory will apparently continue for some time to come. And the Magisterium has left this question of general eschatology, or theology of the "last things," along with its application to Mary's Assumption, open to further dialogue. Regardless of the way it may be definitively answered, if it ever will be in this life, we faithful, and that is all of us in the Church, do not have to wait to have the assurance of our divine Catholic faith that Mary is glorified in her total human personhood, "body and soul." And as ever, this Marian privilege is "for the sake of her Son and for our sake too."

Vatican II, in one other part of Chapter VIII in LG, teaches about Mary's Assumption:

> Finally the Immaculate Virgin, preserved free from all stain of original sin, was taken up body and soul into heavenly glory, when her earthly life was over, and exalted by the Lord as Queen over all things, that she might be the more fully conformed to her Son, the Lord of lords, (cf. Apocalypse [Revelation] 19:16) and conqueror of sin and death. (LG 59)

The two principal theological reasons that Pius XII had given for defining the Assumption in his Papal Bull MD are based upon the fact that the filial love of Jesus for Mary most fittingly calls for their intimate reunion, and that Mary as the New Eve was so closely associated with Christ in the work of our redemption. The Immaculate Conception might be added as a third theological reason for Mary's Assumption, but is really implicit in the other two. She was graced to become the Immaculate Conception and the glorious Assumption only through the redeeming filial love of Christ, who chose to bestow upon her the role of New Eve, helper to him who is the "conqueror of sin and death." How much our world needs to contemplate in faith and hope our loving mother and Lord, her Son, united in glory and making intercession for us that we too may share one day in the resurrection!

CHAPTER X

Mary in the Theology
of the Church's 'Common Doctor'

AT THIS juncture in our meditation upon Mary in the Catholic Tradition, it would be helpful to reflect upon her place in the theological teaching of the Church's *Doctor Communis* or "Common Doctor," St. Thomas Aquinas (1225-1274; cf. TH 343-344). He is frequently also called the "Angelic Doctor" for such appropriate reasons as his angelic intelligence and purity and his outstanding tract on the angels in his monumental synthesis of sacred doctrine, the *Summa Theologiae* or *Summa of Theology* (I, qq.50-64). It seems more fitting, however, to refer to him as the "Common Doctor" in the context of our consideration, because that title emphasizes the fact that his theology has contributed to the elucidation of all the Church's doctrines.

Although the various aspects of St. Thomas's theology of Mary are to be found in several of his works, our consideration will concentrate principally upon his Marian teaching in his most mature writing, the *Summa of Theology* III, qq.27-37. He really does not have a separate tract on Our Lady, but inserts his treatment of her mainly into his Christological section, specifically on Christ's coming into the world. Only where it seems especially in keeping with our purposes will we consider what he has to teach about Mary in other sections of the *Summa of Theology* (ST) as well as his other writings.[1]

To understand better the nature of the ST, there are a few things we ought to know about it. First of all, as one author has very clearly and simply put it: "A *summa* is not an encyclopedia in which one may rummage for information on a particular topic without regard for the adjacent pages."[2] And so one ought to have some idea of the whole before examining the parts. Without knowing the wider context and logical sequence, it is easy to miss the real point that he is making in any particular question. The structure of the ST may be viewed as divided into three parts with the second further subdivided into two: I, II (I-II, II-II), and III. Each part is made up of many questions which, in turn, consist of a number of articles. Each article, in fact, is a question posed by St. Thomas, who begins by raising objections against the true answer, and then proceeds ordinarily to give a proof based upon authority (Scripture, Teaching of the Church or the Fathers) in what is called the *sed contra* or "on the contrary" portion right after the objections. Immediately following this in the "body" of the article is his theological reasoning for the reply to the question, and then the responses to each of the objections which further clarify his answer. The content of the ST under its most general headings is as follows: part I treats of God in the mystery of his one nature and Trinity of Persons from whom proceed all creatures, particularly angels and human beings made to the image and likeness of the triune God; II considers the return of human beings to God through their responsible activity elevated by grace; and III shows that the only way that we can reach God is through Christ and the sacraments.

St. Thomas Aquinas was a Dominican priest of the thirteenth century. He belonged to a religious order, officially titled the Order of Preachers, that has served the Church primarily through its ministries of the preaching and teaching of sacred truth ever since its foundation by St. Dominic in 1216. We should keep in mind that Aquinas wrote his theology during a period of the Church's history when reason was looked upon as inimical to the faith. And so, as a saint as well as a scholar, he wished to demonstrate that when reason is used rightly it can only serve the good of the faith, because the truth about natural things certainly cannot contradict the truth that we can know only through divine revelation. After all, God who is Truth is the Author of both grace and nature. Aquinas wished to make philosophy a particularly useful handmaid of theology, so that the truth of our Christian faith might be defended and nourished. If this is not kept in mind, then St. Thomas's theology might often appear to be rationalistic.

Our Lady is first considered in the ST when Aquinas asks whether God could have made things better than they are (I, q.25, a.6). The context of this particular question is the divine omnipotence. Although his answer to the question is basically affirmative, namely: absolutely speaking, God, whose power is infinite, can always increase the goodness of his creatures, e.g., he can always make a human being more virtuous, still St. Thomas further nuances his answer in his response to the fourth objection (ad4): "Christ's humanity, from being united with God, heaven, from being the enjoyment of God, and the Blessed Virgin, from being the mother of God, have a certain infinite dignity deriving from the infinite good, which is God; in this respect there can be nothing better, just as there can be nothing better than God" (I, q.25, a.6, ad4).

Along with what he teaches more specifically about the grace of Mary's calling to be truly the mother of God (III, q.35, a.4), this seems to be the most sublime and significant theological statement that the "Common Doctor" makes about her. He is saying that God has united humanity so closely with divinity in the Incarnation, the beatific vision (or seeing God face-to-face in glory), and in Mary's motherhood of God incarnate, that not even he himself can do better in his creative works; they have already brought Christ, Mary, and the blessed in heaven into such an intimate union with God, who is Goodness without limit. Such a reflection upon the "infinite dignity" of the divine maternity may well have inspired these words of Pius IX in his apostolic constitution on the Immaculate Conception:

> Wherefore, far above all the angels and all the saints so wondrously did God endow her with the abundance of all heavenly gifts poured from the treasury of his divinity that this Mother, ever absolutely free of all stain of sin, all fair and perfect, would possess that fullness of holy innocence and sanctity than which, under God, one cannot even imagine anything greater, and which, outside of God, no mind can succeed in comprehending fully. (PTOL 31)

The focal point of all his teaching about Mary is her grace to be a worthy mother of God. In the spirit of the New Testament writers and the great Fathers of the Church in Tradition, Aquinas contemplates Mary's motherhood as much more than a physical motherhood, but as a relationship with her Son which most fittingly called for a unique holiness and discipleship in the Christian life.

Sanctification of the Blessed Virgin

In the wider context of the ST, the Common Doctor begins his discussion about Mary between the general consideration of the Incarnation (III, qq.1-26) and his special examination of the main events in the life of her Son (III, qq.31-59). She is a bridge in his construction of the theological edifice that is the ST. That was her very role in salvation history, the woman who bridged the Old and New Covenants and stood at the beginning of her Son's redemptive activity. The work of our salvation began with the virginal conception of Christ in his mother's womb. In this part of his theological synthesis of Christian doctrine, Aquinas appeals to the authorities of our faith in a special way, first the sacred Scriptures and then the witness to Tradition of the Fathers, especially Augustine, Ambrose, Jerome, and Bede in the West, and in the East, Basil the Great, John Chrysostom, and John Damascene. Also he makes abundant use of theological reasons of fittingness which offer intelligibility and meaningfulness to the various mysteries of our faith, resting upon the fittingness of God's saving activity. He does all things wisely, and the human intelligence seeks to savor the divine wisdom. At the same time, we must always be mindful of our limitations and that such reasons of fittingness can never replace our need for faith, but should only deepen our faith-understanding.

Concerning Mary's sanctification in preparation for the Annunciation, when she is invited to be the mother of God's Son made flesh, Aquinas begins by teaching that she was sanctified before her birth while in her mother's womb (III, q.27, a.1). He points out as his reason the authority of the liturgical practice of the Church, celebrating only the feasts of holy people. And, since the Church celebrates the feast of Mary's birthday, she must have been already holy at the time of her birth, and so sanctified in the womb. Even though nothing is said in the canonical Scriptures on the subject, he argues that Augustine taught Mary's body was assumed into heaven without anything in the Scriptures on the Assumption. Here we must call your attention to the fact that St. Thomas, as a thirteenth-century theologian, would have been referring to the *Pseudo-Augustine* (cf. TH 299), which appeared about the beginning of the twelfth century in favor of the Assumption and was falsely attributed to St. Augustine. This does not nullify, however, the force of his theological reason of fittingness based upon the fact that she who gave birth to "the only Son of the Father, full of grace and truth" (John 1:14) should receive the greatest gifts of all. Besides, the angel greeted her at the Annunciation: "Hail, full of grace" (Luke 1:28). Since Aquinas believed on the basis of the Bible that Jeremiah (1:5) and John the Baptizer (Luke 1:15) were sanctified before birth, he considered it that much more reasonable to believe that Mary was made holy in her mother's womb.

In the second article of q.27, he asks: "Was the Blessed Virgin sanctified before animation?" As we have already discussed in Chapter VIII on the Immaculate Conception, St. Thomas answered this question in the negative. He said: "Now it is simply not fitting that Christ should not be the Savior of the whole human race (cf. 1 Timothy 4:10). Hence it follows that the sanctification of the Blessed Virgin was after her animation." Like his fellow great Doctors of the thirteenth century, St. Bonaventure and St. Albert the Great, his Dominican teacher, he could not see how Mary might be redeemed by her Son unless she had inherited original sin, at least for an instant after animation. He followed Augustine's theory that original sin was inescapably contracted in one who was conceived as a result of conjugal intercourse. And he also accepted Aristotle's genetic theory that animation, or human conception by the infusion of the soul, did not take place until the matter of the embryo and fetus was adequately disposed to be so "animated," which was well after the pregnancy had begun. The real reason, however, why he did not accept the doctrine which would eventually be defined as Mary's Immaculate Conception, namely that she was sanctified in the first instant of animation, is theological. Although he did not come to the concept of "preservative" redemption as did Duns Scotus, still his theological concern about the more important truth of the universality of our salvation through Christ had its influence upon the careful wording of the dogma, namely, that Mary was preserved from original sin ". . . in view of the merits of Jesus Christ, the Savior of the human race. . . ." There is some question whether Aquinas actually did come to hold the doctrine, as seems to be indicated in a sermon that he preached on the "Hail Mary" about a year before he died. We shall discuss this after completing our consideration of his Marian teaching in the ST.

The remaining four articles of q.27 (aa.3-6) may be summarized quite briefly for our purposes. It is worth taking note of the fact that the Common Doctor, deeply devoted personally to our Lady, wished to attribute to the mother everything that would not seem to interfere with the glory of the Son. His Mariological doctrine is completely Christocentric. He believed that the inflammable element within human passions that remains even after sin is removed, and which can burst into flames at the slightest provocation, was "rendered harmless" by reason of her abundance of grace received in the womb of her mother. Then this "inflammation of sin" was removed altogether when she conceived Christ, whose own complete freedom from it passed over to his mother. The Common Doctor, invoking the great authority of Augustine, the Doctor of Grace, taught that Mary was free from all actual sin, mortal and venial. His main theological reason is based upon 2 Corinthians 3:6 where St. Paul teaches that God gives the requisite graces to those whom he chooses for special ministries in salvation history. And so, Aquinas argues, since Mary was chosen to be the mother of God, God must have made her worthy of the office. This is primarily for the sake of Christ's honor, which would have been hindered even by a slight sin on his mother's part.

In a.5 Aquinas reasons theologically that it was fitting for Mary to receive a fuller intensity of grace than others because of her closeness to Christ, who "in his Godhead is the authoritative principle of grace and in his humanity is the instrumental principle of grace." In this context he gives his teaching that Mary brought grace to all, "in a certain way," by giving birth to her Son. We must be careful to take seriously his qualification, "in a certain way" (*quodammodo*). This text seems to have been misinterpreted often enough to mean that Mary herself has become a "principle" or source of grace which would put her on a level with Christ. Rather, no matter what theological categories we may use to describe Mary's role in the distribution of her Son's graces, we must be clear that her contribution comes completely through him, based upon her unique role of Theotokos, or Birth-Giver of God. In the same context of a.5, Aquinas attributes to Mary a threefold perfection in her spiritual development: first, her sanctification in the womb when she was disposed to become worthy mother of God; second, at the virginal conception of her Son, who completely freed her from any remains of original sin, and confirmed her in holiness; and third, the complete finalization of her grace in her glorious Assumption, when she entered into the delight of all goodness. St. Thomas also held that Mary's fullness of grace included to an intense degree the gift of wisdom, the charism of prophecy, and the power to work miracles. While it was not consonant with her calling to use all of these gifts as did Christ and the Apostles, still she did use the gift of wisdom in her contemplation (cf. Luke 2:19, 51) and the charism of prophecy in the *Magnificat* (cf. Luke 1:46-55).

Finally, in a.6 he draws a distinction between Mary and Jeremiah along with John the Baptizer, whom he believed were also sanctified in the womb. Only Mary was preserved from committing venial as well as mortal sin by her fullness of grace. The prophet and the precursor were kept free from mortal sin alone. He makes an interesting observation that, were there any other such "prodigies of grace" in salvation history, God would have made them known to his Church, since they are always for the sake of the redemption of others. This is indeed indicative of the Common Doctor's conviction that God's gifts, bestowed upon Mary or upon anyone called to serve his divine plans, are always for the good of all. God's most highly favored one is for the sake of everyone.

The Virginity of the Mother of God

The first three articles of III, q.28, treat of the mystery in accord with the traditional threefold division: virginal conception (a.1), virginal parturition (a.2), and perpetual virginity (a.3). The teaching of a.4 is of secondary importance as far as our Catholic faith is concerned. But it does provide an enlightened approach to the question about Mary's vow of virginity.

He appeals to Isaiah 7:14 just by quoting it as the basis of our faith about the virginal conception. He quotes only the words that are pertinent — namely, "Behold a virgin shall conceive. . ." — without adding any comment in the section called "on the contrary." He begins his theological argumentation in the body of the article with his asser-

tion that a denial of the virginal conception belongs to the heresy of the
Ebionites and Cerinthus in the early Church; they held that Jesus was
only a man, having been born of both sexes. Then Aquinas proposes
several theological reasons of fittingness for our believing the mystery
of Jesus' virginal conception: for the sake of his heavenly Father's
dignity, since, if he had a human father as well, there would be the
danger of attributing a divine dignity to him; as a testimony to the Son
sent into the world, that he is truly the Word of God, who proceeds
from the Father without any spiritual lessening, and so appropriately
proceeds from the Virgin Mary as the Word made flesh without any
physical loss of her virginal status; as a witness to the very purpose of
the Incarnation, that we might be born again as the children of God,
not out of the "urge of the flesh or will of man but of God himself"
(John 1:13). For this third reason of fittingness, he also appeals once
again to the authority of Augustine, who taught that it was appropriate
for the head to be conceived physically of a virgin to signify that his
members should be born spiritually of a virgin Church (cf. ML 40,
399).

Concerning her virginal parturition, Aquinas again invokes Isaiah
7:14, adding the words in this context, ". . . and bear a child." One of
the reasons of appropriateness that he proposes is based upon the effect
of the Incarnation, which is to heal humanity. How unfitting, therefore, if he who came to heal would harm his own mother's virginal integrity by coming forth from her. He also sees a reason of fittingness
for Mary's virginity in childbirth in the unique character of the Child
as the Word of God (cf. second reason, above, for the virginal conception). He explains the fact of Christ's coming forth from a closed womb
as having happened "miraculously by divine power" akin to the risen
Lord's passing through closed doors.

Concerning the doctrine of Mary's perpetual virginity (a.3), St.
Thomas offers four reasons of fittingness in its favor. He explains
them, however, only after invoking the authority of Ezekiel 44:2,
"This gate shall remain shut; it shall not be opened, and no one shall
enter by it; for the LORD the God of Israel has entered by it." And
once again he quotes from Augustine, who interprets the gate that will
be kept shut in terms of Mary's perpetual virginity. The first reason of

fittingness is in opposition to the error of Helvidius, who held that Mary and Joseph had other children after the birth of Christ. Aquinas points out how appropriate it is that the "only Son of the Father" (John 1:14), "the Son who has been made perfect forever" (Hebrews 7:28), "that he be the only Son of his mother, her utterly perfect child." On the other hand, how unfitting that the virginal womb, the temple of the Holy Spirit (the Holy of Holies) be "violated by sexual intercourse"! Thirdly, it would have been most unbecoming to the dignity and the holiness of the mother of God, since she would have been most ungrateful to want other children besides her Son, or to surrender her virginity, which had been miraculously preserved by God in the conceiving and bearing of her Son. Finally, it would have been extremely reckless of Joseph to have had relations with Mary after learning that she had come to be with child by the Holy Spirit. In addressing the scriptural difficulty about the "brothers of the Lord," he follows the opinion of St. Jerome that they were his cousins and not the children of Joseph by a previous marriage. Aquinas believed too that St. Joseph also remained a virgin.

In a.4 of the question on Mary's virginity, St. Thomas states that we should not think that she made an irrevocable vow before she was betrothed to Joseph, even though she may have been so inclined. Before Christ was conceived virginally in her womb, Mary would have considered the law which insisted that men and women have children to spread their religion as God's will for her. She waited upon God's good judgment, which came at the Annunciation. "Afterwards, when she had taken a husband, the acceptable thing to do in those days, she with her husband took a vow of virginity." Apparently, Aquinas was sensitive to the pious tradition that Mary had vowed her virginity to God at a very early age. And so he does admit that there could have been a "conditional" vow, i.e., on the condition that it would be pleasing to God. Only when she came to learn through revelation that such a vow was part of God's plans for her did she make it absolute.

Mary, the Betrothed Virgin Mother
of God and True Spouse of St. Joseph
St. Thomas offers several reasons of appropriateness for the fact,

clearly revealed in Scripture (cf. Matthew 1:18 and Luke 1:27), that Mary was betrothed to Joseph. It was fitting for the sake of Christ to head off his being rejected as illegitimate by unbelievers, to allow his genealogy to be traced through the male line, and to make Joseph his provider so that he might be called his father. The betrothal was also right for Mary's sake, to prevent her from being stoned to death as an adulteress, to preserve her reputation, to provide her with a helper. It was also helpful to us because Joseph became a witness to the virginity of his spouse in giving birth to Christ. It also makes her statement of virginity more credible, since she certainly had no reason to lie about the way she had become pregnant on account of the fact that she was betrothed. Both of these reasons, Aquinas asserts, "strengthen our faith."

The betrothal also symbolizes for us the whole Church, which is a virgin betrothed to one man, Christ, as Augustine teaches (ML 40, 401). Aquinas states the final reason for our sake thus: "The mother of the Lord as a betrothed virgin testifies to the good of both marriage and virginity. In this way the lie is given to those who would disparage either one" (III, q.29, a.1). In this a.1 he also explains that the virginity of Mary in giving birth to Christ, like the resurrection, is a miracle that is the direct object of our belief, and not the kind of miracle that confirms our faith, which is always more evident to us.

Having invoked Augustine's authority once again, this time to support his own teaching that the marriage between Mary and Joseph was a true marital union (cf. ML 34, 1071), Aquinas argues in a.2: "The form of matrimony . . . is an inseparable union of souls in which husband and wife are pledged in an unbreakable bond of mutual love, and the purpose is the birth and training of children. . . . [But] both [Mary and Joseph] consented to the marital bond . . . not expressly to sexual union. . . ." In the case of Mary and Joseph, he concludes that their union had the three good things requisite for a true marriage, and again he quotes Augustine: "Each marital good is found in the marriage of Christ's parents; the child, fidelity, and the sacred element. The child is the Lord Jesus, as we know; there was no adultery to destroy fidelity; or divorce to destroy the sacred element. The only element missing was sexual intercourse" (ML 44, 421).

The Appropriateness of the Annunciation to the Blessed Virgin

The Common Doctor's Mariological teaching in III, q.30, is particularly important for the spiritual significance of Mary's motherhood of God. His first question is: "Was it right for her to be told about who would be born of her?" (a.1). First of all, he points out how appropriate it was to "put first things first in this union of the Son of God with the Virgin, i.e., the enlightenment in her mind before the conception in her body." Here he makes two references to Augustine in support of this reason: "Mary is better for having conceived Christ in faith than in the flesh. . . . Mary would have gained nothing from her physical and maternal nearness to Christ if she had not first, and in a better way, conceived Christ in her heart" (ML 40, 398). The Annunciation gave Mary the opportunity to obey freely, and it shows that, at the moment of the Incarnation, a kind of spiritual marriage took place between the Son of God and human nature, and so Mary's consent, which was asked for, represented the consent of us all. Although Aquinas makes no explicit references to a homily, "In Praise of the Virgin Mary," by St. Bernard, apparently this reason of fittingness for the Annunciation was influenced by it. To quote briefly from St. Bernard's homily: "The price of our salvation is offered to you [i.e., Mary]. We shall be set free at once if you consent. In the eternal Word of God we all came to be, and behold, we die. In your brief response we are to be remade in order to be recalled to life" (*The Liturgy of the Hours* for the Advent season, December 20).

We pass over to a.4, which reflects theologically upon the fittingness of the actual account of the Annunciation (Luke 1:28-38). His general response, based upon the authority of Romans 13:1, is that all things coming from God are well planned, and the angel was sent by God. Aquinas points out that the angel had three things in mind: to call Mary's attention to an important announcement, which he did by greeting her in a new and strange manner; to instruct her on the mystery of the Incarnation, which he did by telling her about the Child's conception and birth from her, by revealing the importance of the Child, and even by indicating the mode of the conception; the third, by bringing her to consent, which he did by bringing in Elizabeth and the omnipotence of God. Responding to one of the objections about the apparent lack of faith or doubt in Mary's question to the angel — "How can this be?" — Aquinas primarily follows the interpretation of St. Ambrose. He considered that she was not doubting *that* the conception would take place, but was asking *how* it would (ML 15, 1558C).

These four questions in the ST (III, qq.27-30) come closest to what might be called a Mariological treatise or tract in the theology of Aquinas. And yet they are really more a part of his Christology and soteriology (or theology of our redemption). Of course, this does not make them any less genuinely Marian, but even more so. Her real meaning can be seen only in relationship to the mystery of Christ and our redemption by him in the Church. So Aquinas had anticipated the kind of Mariology taught in Vatican II. Obviously there have been many developments in Marian doctrines since the thirteenth century, especially in the development of the dogmas of the Immaculate Conception and Assumption. We still can learn much, however, from his content and approach in his theology of Mary.

The Common Doctor's Theological Elaboration of the Theotokos

Aquinas's Marian teaching in III, q.35, "the birth of Christ," appears principally in aa.3-6. In a.3 he wishes to affirm the fact that Mary is truly Christ's mother in his being born of her in time, which is opposed to the Gnostic heresy in the early Church, which held that his body was brought down from heaven and not really assumed from the Virgin Mary.

Having affirmed the reality of Christ's human nature, he then addresses the realism of his divinity in a.4 by asking: "whether the Blessed Virgin should be called the Mother of God?" In my opinion, his teaching here, taken in conjunction with I, q.25, a.6, is the most sublime and significant in St. Thomas's theology of Mary, as I pointed out earlier in this chapter. So let us examine it in some detail.

In his objections, he poses the problem that the Scriptures do not explicitly call Mary the "mother of God," and we should say nothing about divine mysteries that are not contained in biblical revelation. Furthermore, Christ is called God because of his divine nature, which in no way originates from the Virgin. Finally, it would make Mary mother of the Father and the Holy Spirit as well as the Son, since "God" is predicated of the three divine Persons.

Aquinas quotes from the writings of St. Cyril of Alexandria, whose teaching about Mary as "Theotokos" in his Christological controversy with Nestorius was approved as defined dogma at the Council of Ephesus (431). We have discussed all this in Chapter VII. His theological reasoning proceeds on the basis of Chalcedonian Christology:

> Now to be conceived and to be born are attributed to the person of hypostasis in respect of that nature in which it is conceived and born. Since therefore the human nature was assumed by the divine Person at the very outset of conception, as was stated above (III, q.33, a.3), it follows that it can truly be said that God was conceived and born of the Virgin. Now a woman is considered a man's mother when she has conceived and given birth to him. Therefore, the Blessed Virgin is truly called the mother of God.

The force of the "truly" (*vere*) here would seem to be that Mary is the Theotokos (*mater Dei*) in the proper sense and not in an extended meaning because motherhood is always a relationship to the *person* conceived and born of a woman. Mary's maternal relationship to Christ, therefore, is precisely to the second Person of the Blessed Trinity, the Son of God who became incarnate in her at the virginal conception and birth. Aquinas concludes by clearly asserting that the rejection of this doctrine inevitably leads to one or the other of two Christological errors: either the complete denial of the hypostatic union, i.e., the union of the divine and human natures of the one Person of the Word made flesh, or to the belief that the humanity of Christ was first conceived and born of Mary before becoming the Son of God. Both are utterly opposed to the teaching and faith of the Catholic Tradition.

In replying to the objections, he states that, although the Scriptures do not explicitly call Mary "mother of God," still they do affirm both that Christ is God and that Mary is his mother. And this responds to the objection of Nestorius. The reply to the next objection, another one from Nestorius, is the explanation that Mary is the mother of God, ". . . not because the mother of the divinity, but because she is mother of a person who has divinity and humanity." And although "God" is commonly attributed to all three Persons, we must determine from the context whether it is being predicated of the Father, or of the Son, or of the Holy Spirit. When we call Mary the mother of God, therefore, "God" can apply only to the Son, who alone became incarnate.

Other Marian Doctrines in the Theology of St. Thomas Aquinas

The two dogmas of faith from the Catholic Tradition about Mary at the time of Aquinas were her virginity and her motherhood of God. In keeping with the best in that Tradition, he reflected theologically upon these truths of divine revelation in such a way as to underscore their spiritual significance. For instance, he contemplated her graced consent at the Annunciation as representing the whole human race, since our salvation rested upon her consent to the wedding between divinity and humanity in the Incarnation (III, q.30, a.1). In the same context, it was the grace of her faith making her free consent possible that was emphasized. Here he is following the great tradition of the Fathers, epitomized in St. Augustine, that it was Mary's conception of Christ in her heart through faith that really gave dignity to her experience of being his mother in the flesh. Now let us glance briefly to see what other insights about Our Lady he may have to share with us.

Concerning Marian devotion, Aquinas is clear in his teaching that a very special form of honor or veneration called *hyperdulia* is due to Mary. He says that this kind of reverence "is offered to creatures having some exceptional closeness to God, e.g., to the Blessed Virgin, his mother" (II-II, q.103, a.4). At the same time he is very careful to avoid the error that *latria*, or divine worship, be given to Mary by reason of her divine maternity. This is due to the triune God alone and to Christ by reason of the hypostatic union, or the unity of his human nature with the divine in the one Person who is God the Son. And the *latria* shown for likenesses of Christ, e.g., a crucifix, does not terminate in the inanimate object but in the Person of the Word incarnate imaged by the crucifix. If one were to argue in favor of giving such worship to Mary, since the *latria* would not terminate in her but in her Son, Aquinas replies that this cannot be done in the case of rational creatures who are venerated in their own right. And so there would always be the risk of our falling into "Mariolatry" or some form of "idolatry" with any of the saints if we were to offer to them the worship or adoration of *latria*, which can be given only to God, Christ, or likenesses of the Lord. Aquinas teaches: "Accordingly, since the Blessed Virgin is no more than a creature and is rational, she must not be paid divine worship, but simply the veneration known as *dulia*; however, since she is Mother of God, this should be of a higher form than that given other creatures. For this reason the veneration paid her is termed *hyperdulia*, to indicate that it is more than ordinary *dulia*" (III, q.25, a.5).

In commenting upon the *Sentences* of Peter Lombard (Book III, distinction 4, article 1), St. Thomas explains why the virginal conception of Christ is appropriated to the Holy Spirit. Although, as with all works of nature and grace in creation, the three divine Persons as the one true God really act as one in bringing the effects into being, still it is salutary to speak as though certain works were proper to this or that Person, i.e., "appropriation." And so it is fitting to appropriate the work of the Incarnation to the Holy Spirit, who proceeds from the Father and the Son as their infinite Love One for the Other, because the Word becoming flesh for our salvation is the greatest revelation of God's love for us.

In his *Commentary upon Matthew's Gospel* (12:46-50), "Who is my mother? Who are my brothers? . . . Any one who does the will of my Father," he rules out any possibility that Mary was among the members of his natural family who may have been trying to "rob" the glory due to Christ alone. It is impossible to accuse her of this, since she never sinned even slightly. Christ in this passage from Matthew's Gospel, according to Aquinas, is not calling into question his mother's virtue, but is rather giving priority to spiritual generation over physical ("eschatological" family over the natural family), and is warning against inordinate attachment to relatives.

In his *Commentary upon John's Gospel*, the Cana scene, St. Thomas makes a number of significant observations about Mary. He suggests that Mary was invited as a neighbor and was asked about the appropriateness of also inviting her "religious" son to such a celebration. She assured them that a marriage feast would not be opposed to his "religious" spirit. Perhaps, he proposes, this is the reason why the evangelist mentions Mary first before speaking about the invitation to

Jesus. In it he perceives a mystical meaning, namely, that Mary's role in the spiritual marriage between God and a soul is to serve as counselor (*consolatrix*), because through her intercession the soul is united to Christ by grace. In the "sign" of changing the water into wine, Aquinas sees Mary's meditation involved in obtaining it, her own reverence for Christ in simply pointing out the need to him without demanding anything from him as a mother might do, and also alertness in noticing the need in time, as well as her being merciful in having compassion upon the host's predicament. Aquinas also seems to reject any interpretation of the words "O woman, what have you to do with me?" (John 2:4) as a rebuff of the mother by her Son. "Woman" is not a harsh form of address, since it is used elsewhere in Scripture.

Let us return for a moment to his teaching in the ST (III, q.2, a.11), where he inquires whether any merits preceded the Incarnation. This is a very important ecumenical question, since our sisters and brothers in the Protestant Churches often think that Catholic doctrine maintains that Mary merited becoming the mother of God by her free consent at the Annunciation and so, in effect, we believe that she "merited" the Incarnation. St. Thomas is very clear in his explanation why no one, not even Christ himself, could have merited the Incarnation. The simplest and most profound reason is that the Word made flesh, a completely gratuitous gift of God's redeeming love of the human race, is the source of all grace. And if we cannot merit grace itself, but only the growth in grace and its final reward in heaven once we've been given grace as a completely free gift of God's love, then certainly the very source of all grace in the redemptive Incarnation cannot itself be merited. Strictly speaking, it can be said that Mary, having been filled with grace at her Immaculate Conception, did merit becoming a worthy mother of God by freely and generously cooperating with the abundance of graces gratuitously given her by God in view of the foreseen merits of Christ's redemptive act. But she cannot be said to have merited the grace of that motherhood itself, which would be equivalent to saying that she merited the Incarnation of her Son. Aquinas does concede that Mary, and other holy people of the Old Covenant, may be said to have merited the Incarnation in the wide sense of "congruous" or "suitable" merit, whereby it was fitting that God responded to their prayers and yearnings for salvation by sending the promised Messiah into the world.

Finally, let us look briefly at the series of sermons or Lenten instructions that the Common Doctor probably preached in Naples about one year before his death on March 7, 1274. One set was a commentary upon the Apostles' Creed and the other his commentary upon the Angelic Salutation, or the first part of the "Hail Mary" as we know it. Both works reflect St. Thomas the preacher more than the teaching of the scientific theologian. Of course this does not mean that there was not solid theological doctrine behind his homiletic writings. I mention this precisely because in his preaching on the "Hail Mary," he seems to hold for the Immaculate Conception. He mentions it, if the emended text of the Tossi edition of the work is authentic, in the context of explaining Mary's preeminent purity. She incurred neither original, nor mortal, nor venial sin. He refers to Mary's glorious Assumption as expressing her freedom from the penalty of sin. Aquinas follows the tradition that she died before being taken up bodily into heaven. Commenting upon what was the final phrase of the "Hail Mary" in his day, "Blessed is the fruit of thy womb," Aquinas applies the antithesis of the Eve-Mary analogy. Mary found in her womb the true good that Eve sinfully desired to find in the forbidden fruit of the tree. He concludes his little commentary in a way that is characteristic of the Christocentric emphasis in all of the Common Doctor's theological teaching about Mary: "The Virgin, therefore, is thus blessed; [but] more blessed [is] the fruit of her [womb]."

CHAPTER XI

Mary and Joseph
in the Communion of Saints

We fly to thy patronage, O holy Mother of God,
despise not our petitions in our necessities,
but deliver us from all danger,
O ever glorious and blessed Virgin. Amen.

IN THE Catholic Tradition, this is the earliest prayer to our Blessed Mother which expresses belief in her intercessory role in heaven (cf. TH 336). It is most often called the "*Sub Tuum,*" the first words of the Latin version. Some scholars date the Greek version of the prayer as early as the third century. The *Sub Tuum* invokes Mary as "Theotokos," and so, if the third-century dating is correct, then this prayer would witness to the use of this title "Mother of God" sometime during the century before Alexander, the Patriarch of Alexandria, who first used it in his writings in 325 (cf. Chapter VII). Also that would mean that "Theotokos" was on the lips of the faithful for about two centuries before its definition as a dogma of our faith at the Council of Ephesus (431). What mainly interests us now, however, is its very early testimony to the belief of the faithful regarding Mary's power of intercession. The fact that the word "deliver" appears in the prayer, the very same one in the original Greek New Testament that is used in the "Our Father" (cf. Matthew 6:13), emphasizes their confidence in the ministry of Mary in glory, not only to pray for them but even to mediate protection (salvation) to them.

At this point it would be helpful to clarify just how we are using certain terms that will appear frequently throughout this chapter and most of the remainder of the book. "Veneration" is a broad term that applies to any form of devotion to the saints, whether it be expressed through imitation of their inspiring example of Christian virtue or by invoking them to pray for us. "Intercession" refers primarily to the prayers of the saints in heaven on our behalf. "Mediation," closely connected with intercession, is used to emphasize the salutary effects that the intercessory prayers of the saints have upon us. And so, for example, Mary is called "Mediatrix" because of her special role in the distribution of her Son's graces for the sake of our salvation. Finally, "invocation" is the technical term for "calling upon" or "praying to" the saints beseeching their intercession and mediation on behalf of us and those for whom we are invoking them. Obviously our "veneration" of Mary, Joseph, and all the saints is expressed this way also, but goes beyond it and includes our praise of them, our thanksgiving to them for favors received through their intercession, and our imitation of them by following the inspiring example of their lives. The nuances of these terms should be clear from their usage in the various contexts of our consideration of the Communion of Saints.

Although in this chapter we shall be concentrating primarily on Mary's place in the Communion of Saints, and then upon the special role of St. Joseph in heavenly glory, our initial discussion concerns the doctrine generally as an article in the Apostles' Creed. We wish to emphasize the truth that Mary is not "above" the Communion of Saints but "in" it, although her place is preeminent. This concurs with the teaching of Vatican II, which emphasized that Mary is a "preeminent" and "wholly unique member of the Church," but a member nonetheless, and not outside or beyond the Church (cf. LG 53). If she is to have the role given her by God in our redemption, then we must see Mary in solidarity with all of us members of her Son's Body. In order for us to grasp more fully Mary's special power of intercession and mediation for the sake of Christ and the Church, it will be necessary first to make a few general observations about the unique role that she had as the New Eve by sharing in the redemptive activity of the New Adam. The vocation of her true spouse, St. Joseph, foster-father of God's own Son, and hers, the highest calling in salvation history among the redeemed after that of his wife, will also be discussed briefly as the basis for his universal patronage in the Church today. The chapter also includes some suggestions about ways in which to approach the mystery of the mediation and intercession of the saints, of St. Mary especially, so as not to confuse it with the unique Mediatorship of Jesus Christ, the one eternal High Priest.

The Communion of Saints in the Catholic Tradition

Vatican II's teaching about this traditional doctrine is found principally in Chapter VII of LG: "The Eschatological Character of the Pilgrim Church and Her Union with the Heavenly Church." It sums up the substance of the Tradition succinctly: "This sacred Council accepts loyally the venerable faith of our ancestors in the living communion which exists between us and our brothers who are in the glory of heaven and who are yet being purified after their death; and it proposes again the decrees of the Second Council of Nicea, of the Council of Florence, and of the Council of Trent" (LG 51). The doctrine of the Communion of Saints in its entirety, therefore, includes the threefold state of Christ's Church: the Pilgrim Church upon earth (formerly called the "Church Militant"); the Heavenly Church (formerly the "Church Triumphant"); and, the Expectant Church in purgatory (customarily called the "Church Suffering"). The doctrine also embraces the dynamic living spiritual bond of unity in prayer and love that exists among the members of the one Church in the three states of the Church. Chapter VII of LG focuses mainly upon the relationship between the Pilgrim and Heavenly Church, which is also our chief consideration of the mystery. It provides a general introduction to Chapter VIII of LG, especially those sections that treat of Mary's mediation.

The three ecumenical councils whose decrees Vatican II proposes again, particularly regarding the invocation and intercession of saints in the Heavenly Church, are: II Nicea in 787; Florence, 1431-1445; and Trent, 1545-1563. As with its teaching generally, however, Vatican Council II saw the need to propose traditional doctrines not merely by repeating them but by formulating them in a way that could address the questions that people are asking about salvation today. In Chapter VII of LG there are some fresh insights into the connection between ecclesiology (theology of the Church) and eschatology (theology of the so-called "last things," death, judgment, heaven, and hell). It is important to note that the emphasis is upon looking at heaven not purely as a future reality but as a mystery that has a profound influence upon us in the Pilgrim Church. The title of Chapter VII clearly indicates this emphasis, "The Eschatological Character (Nature) of the Pilgrim Church and Her Union with the Heavenly Church." It and the chapter on Mary were not a part of the original *schema* on the Church at Vatican II.[1] But while the Council planned to include its Marian teaching somewhere in its documents, there had been no provision made for its eschatological doctrine. This indeed would have been an unfortunate omission, but placing it in the document on the Church proved to be of great importance. The Church, even in its institutional aspects, cannot be sufficiently understood apart from her eschatological dynamism, i.e., her inherent thrust towards the *eschaton* or heavenly state which profoundly influences her very nature upon earth. Although this theme had been briefly mentioned in the first two chapters of LG (e.g., the end of art. 5), the veneration of the saints as a concrete expression of the Pilgrim Church's eschatological nature had not been adequately treated.

Consequently there are two sections in Chapter VII of LG: articles 48-49, which explain the eschatological nature of the Pilgrim Church; and, articles 50-51, which show how this essential character of the Church is actually expressed by the devotion of the faithful to the saints in heaven. The chapter opens with the words: "The Church to which we are called in Christ Jesus, and in which by the grace of God we acquire holiness, will receive its perfection only in the glory of heaven, when will come the time of the renewal of all things (Acts 3:21)" (LG 48).

Despite the provisional character of the Pilgrim Church, which can never reach its full perfection upon earth, the *eschaton* has entered time "in Christ Jesus," and through the Pentecostal Spirit of our risen Lord the Church is being gradually prepared, as is efficaciously symbolized by the Sacraments, especially the Eucharist, for her final transformation at the Second Coming of Christ. The teaching of Vatican II, therefore, resumes: "When the Lord will come in glory, and all his angels with him (cf. Matthew 25:31), death will be no more and all things will be subject to him (cf. 1 Corinthians 15:26-27)" (LG 49). Because this passage is particularly important for the proper understanding of the Communion of Saints, let us listen to its teaching carefully and in some detail:

> But at the present time some of his disciples are pilgrims on earth. Others have died and are being purified, while still others are in glory, contemplating "in full light, God himself triune and one, exactly as he is." All of us, however, in varying degrees and in different ways share in the same charity toward God and our neighbors, and we all sing the one hymn of glory to our God. All indeed who are of Christ and have his Spirit form one Church and in Christ cleave together (Ephesians 4:16). So it is that the union of the wayfarers with the brethren who sleep in the peace of Christ is in no way interrupted, but on the contrary, according to the constant faith of the Church, this union is reinforced by an exchange of spiritual goods. Being more closely united to Christ, those who dwell in heaven fix the whole Church more firmly in holiness, add to the nobility of the worship that the Church offers to God here on earth, and in many ways help in a broader building up of the Church (1 Corinthians 12:12-27). Once received into their heavenly home and being present to the Lord (cf. 2 Corinthians 5:8), through him and with him and in him they do not cease to intercede to the Father for us, as they proffer the merits which they acquired on earth through the one mediator between God and men, Christ Jesus (cf. I Timothy 2:5), serving God in all things and completing in their flesh what is lacking in Christ's afflictions for the sake of his Body, that is, the Church (cf. Colossians 1:24). So by their brotherly concern is our weakness greatly helped. (LG 49)

In Christ Jesus, therefore, the three states of the one People of God, the Pilgrim Church, the Heavenly Church, and the Expectant Church in purgatory are truly united. As different as the conditions of those in each state may be, they really belong to the one Church of Christ. And as long as these differences perdure, i.e., till the consummation of human salvation history at the Second Coming of Christ, the bond of unity among the members of this Communion of Saints is found in the loving relationship of prayer and worship. The intercessory prayer of the saints in heaven on our behalf is a continuation of their good lives led upon earth. And their lives became worthy of receiving the reward of heavenly glory only because of the redemptive act of Jesus. The merits that they proffer while interceding to the Father for us are all the result of the graces which Christ won for them and us all in accomplishing our redemption.

In no way do the saints in heaven become sources of salvation independently of the one Savior of all, Jesus Christ. The constant and consistent belief in our Catholic Tradition is that to share through faith, and the good works issuing from that faith, in the redeeming activity of Christ, is also to share in the redemptive value of that activity for all the People of God.

By calling upon the saints in heaven, the Pilgrim Church both glances backward to her historical past and gazes forward and upward to her eschatological future. Contemplating the lives of her heroes and heroines in salvation history to learn from the inspiration of their example has been the practice of the Church "from the very earliest days of the Christian religion," first the apostles and martyrs, whom "she has always venerated . . . together with the Blessed Virgin Mary and the holy angels, with a special love," and later on in her history "others who had chosen to imitate more closely the virginity and poverty of Christ, and still others whom the outstanding practice of the Christian virtues and the wonderful graces of God recommended to the pious devotion and imitation of the faithful" (LG 50). The teaching about the mystery of the Communion of Saints in this context also includes the exemplary lives of the holy people upon earth who, in company with the saints in heaven, go to make up "so great a cloud of witnesses . . . (cf. Hebrews 12:1) and such a witness to the truth of the Gospel" (LG 50). Vatican II continues to teach concerning this consoling mystery that our devotion to the saints in heaven is not practiced only through studying their example, but by belonging to the same communion of love we venerate them for helping to deepen our mutual union in Christ:

> It is most fitting, therefore, that we love those friends and co-heirs of Jesus Christ who are also our brothers and outstanding benefactors, and that we give due thanks to God for them, "humbly invoking them, and having recourse to their prayers their aid and their help in obtaining from God through his Son, Jesus Christ, our Lord, our only Redeemer and Savior, the benefits we need." Every authentic witness of love, indeed, offered by us to those who are in heaven tends to and terminates in Christ,

"the crown of all the saints," and through him in God who is
wonderful in his saints and is glorified in them. (LG 50)

Christ himself can be contemplated as our risen Lord in glory only in
the company of his redeemed Body the Heavenly Church. And only
through Christ is the triune God eternally revealed in the vision of
glory which is the very heart of heavenly happiness. Here we must recall the distinction between the *latria*, or worship and adoration due to
the triune God and Christ alone, and the *dulia*, or veneration paid to
created saints, including the *hyperdulia*, or special veneration given to
St. Mary (cf. Chapter X). If we grasp the Communion of Saints, then
we should recognize that *dulia*, far from distracting us in our *latria*, actually enriches our worship of the Blessed Trinity and the Word incarnate, Jesus Christ. Authentic veneration of Mary, Joseph, and all
the angels and saints, therefore, must mean a greater honor and glory
given to God since all devotion to them is praise of the one Redeemer,
Christ, "the crown of all the saints," and through him, the one Mediator, the praise of the triune God, the sole source of all sanctity.

And it is in our liturgical celebrations that we are most intimately
united with our brothers and sisters in heaven, offering together with
them our loving adoration and one perfect sacrifice of praise through
our eternal high priest, Jesus Christ:

> It is especially in the sacred liturgy that our union with the heav-
> enly Church is best realized; in the liturgy, through the sacra-
> mental signs, the power of the Holy Spirit acts upon us, and with
> community rejoicing we celebrate together the praise of the di-
> vine majesty, when all those of every tribe and tongue and people
> and nation (cf. Apocalypse 5:9) who have been redeemed by the
> blood of Christ and gathered together in one Church glorify, in
> one common song of praise, the one and triune God. When,
> then, we celebrate the Eucharistic sacrifice we are most closely
> united to the worship of the heavenly Church; when in the fel-
> lowship of communion we honor and remember the glorious
> Mary ever virgin, St. Joseph, the holy apostles and martyrs and
> all the saints. (LG 50)

The liturgical worship of the Pilgrim Church is a participation in the
perfect liturgy of the heavenly Church. What we are called to do upon
earth through faith and sacramental signs, the saints in glory do

through direct vision in adoring the triune God, who is immediately present to them, and not through the symbols that we require in space and time. But the most important conviction for us is to believe that, by belonging to the great Communion of Saints, our worship becomes one with theirs "through Christ, with Christ, and in Christ," according to the conclusion of the Eucharistic Prayer.

Vatican II draws Chapter VII of LG to a conclusion by warning against abuses in the practice of venerating the saints either through excess or defect. Especially does the Council urge that the faithful be taught ". . . that the authentic cult of the saints does not consist so much in a multiplicity of external acts, but rather in a more intense practice of our love, whereby . . . we seek from the saints example in their way of life, fellowship in their communion, and the help of their intercession" (LG 51). It is important for us to bear in mind the old proverb: "Abuse does not destroy the use." Just because there has been a tendency to abuse a certain practice does not necessarily mean that it can never be done right. If superstitious beliefs and practices have distorted devotion to the saints in heaven, that does not mean there cannot be a reform and renewal which helps to purify popular piety. Of course this is especially so, as is generally true, when the people concerned are performing such practices with good intentions. They must be gently, kindly, but clearly and firmly liberated from their excesses. At the same time, those who have erroneously dismissed devotion to the saints altogether from their practice of prayer must be helped in their state of spiritual deficiency.

Mary's Unique Share in Her Son's Work of Redemption

In the Catholic Tradition's general teaching about the Communion of Saints, particularly as it has been formulated by Vatican II, there is a clear affirmation of the basic continuity between one's life in the Pilgrim Church and in the Heavenly Church. The holy person who enters into the fullness of eternal life takes along, so to speak, the results of his/her part in the Tradition of the Church's salvation history. In other words, the role that one has in Christ's redemptive work upon earth seems to ready him/her for the intercessory role in heaven. And we Catholics have traditionally believed that to be redeemed by Christ means not only to assume a responsible role in receiving the free gift of Christ's saving grace but also to become a channel of redemption to others.

As Mary was uniquely redeemed by the foreseen merits of her Son in her Immaculate Conception, the way in which she so fully accepted the free gift and also freely and generously entered into his work of redeeming humanity is also unique.[2] We are all redeemed both *by* Christ and *in* Christ. Jesus Christ, the New Adam, is truly in solidarity with the whole human race. As Son of Mary, he truly became one of us, and as Son of God, he perfectly redeemed us and represents that redemption before the Father. Our one eternal high priest, Jesus, always makes intercession for us in heaven (cf. Hebrews 7:25). The Father beholds in him, the Head of the Church, that all the members *are* redeemed.

This embraces all. He suffered, died, and rose for all, and so every human person is called to belong to his redeemed Body. We are the redeemed People of God. This is "objective redemption." Redemption is a fact. The precious blood of Christ has already paid the price of ransoming us from the powers of sin and death. The work of our redemption has been completely accomplished by Christ and in Christ.

The application of the saving gifts of Christ to each one of us personally is called "subjective redemption." It is first of all a gift to us from the triune God through Christ. We receive a share in the fruits of redemption through no merits of our own but entirely through the merits of our one Redeemer, Son of God, Son of Mary. Mary's Immaculate Conception, as we have considered (cf. Chapter VIII), was a pure gift bestowed in view of the foreseen merits of her Son. The grace of our baptism as infants was completely gratuitous. Even those who seek the sacrament of baptism after reaching the use of reason do so as a result of the free gift of grace. And those who, through no fault of their own, never come during this life to see the necessity of the sacrament of baptism for salvation can still be saved by what is called the "baptism of desire." In God's providence, they have done all that can be expected of them to find the truth, and this itself is possible only because they are redeemed by Christ and have accepted and cooperated with his grace in good faith and according to the best lights of their own consciences, even though they do not come to recognize Christ and his Church upon earth.

Those of us who are blessed with the gift of an explicit faith in Christ and his Church, from the beginning or sometime during the course of our lives, must in due time affirm our free acceptance of this gift. This responsibility is in accord with the personal development of each one of us amid the providential circumstances of life. According to divine revelation as recorded in Luke's Gospel, a most significant affirmation by Mary of her great gifts of grace took place at the Annunciation (cf. Luke 1:26-38). Her response, "Behold, I am the handmaid of the Lord; let it be to me according to your word" (Luke 1:38), reflects the profound appropriation of the fullness of grace bestowed upon her by divine favor beginning with her Immaculate Conception. All her graces were bestowed in preparation for this moment when God was calling her to be the Theotokos, the Birth-Giver of God's own Son. And her wholehearted "Yes" to the Father's will was not only an affirmation of her free acceptance of the unique gift of redemption for herself, but also her consent to share uniquely in her Son's work of redeeming us all.

As we have already seen (cf. Chapter X), St. Thomas teaches that Mary gave her free consent at the Annunciation "in place of the whole human race" (III, q.30, a.1). She accepted, as it were, the divine proposal for humanity to be wedded to divinity in the Person of God's own Son and hers. Because Mary did say "Yes" to the divine will for her, it has become possible for us to accept the fruits of Christ's redemption into our lives.

But did Mary really realize at the time of the Annunciation that her "*fiat*" or "let it be" was consenting to the beginnings of our redemption in Christ? Just what she knew explicitly is not possible for us to say on the basis of what has been revealed. Called to journey through life on a "pilgrimage of faith" (LG 58), she would not seem to have had the details leading to the passion, death, and resurrection of her Son revealed to her. Like us, she had to walk amid the ambiguities of a life of faith that is led in complete openness to the gradual manifestation of the Father's will for us. At the same time, however, there would have been enough understanding to make her act of obe-

dient and loving faith at the Annunciation an intelligent and meaningful acceptance of her calling to be the mother of the "Suffering Servant of Yahweh" (cf. Isaiah 40-55). At least implicit in her "Yes" was
the consent to share in what her Son would have to do in order to accomplish the redemption of the human race, even though she did not
know all that it actually would imply. And her vocal *"fiat"* at the Annunciation was never taken back, but rather prolonged till it led her to
the silent *"fiat"* spoken in her heart at the foot of the cross on Calvary.
It was the *"fiat"* of her compassion which confirmed her calling to
share uniquely in the work of her Son's redemption. That was his
"hour" and hers, according to John's Gospel, when the sword of sor-
row foreshadowed in the prophecy of Simeon (cf. Luke 2:35) would
pierce her own soul most deeply. But out of this suffering with her Son
for the sake of our salvation came the gift of her spiritual motherhood
to us all: "Behold, your mother!" (John 19:27). And we are represented by the "beloved disciple."

Following upon her Son's ascension to the right hand of his Father
in heaven, Mary was in the midst of the community of his disciples:
"All these with one accord devoted themselves to prayer, together with
the women and Mary the mother of Jesus, and with his brethren"
(Acts 1:14). This final explicit reference to Mary in the New Testament completes the Madonna of Luke/Acts (cf. Chapter III). Her own
discipleship of prayer and ministry reaches a certain climax in this preparation for the first Pentecost in the upper room, the Cenacle. She was
the most responsive to receive from her risen and ascended Son's Holy
Spirit the special enlightenment and inspiration to penetrate more profoundly into the meaning of Christ's saving mysteries. Her motherly
presence in the midst of the infant Church was a prophetic prelude to
the spiritual motherhood that Mary would have in relationship to the
members of the Pilgrim Church after her glorious Assumption.

Universality of Mary's Mediation and Intercession

Having considered Mary's unique relationship to her Son in his
work of accomplishing our redemption, we now turn to contemplate
the mystery of her unique role in interceding for us in heaven as well as
mediating the fruits of his redemption to us upon earth. Since she

seems to have been divinely predestined to share in the universality of God's saving deed in Christ through her graced consent to be the Theotokos and to suffer with him on Calvary, then Mary would also fittingly participate in her risen Son's distribution of the graces of redemption to all. Her heavenly role of intercessory prayer and mediation of graces embraces everyone because her Son has saved everyone. This is the exercise of her spiritual motherhood in the Communion of Saints. Because the teaching of Vatican II about the mystery of Mary's mediation helps us understand how it does not interfere with the unique Mediatorship of Christ but actually enhances it, let us listen to that teaching at some length:

> In the words of the apostle there is but one mediator: "for there is but one God and one mediator of God and men, the man Christ Jesus, who gave himself a redemption for all" (1 Timothy 2:5-6). But Mary's function as mother of men in no way obscures or diminishes this unique mediation of Christ, but rather shows its power. But the Blessed Virgin's salutary influence on men originates not in any inner necessity but in the disposition of God. It flows forth from the superabundance of the merits of Christ, rests on his mediation, depends entirely on it, and draws all its power from it. It does not in any way hinder the immediate union of the faithful with Christ but on the contrary fosters it. (LG 60)
>
> . . . in a wholly singular way she cooperated by her obedience, faith, hope, and burning charity in the work of the Savior in restoring supernatural life to souls. For this reason she is mother to us in the order of grace. (LG 61)
>
> This motherhood of Mary in the order of grace continues uninterruptedly from the consent which she loyally gave at the Annunciation and which she sustained without wavering beneath the cross, until the eternal fulfillment of all the elect. Taken up to heaven she did not lay aside this saving office but by her manifold intercession continues to bring us the gifts of eternal salvation. By her maternal charity, she cares for the brethren of her Son, who still journey on earth, surrounded by dangers and difficulties, until they are led into their blessed home. Therefore the Blessed Virgin is invoked in the Church under the titles of Advocate, Helper, Benefactress, and Mediatrix. This, however, is so understood that it neither takes away anything from nor adds anything to the dignity of Christ the one Mediator. (LG 62)

These excerpts from the section of Vatican II's Chapter VIII of LG, entitled "The Blessed Virgin and the Church," call for very careful and prayerful reflection.[3] Mary's spiritual motherhood, her motherhood "in the order of grace," is a continuation in heaven of her unique role in Christ's redemption of the human race while upon earth. What she did upon earth in close connection with her Son is eternally present before the Father as a powerful intercession of motherly care for the spiritual welfare of us all. The way in which the original Latin text expresses this intercession, "*multiplici intercessione,*" seems to convey in the context the concept of a continuation of her share in the saving office of Christ upon earth which is "manifold" in its outreach to all of the redeemed.

The Marian title of "Mediatrix" is included among the four listed. It is noteworthy that this is the only time that the Council uses the term, and only after carefully distinguishing Mary's mediation from that of Christ, our one eternal high priest, who always makes intercession for us in heaven (cf. Hebrews 7:25). Although God has endowed her mediation with a universal efficacy, it is completely dependent upon her Son's unique Mediatorship and must never be placed upon the same level as his. Her Son alone is the eternal high priest who continuously reconciles the world with the Father in the Holy Spirit. On earth this ministry is exercised by those of us who are called to represent Christ in the ordained priesthood. The maternal influence of Mary's mediation is an exercise of her sublime share in the general priesthood of Christ in the Church. Mary, a preeminent member of the Church, belongs to the communion of all the faithful called to share in the life of Christ and to share that life with others. There is no indication in our Catholic Tradition that Mary's vocation included the ministerial priesthood. This is certainly not to lessen the dignity of her calling, but to distinguish her role carefully from that of her Son, who gives redemptive meaning and efficacy to the ministry of word and sacrament exercised by his ordained priests in the Pilgrim Church. Mary's salutary influence upon us all in the exercise of her spiritual motherhood in the order of grace is to be interpreted in a different way, a way that does not "compete" with her Son's mediation of all graces. Her role seems to be the motherly one of helping dispose us to receive and grow in the life of grace, a share in God's own life that can be caused in us only by God through the mediation of Christ.

While we are carefully considering the differences between the manner in which Mary mediates her Son's redeeming love to us and the way in which he alone as our redeemer does so, it would be helpful to point out that Vatican II does not call her our Co-Redemptrix. This is a Marian title that had been frequently heard before the Council. One hardly hears it used any longer. It is not that the term "co-redemption" cannot be interpreted correctly to describe the mystery that Mary and all of us redeemed become associated with the redemptive activity of Christ. As members of his redeemed-redeeming Body the Church, of which he is the Head, we are called to be channels of redemption to one another and to our world. Always dependent upon the grace of Christ, we are able to help build up the Body of Christ in love through our prayers, sufferings, and good works flowing from our faith. The term "co-redemptrix" has become confusing, however, especially in our language, where the prefix "co-" does not have the same connotation as it does in the Latin *con* whence it is derived. A *Con-Redemptor* or *Con-Redemptrix* merely associates another or others with the one Redeemer but always in a completely dependent and subordinate role. But usually in English "co-" makes the other an equal partner in an enterprise or relationship, e.g., the co-signer of a checking account. And so the Council did not call Mary "Co-Redemptrix" to avoid confusion as well as to prevent any ecumenical misunderstanding, since our Protestant brothers and sisters find it offensive. Whether the term is used or not, the Catholic sense can never mean that Mary is a fellow redeemer with Christ!

Finally, a few comments should be made about the conciliar teaching that Mary's mediation "does not in any way hinder the immediate union of the faithful with Christ but on the contrary fosters it" (LG 60). Mary's mediation ought not to be imagined and interpreted as though she were a go-between or a bridge between us and a remote Christ. In the words of the American bishops:

> Pope Paul [VI] put it this way: "Since Mary is rightly to be regarded as the way by which we are led to Christ, the person who encounters Mary cannot help but encounter Christ like-

wise." Father Frederick Jelly explains how Mary's mediation . . .
fosters "immediate union of the faithful with Christ." Father Jelly writes: "Mary is not a bridge over the gap that separates us
from a remote Christ. . . . Such an approach to Marian devotion
and doctrine would minimize the deepest meaning of the Incarnation, the fact that he has become a man like us, and that his
sacred humanity has made him the unique mediator between
God and us. Mary's greatness is that she brought him close to us,
and her mediation continues to create the spiritual climate for our
immediate-encounter with Christ." (BYM 67)

Mary's mediation, therefore, must not be misconstrued to mean that
she tries to bring Christ and us together as one mediates between labor
and management during a dispute over wages or working conditions.
Such an image is far removed from the mystery that we are contemplating. We do not have to go to Mary or invoke her help because Christ
cannot be approached directly. After all, Christ is the incarnate Son of
God, the nearness of God to us. In him and through him the Blessed
Trinity, infinitely beyond us, has become accessible to each one of us.
So Mary's intercessory and mediating role in glory is not to make God
approachable to us, but to help make us more aware of the abiding
presence of the triune God in and through Christ. She is like a loving
mother with a son who can help others if only they really believe in
him. And so she prepares a meeting where they can come to see and
hear him, knowing just how to make her home pleasant for the meeting. She does not stand between them and her son, but stays in the
background always ready to serve. Mary's mediation or motherhood in
the order of grace is something like this. She knows just how to help
prepare for our direct or immediate encounters with her saving Son by
disposing us to open up our eyes of faith more fully to behold him always there to offer us the graces that we need when we need them. If
we allow her to have this salutary influence upon our spiritual lives,
then we shall be much better disposed for the direct meeting with her
Son and God's Son, who ever comes with the Father and the Holy Spirit to dwell in us and make us holy. When we invoke Mary, therefore,
we are asking her to act upon us and not upon God. We are calling
upon her to help us become more open to the gifts of God, to God himself.

Devotion to St. Joseph, Mary's Husband and Foster Father of Jesus

The intercessory role of St. Joseph in the Communion of Saints is also a continuation of the very special calling that he had in relationship to Jesus and Mary upon earth. We have already seen what the New Testament tells us about his role in the Incarnation (cf. Chapter III) as well as the theological explanation of why he can truly be called Mary's husband, since theirs was a real marriage even though virginal (cf. Chapter X). As guardian of the Holy Family, he was brought by God most intimately into the mystery of the origins of our redemption in Christ.[4] Now let us look at the historical development of devotion to St. Joseph in the Church, as well as at the theological understanding of his special place in the Communion of Saints as Patron of the Universal Church (cf. TH 206-209; NCE 7, 1106-1113).

Devotion to St. Joseph caught on relatively late in the history of the Church. The main reason seems to have been the fear that his unique role, as the virginal husband of Mary and father of Jesus through a spiritual relationship, might have caused some confusion concerning the virginal conception of Christ and Mary's perpetual virginity. The apocryphal legends about the childhood of Christ also contributed toward the lack of appreciating Joseph's real role in the mystery of the Incarnation. For instance, they portrayed him as a man of advanced age in order to make certain that he would not be mistaken as the natural father of Jesus. But the canonical Gospels indicate that he was considered to be *just that* by the people of the time in order to protect the reputation of Jesus and Mary. If he had been a very old man, they would not have looked upon him as the natural father of the child. Likewise, the apocryphal legends wished to portray Joseph as an elderly widower with six children from a previous marriage to attempt an explanation of the references to the "brethren of Jesus" (Matthew 12:46; John 2:12; 7:10). Such legends were kept alive in the tradition through medieval drama, art, and poetry. But gradually the true image of St. Joseph emerged in the Church and his proper role in the Holy Family came to be appreciated. The belief that he himself was a virginal husband and father has prevailed since Sts. Jerome and Augustine defended it in the early part of the fifth century.

In an eighth-century martyrology from an unknown church in

northern France or Belgium is found the first known independent commemoration of St. Joseph on March 20 as "spouse of Mary." In the
early part of the next century, St. Joseph appears in the martyrologies
of monasteries, which list March 19 as the day of his death. The desire
to know more about Jesus and Mary during the Middle Ages inspired
the beginnings of an independent devotion to St. Joseph. In the early
fourteenth century we find the first observances of March 19 as his
feast day, more than a mere commemoration, among the Servites,
Franciscans, and at Bologna. Pope Sixtus IV introduced the feast at
Rome about 1479, which seems to have inspired the spread of the celebration of the feast in many places throughout Europe. St. Bernadine
of Siena (d. 1444) and St. Teresa of Avila (d. 1582) contributed greatly to spreading devotion to St. Joseph. During the seventeenth century,
St. Francis de Sales and Bossuet were outstanding among those who
were preaching and writing about him. A decline in the promoting of
the devotion set in during the eighteenth century, but St. Alphonsus
Liguori was a notable exception.

The developments in devotion to St. Joseph throughout the
Church are especially significant during the nineteenth and twentieth
centuries. On December 8, 1870, Pope Pius IX proclaimed him the
Patron of the Universal Church. Pope Leo XIII has given us the most
important papal document on St. Joseph, in which he teaches: "For he,
indeed, was the husband of Mary, and the father, as was supposed, of
Jesus Christ. From this arise all his dignity, grace, holiness, and glory"
(encyclical letter *Quamquam Pluries*, August 15, 1889). Pope St. Pius
X (Pope 1903-1914) approved the Litany of St. Joseph. Pope
Benedict XV issued a special papal document that marked the fiftieth
anniversary of the proclamation of St. Joseph's universal patronage of
the Church on July 25, 1920. Pope Pius XI (Pope 1922-1939) frequently praised St. Joseph in his addresses, and considered him a special
protector against atheistic communism. On May 1, 1955, Pope Pius
XII instituted the special feast of St. Joseph the Worker to counteract
the "May Day" celebration of the communists, and to celebrate the
true dignity of the working class in accord with the Christian Tradition. By indult, this Mass may be celebrated on Labor Day in the United States and Canada. The feast of the Holy Family, the Sunday within

the Octave of Christmas, celebrates the mystery of Jesus' hidden life and of course includes Joseph. His main feast, however, is the Solemnity of St. Joseph, Husband of Mary, on March 19. Pope John XXIII (1958-1963) named him "Protector of the Second Vatican Council" and also inserted St. Joseph into the *Communicantes* of the Roman Canon in 1962.

As we reflect theologically upon these historical developments in the devotion to St. Joseph, the first thing to strike us is that it began to catch on in the Church only when his proper role in salvation history came to light. As long as the apocryphal legends obscured the simple but profound and true portrait of him in the canonical Gospels, especially Matthew's infancy narrative, his special relationship to Jesus and Mary remained somewhat obscured. It is small wonder that St. Jerome, the Scripture scholar among the Fathers and Doctors of the Church, treated the apocrypha with such contempt! Of course, they still do have the value of reflecting certain beliefs and practices of the times. As Pope Leo XIII taught, however, "all his dignity, grace, holiness, and glory" arise from his special relationship, indeed unique relationship, to Jesus and Mary. The clarification of his real role in the Holy Family, therefore, coupled with the wishes of the Middle Ages to know more about Jesus and Mary, were the providential foundations for the spread of devotion to St. Joseph.

St. Augustine, as in so many other matters of doctrine in the Western Church, bequeathed to the Catholic Tradition the beginnings of a theology of St. Joseph (Josephology). He provided clear convincing explanations of the true marriage between Mary and Joseph as well as the nature of Joseph's fatherhood of Jesus. Depending largely upon Augustine, Aquinas, as we have seen, gave a synthesis of the traditional teaching about the marriage. In 1522 another Dominican theologian, Isidore of Isolanis, published a *Summa de donis Sancti Joseph (Summa about the Gifts of St. Joseph)*. And Suárez, in his work *On the Mysteries of the Life of Christ* (1592), treated in a scientific way questions about St. Joseph.

In the context of such a theological tradition, recent Josephologists have tried to clarify the precise nature of his fatherhood of the Son of God, the Son of Mary. "Foster father" is the most common way of designating this relationship, but it must not be interpreted as though Joseph were merely the "adoptive" father of Jesus. Jesus was a member of Joseph's own family, truly the Son of his real wife. He was not "adopted" into the Holy Family, of which Joseph was truly the guardian and protector. Surely he was the "legal" father, which was important in establishing the descent of Jesus as "Son of David." But it seems that no theologian has been able to come up with an apt title that expresses the mystery of his paternal relationship to the Son of God incarnate, conceived and born of his wife Mary. Many recent writers accept "virgin father," which originated with St. Augustine, but it was not just as a virgin that he entered the mystery, since he was truly Mary's husband. This title does, however, emphasize his calling to serve the Word incarnate.

What is most significant in our devotion to St. Joseph is its spiritual power to draw us closer to Jesus through Mary. His unique role in the Holy Family has prepared him for a very special place in the Communion of Saints. He continues to protect by his intercessory prayer the holy family of God that is the Church. His virtues of justice, patience, prudence, faith, obedience, etc., based upon the little explicitly revealed about him in the New Testament, are a special inspiration to the fathers of families. The tradition that he was a carpenter or craftsman in the village of Nazareth, and that Jesus most likely learned the trade from him to help support the Holy Family, has made Joseph a special model for working people. The belief that he died sometime during the "hidden life" of Jesus has inspired the devotion to him as the patron of a happy death, since his life upon earth came to a conclusion in the intimate, consoling presence of both Jesus and Mary. Because of his closeness to Our Lady, he is also invoked as patron of devotion to Mary. Papal documents, popular acclaim, and the Litany of St. Joseph hail him as the patron of prayer and the interior life, of the poor, of those in authority, of priests and religious, of travelers, of the sick, of virgins, and numerous special causes.

But, as with all devotion in the Church, the liturgy is the most efficacious way of expressing it. In liturgical practice, the Church, i.e., all the faithful, venerate St. Joseph as second in holiness only to Mary. It has been said that he is given the honor of *"protodulia"* in the Communion of Saints in heaven, i.e., a "first veneration" above all the other saints except our Blessed Mother. Pope John XXIII's decision to place him in Eucharistic Prayer I immediately after Mary is especially significant, since it makes possible his veneration in the liturgy that much more often. Even more importantly, this places him in a part of the celebration of the Eucharistic liturgy that particularly honors Joseph right after Mary and before the apostles in our communion with the saints: "In union with the whole Church we honor Mary, the ever-virgin mother of Jesus Christ our Lord and God. We honor Joseph, her husband, the apostles and martyrs Peter and Paul. . . ."

CHAPTER XII

Mary in the Liturgical Year

THE FOLLOWING magnificent hymn is taken from the *Liturgy of the Hours*, Morning Prayer in the "Common of the Blessed Virgin Mary." It expresses beautifully the Christocentric emphasis of Mary's place in the liturgy of the Church.

> Mary the dawn, Christ the Perfect Day;
> Mary the gate, Christ the Heavenly Way!
>
> Mary the root, Christ the Mystic Vine;
> Mary the grape, Christ the Sacred Wine!
>
> Mary the wheat, Christ the Living Bread;
> Mary the stem, Christ the Rose blood-red!
>
> Mary the font, Christ the Cleansing Flood;
> Mary the cup, Christ the Saving Blood!
>
> Mary the temple, Christ the temple's Lord;
> Mary the shrine, Christ the God adored!
>
> Mary the beacon, Christ the Haven's Rest;
> Mary the mirror, Christ the Vision Blest!
>
> Mary the mother, Christ the mother's Son
> By all things blest while endless ages run. Amen.

Pope Paul VI, in his *Apostolic Exhortation for the Right Ordering and Development of Devotion to the Blessed Virgin Mary (Marialis Cultus — MC)*, issued February 2, 1974, teaches: "The Church's reflection today on the mystery of Christ and on her own nature has led her to find at the root of the former and as a culmination of the latter the same figure of a Woman: the Virgin Mary, the Mother of Christ and the Mother of the Church" (MC Introduction). This papal document, which develops nicely the doctrine of Vatican II, primarily considers the connection between the revised Roman liturgy and the renewal of devotion to Mary. It also addresses private Marian devotions, especially the Rosary in relationship to the liturgy of the Eucharist, which we shall discuss in the next chapter.

In Vatican II's *Constitution on the Sacred Liturgy*, one of the first conciliar documents to be issued (December 4, 1963), there is a brief but very important paragraph about Mary in the liturgical year:

> In celebrating the annual cycle of the mysteries of Christ, Holy Church honors the Blessed Mary, Mother of God, with a special love. She is inseparably linked with her Son's saving work. In her the Church admires and exalts the most excellent fruit of redemption, and joyfully contemplates, as in a faultless image, that which she herself desires and hopes wholly to be. (SC 103)

The entire liturgical year celebrates all the mysteries of our redemption by and in Christ from his Incarnation to Pentecost and our blessed hope of his Second Coming (cf. SC 102). The prayers and actions of the liturgical rites symbolize for us the efficacious means of our receiving the grace of Christ, who alone can save us. Although the paschal mystery of Christ's passion, death, and glorification is always the center of our liturgical celebrations of redemption, the feasts of saints are included in the calendar of the Church's year because they are such inspiring examples of the achievement of the paschal mystery in those who have suffered and been glorified with Christ (cf. SC 104).

Before examining the various liturgical celebrations in honor of Our Lady during the course of the Church's year, which begins with the First Sunday of Advent, let us take a "bird's-eye view" of their dates and different ranks:

December 8	Immaculate Conception	Solemnity
December 12	Our Lady of Guadalupe	Memorial
January 1	Mary, Mother of God	Solemnity
February 2	Presentation of the Lord	Feast
February 11	Our Lady of Lourdes	Optional Memorial
March 25	Annunciation of the Lord	Solemnity
May 31	Visitation	Feast
Saturday following the Second Sunday after Pentecost	Immaculate Heart of Mary	Optional Memorial

July 16	Our Lady of Mount Carmel	Optional Memorial
August 5	Dedication of St. Mary Major	Optional Memorial
August 15	Assumption	Solemnity
August 22	Queenship of Mary	Memorial
September 8	Birth of Mary	Feast
September 15	Our Lady of Sorrows	Memorial
October 7	Our Lady of the Rosary	Memorial
November 21	Presentation of Mary	Memorial

Of the sixteen liturgical celebrations of the Blessed Virgin in the revised Roman Rite there are four solemnities, three feasts, five memorials, and four optional memorials. The Solemnity of the Assumption has a special Vigil Mass with its proper prayers and Scripture readings. Also contained in the *Sacramentary* are several Masses in the section called "Common of the Blessed Virgin Mary." These may be used for Saturday celebrations or Votive Masses when permitted. And the *Lectionary* has both the proper Scripture readings for the special Marian feasts and a number to choose from in the Common. Three of the Saturday or Votive Masses are designated for the Advent, Christmas, and Easter Seasons. Paul VI pointed out: ". . . it should be noted that frequent commemorations of the Blessed Virgin are possible through the use of the Saturday Masses of Our Lady. This is an ancient and simple commemoration and one that is made very adaptable and varied by the flexibility of the modern Calendar and the number of formulas provided by the Missal" (MC 9). There seems to be no basic reason why Saturday has come to be dedicated to Mary in the Catholic Tradition, unless it be to commemorate her faith that remained undaunted on that first Holy Saturday while her Son was in the tomb.

Inseparable Link between the Mother and Son in the Liturgical Year

The reform of the Roman liturgy and the restoration of its General Calendar ". . . makes it possible in a more organic and closely-knit fashion to include the commemoration of Christ's Mother in the annual cycle of the mysteries of her Son" (MC 2). During the liturgical season of Advent there are numerous references to Mary in addition to the Immaculate Conception on December 8. These references to Mary appear particularly on December 17-24, especially the Sunday preceding Christmas, which recalls the prophecies of old about the Virgin

Mother and the Messiah and has Gospel readings about the birth of Christ and his Forerunner (cf. MC 3). The celebration of the Immaculate Conception fits very nicely into the spirit of the Advent season. Mary in this mystery is given to us as the model of readiness for the coming of Christ. She is the prototype of the sinless Church that is preparing to celebrate anew its beginnings in her Son, the Word made flesh. And in doing so, we are truly awaiting the complete transfiguration of the Church at the glorious return of the Lord. Pope Paul considered this linking Mary and Jesus in the Advent liturgy to be ". . . a happy balance in worship. This balance can be taken as a norm for preventing any tendency (as has happened at times in certain forms of popular piety) to separate devotion to the Blessed Virgin from its necessary point of reference — Christ" (MC 4). In this context he confirmed the proposal of liturgy experts that the Advent season is most suitable for devotion to the Mother of Jesus.

Throughout the Christmas season there is a continuous veneration of the Mother linked with the adoration of her Son, especially on Christmas day itself, when the liturgy celebrates the birth of Christ. The Church contemplates the holy life of Jesus, Mary, and Joseph on the feast of the Holy Family, the Sunday within the octave of Christmas. And on Epiphany, we are called to celebrate the fact that the Child came to save all, and we see the Mother presenting him to the Magi, who represent the call of the pagan Gentiles to redemption (cf. Matthew 2:11). On the very first day of the New Year, the restored Solemnity of Mary the holy Mother of God (Theotokos) is celebrated. It is meant to commemorate the intimate role of Mary in the mystery of our salvation. It has restored the wisdom of the ancient Church regarding the inherently Christocentric character of Mary's most glorious title and the dogma of Ephesus (431). Pope Paul VI calls our attention here to his institution of the Octave of Christmas, New Year's Day, as "World Day of Peace." How fitting to pray to the Prince of Peace through the Queen of Peace for this supreme gift in the liturgy of the day (cf. MC 5)!

The solemnity of the Annunciation of the Lord is a joint feast of Jesus and Mary. The liturgies of both the East and the West celebrate the "*fiats*" of both Son and mother. Christ said, upon coming into the world: "Lo, I have come to do your will, O God" (Hebrews 10:7). It commemorates the beginning of our redemption and the unbreakable bond between divinity and humanity in the incarnate Word. In reference to Mary, they celebrate this solemnity as a feast of the "New Eve" whose "*fiat*" (cf. Luke 1:38) made her both Mother of God and true mother of the living. By receiving into her virginal womb, through the working of the Spirit, the one Mediator (cf. 1 Timothy 2:5), Mary "became the true Ark of the Covenant and true Temple of God" (MC 6).

The solemnity of the Assumption on August 15 celebrates the mystery ". . . of the glorification of her immaculate soul and of her virginal body, of her perfect configuration to the Risen Christ" (MC 6). This feast also presents to us all the fulfillment of our final hope to be glorified with Christ in our complete humanity. The Queenship of Mary takes place seven days later, and extends the mystery of the Assumption, as we are called to celebrate our heavenly mother's royal role in the spiritual kingdom of her Son, the Lord of the universe. It is a kingdom of grace, of love, of peace, of justice, of mercy, and of all the virtues that the redemption has made possible for us to practice. And Mary's function as Queen, alongside her Son the King, is really to exercise her spiritual motherhood of intercessory prayer for all and mediation of his graces to all who will come under their sweet dominion.

The four solemnities of the Immaculate Conception, the holy Mother of God, the Annunciation of the Lord, and the Assumption celebrate the main Marian mysteries in the dogmatic truths about Mary. After the solemnities come those celebrations that call to mind and relive today saving events in which Mary was closely associated with Christ. Her own birth on September 8 has a feast commemorating the nativity of the mother in close connection with that of her Son, the hope and salvation of the world. The feast of the second joyful mystery, the Visitation, makes present to us the saving event of Mary's carrying her Son within her to the home of Elizabeth, whose child within her own womb leaped with joy in the presence of the Messiah. And on September 15 the commemoration of Our Lady of Sorrows calls us to relive that decisive moment of our redemption by contemplating the mystery of the mother's compassion with her crucified Son (cf. MC 7).

The feast of the Presentation of the Lord (February 2) is another joint celebration of the Son and the mother. This commemorates the prophecy of Simeon, who foretold that Mary would be called upon to suffer because of her Son's messianic mission (cf. Luke 2:34-35). Although it is counted among the joyful mysteries of the Rosary, one might say that it provides a prelude to the sorrowful mysteries.

The remaining feasts found in the General Calendar of the universal Church of the Roman Rite are either associated with local devotions that have attracted worldwide interest, e.g., Our Lady of Lourdes (February 11) and the Dedication of the Roman Basilica of St. Mary Major (August 5); or they were originally celebrated by particular religious families but have become popular in the Church as a whole, e.g., Our Lady of Mount Carmel (July 16), and Our Lady of the Rosary (October 7); plus one that inspires exemplary values in the Christian life despite its apocryphal origins — the Presentation of the Blessed Virgin (November 21) — and one that manifests certain characteristics of contemporary devotion, the Immaculate Heart of the Blessed Virgin, which is celebrated on the Saturday following the second Sunday after Pentecost (cf. MC 8).

Finally, as far as Marian feasts are concerned, there is the memorial of Our Lady of Guadalupe, celebrated in the United States on December 12. In the next chapter we shall be briefly telling the story behind Mary's apparition at Guadalupe, along with other authenticated appearances of Our Lady. The shrine of Our Lady of Guadalupe in Mexico City is a very popular center of devotion, but it does not possess the wide international appeal of Lourdes, and so the feast is not celebrated in the universal Church.

Concerning Mary's daily commemoration in each one of the Eucharistic Prayers, Pope Paul VI comments: "This daily commemoration, by reason of its place at the heart of the divine Sacrifice, should be considered a particularly expressive form of the veneration that the Church pays to the 'Blessed of the Most High' (cf. Luke 1:28)" (MC 10). While the Marian feasts manifest a continuity with the past liturgical celebrations in the Catholic Tradition (e.g., the themes of her Immaculate Conception, Motherhood of God, Assumption into heaven, etc.), there are new themes in accord with contemporary theological developments. The main one is that of Mary and the Church, which might be called a *renewed* theme more properly than a new one. Because of the many relationships between Mary and the Church, this theme has been introduced into the liturgical texts in a variety of ways. In the Immaculate Conception, the beginning of the sinless Church is celebrated. In the Assumption, the image of what is yet to come to pass for the whole Church at its completion is celebrated. "In the mystery of Mary's Motherhood they confess that she is the Mother of the Head and of the Members — the holy Mother of God and therefore the provident Mother of the Church" (MC 11). Whether the liturgy turns its gaze toward the ancient Church or the contemporary Church, Mary is always present. She is either praying with the first disciples or helping us to live with her the saving mysteries of her Son.

In the *Lectionary* since the postconciliar reform, a greater number of Old and New Testament readings concerning Mary may be found. These have been carefully selected in accord with good exegesis under the guidance of Tradition and the Magisterium. And so, as we saw in the first chapter of this book, the three channels of communicating God's revealing Word have been used, namely, sacred Scripture as it unfolds in the living Tradition of faith, worship, and mission under the special care of the Church's Magisterium. Therefore chapters II-IV considered Mary in the Bible at some length because of its special importance for more fruitful participation in the liturgical celebrations of Marian feasts (cf. MC 12).

The revised book of the Office, the *Liturgy of the Hours*, also contains excellent expression of devotion to the Mother of the Lord. Some magnificent hymns have been added, e.g., the one quoted at the beginning of this chapter. The ancient and beautiful little prayer *Sub tuum praesidium* (cf. start of Chapter XI) has also enriched this daily liturgical prayer in the Church. The prayers of intercession for the conclusions of Morning and Evening Prayer are filled with confidence in the merciful intercession of Mary. And a wide variety of writings besides the Scripture by authors in the Catholic Tradition over the centuries help make the Office of Readings a fruitful source of Marian meditation (cf. MC 13). It is unfortunate that the *Liturgy of the Hours* seems to be a "closed book" to most of the laity. Vatican II encourages them along with the clergy and religious to take part in the recitation of this liturgical prayer (cf. SC 100).

In addition to the *Sacramentary, Lectionary,* and the *Liturgy of the Hours,* devotional references to Mary in the other revised liturgical books are frequent, e.g., in the baptismal rite, the Sacrament of Reconciliation, etc. (cf. MC 14). All the sacramental moments of our Christian life provide a place for Mary to help dispose us to encounter her Son more closely. The liturgical renewal in the Catholic Church has indeed recognized the unique role of Mary in the saving mysteries of Christ. As Pope Paul put it: "From perennial tradition kept alive by reason of the uninterrupted presence of the Spirit and continual attention to the Word, the Church of our time draws motives, arguments, and incentives for the veneration that she pays to the Blessed Virgin. And the liturgy, which receives approval and strength from the Magisterium, is a most lofty expression and an evident proof of this living tradition" (MC 15).

Mary the Model of Our Worship in the Church

The second section of Paul VI's *Marialis Cultus* is devoted to a reflection upon those special virtues of Mary that make her the model of "the spiritual attitude with which the Church celebrates and lives the divine mysteries" (MC 16). This is an application to our liturgical life of the ecclesiotypical Mariology emphasized by Vatican II. If Mary is to be contemplated as the most excellent exemplar of the Church in the order of faith, of charity, and perfect union with her Son (cf. LG 63), then she must be a special example of the spirit of liturgical worship which is ". . . the summit toward which the activity of the Church is directed . . . [and] the fount from which all her power flows" (SC 10).

The first stroke of the brush in the painting of the Lucan Madonna at the Annunciation certainly portrays Mary as the "attentive Virgin" (MC 17). She was filled with the divine favor of a vibrant faith in both listening and responding to God's word addressed to her (cf. Luke 1:38). We in the Church, especially during our active and intelligent participation in liturgical celebrations, are called to hear God's inspired word in Scripture and to receive the divine Word as the Bread of Life in the Eucharist. Graced with a more living faith by the sacramental presence of Christ, we are summoned like Mary to interpret the events of our times in light of God's word that has addressed us in the liturgy.

The next stroke from the brush of St. Luke shows us the Madonna as the "Virgin in prayer" (MC 18). Mary's prayer is the *Magnificat* (cf. Luke 1:46-55), which we have meditated upon in Chapter III. It beautifully expresses her humility, hope, and faith giving rise to joy in the presence of the Messiah, the saving God. At Cana (cf. John 2:1-12), a special subject of our meditation in Chapter IV, Mary's request for a sign from her Son was indeed a prayerful one. Even if the faith that she showed at the time was still in need of growth, especially in understanding the mission of her Son more maturely, it was relatively advanced for that stage of her spiritual journey; the sign that Jesus worked in response to her prayerful request confirmed the faith of his disciples in him. And in the upper room, or Cenacle, during that period of prayerful preparation for Pentecost, Mary was in the midst of the Church about to be born of the Spirit as was her own Son. The Apostles, disciples, and other holy women were all persevering with one mind in prayer as Mary's motherly presence encouraged them (cf. Acts 1:14). Having been gloriously assumed into heaven, she continues to exercise her spiritual motherhood in the order of grace (cf. LG 62). And that which makes her Mother of the Church through her intercession and mediation also makes her model of the Church which, also as a virgin-mother, intercedes for the needs of all her children and mediates to them the gifts of salvation.

This leads us into a meditation upon Mary "the Virgin-Mother" (MC 19) as the model of the Church at worship. That spiritual motherhood is exercised by the Church in her ministries of Word and Sacrament. By her preaching she proclaims the Good News of our calling to be born again in Christ and incorporated into his Body the Church. By Baptism we are reborn by the power of the Holy Spirit and become the adopted children of the Father. We have seen, especially in Chapter VI, that one theological reason of fittingness for Mary's virginal motherhood, often given in the Tradition, is its symbolism for the Church as a Virgin-Mother. And the Eucharist is the greatest source of nourishing our life of Christ in the Church. Again, Mary's role both as mother and as model is to help dispose us to meet Christ more intimately and in a special way in the liturgical celebration of the Eucharistic Sacrifice.

In the mysteries of the Presentation of her Son in the Temple and of her own compassion at the foot of the cross, we find in Mary the perfect example of entering into the spirit of celebrating the Eucharistic liturgy as a sacrifice. As Abbot Marmion said in relating the saving mystery of the Presentation to the Passion: "It was like the offertory of the Sacrifice that was to be consummated on Calvary."[1] Unless we make our own daily sacrifices, as the cost of our Christian discipleship, a part of the offerings and one perfect sacrifice of Christ renewed in the Mass, we are not truly sharing in the liturgy. We should unite ourselves in the Holy Spirit with Mary and the whole Communion of Saints in heaven under the one eternal high priest in offering perfect praise and adoration to the Father and in receiving the gifts that can transform our lives (cf. MC 20).

Mary inspires the whole Church to have the suitable spirit of worship, not only corporately but also by providing us with instruction for our spiritual lives individually (cf. MC 21-23). In the next chapter we shall be considering how our liturgical worship ought to influence our private devotions to Mary. Liturgy is the purest expression of our faith in prayer and so should have a salutary impact upon all our forms of prayer. In our veneration and love of Mary, this devotion most frequently expresses itself through invocation or directly calling upon her for help. This form of Marian devotion, as with any of the saints, is almost exclusively found in personal prayers outside liturgical celebrations. Since the liturgy is essentially an act of worship or adoration (*latria*), the triune God is invoked or prayed to directly. Ordinarily the Father is addressed *through* the Son *in* the Spirit.[2]

CHAPTER XIII

Mary in Private Devotions
and Apparitions

As WAS pointed out in the first chapter, there is a close interdependence between the biblical and liturgical renewals that have been going on in our Church especially since Vatican II. This is very clearly manifested in the Marian renewal. Devotion to Mary, whether celebrated in the liturgy or expressed in popular forms of piety outside it, should be suffused with the spirit of the Scriptures. Pope Paul VI emphasized: "What is needed is that texts of prayers and chants should draw their inspiration and their wording from the Bible, and above all that devotion to the Virgin should be imbued with the great themes of the Christian message" (MC 30). Then the "Seat of Wisdom" will help us hear the word of God so as to live as faithful disciples of Incarnate Wisdom, her Son.

It is also of paramount importance that the spirit of the liturgical renewal inform the right ordering and development of devotion to Mary that is practiced by the faithful outside the liturgy. Of course, this is true in regard to all forms of extraliturgical or private prayer. Vatican II teaches: ". . . such devotions should be so drawn up that they harmonize with the liturgical seasons, accord with the sacred liturgy, are in some way derived from it, and lead the people to it, since in fact the liturgy by its very nature is far superior to any of them " (SC 13). It is important to note here that two attitudes have to be altered if the conciliar teaching is to be implemented. One is that private devotions are to be eliminated altogether. This is definitely *not* what Vatican II called us to do, since they should be harmonized with the liturgy and not suppressed (cf. MC 31). The other erroneous attitude is based upon a misinterpretation of what the Council means by "harmonize." It definitely does not mean that private devotions are to be inserted into the liturgy. The proper balance between these two extreme attitudes will be exemplified later in this chapter when we discuss the relationship of the Rosary devotion with the Eucharist.

One of the salutary influences of the liturgy upon our private devotions to Mary and all the saints is its practice of "comprecation."[1] This signifies the direct invocation of God asking that the intercessory prayers of the saints in heaven on our behalf be favorably received. On the solemnity of the Immaculate Conception, for instance, we pray: "[that through the prayers of the sinless virgin Mary, God will free us from our sins] — Father, you prepared the Virgin Mary to be the worthy Mother of your Son. You let her share beforehand in the salvation Christ would bring by his death, and kept her sinless from the first moment of her conception. Help us by her prayers to live in your presence without sin." Let us take note that Mary is never directly invoked in the prayer, since the liturgy is primarily an act of worship and adoration (*latria*), as was indicated at the end of the previous chapter. And let us also appreciate the graceful way in which the mystery of the feast, Mary's complete liberation from all sin, is made the special object of our beseeching the Father's help "by her prayers" in heaven. The prayer over the gifts repeats the very same petition directly addressed to the Lord: "Help us by her prayers, and free us from our sins."

When celebrating the Vigil Mass of the solemnity of the Assumption, the presiding celebrant invites us to pray with him: "Let us pray [with Mary to the Father, in whose presence she now dwells] — Almighty Father of our Lord Jesus Christ, you have revealed the beauty of your power by exalting the lowly Virgin of Nazareth and making her the Mother of our Savior. May the prayers of this woman clothed with the sun bring Jesus to the waiting world and fill the void of incompletion with the presence of her child, who lives and reigns with you and the Holy Spirit, one God, for ever and ever. Amen." We are invited to pray "with Mary to the Father" in this alternative opening prayer. It is salutary for us to be reminded from time to time that we often pray *with* Mary and the saints, especially in the liturgy. Even though in our private devotions it seems that we most frequently pray *to* Mary and the saints so that they may intercede or pray *for* us, it is good for us to realize that our companions in the celestial Communion of Saints constantly pray *with* as well as for us, whether or not we are invoking or praying *to* them. This should impress upon our faith-understanding that the triune God, and most precisely the Father, is the primordial source of all blessings received through our prayers. Also the intercessory power of the prayers of Mary and all the saints on our behalf is based upon the sovereignly free and loving will of the Father, who chooses to make them salvific for us. And so, although invocation of Mary and the saints in our private devotions is a well approved practice in the Catholic Tradition, it is still wise to use "comprecation" and to pray *with* them as well as *to* them in such devotions.

The two "exercises of piety" that Pope Paul VI chose to consider for his special observations on private Marian devotions are the Angelus and the Rosary. His reason for selecting them was that they are widespread in the West and the Apostolic See has on a number of occasions brought them to the attention of the faithful (cf. MC 40). He gave a much more detailed consideration to the Rosary, especially as it relates to the Eucharistic Liturgy (cf. MC 42-45), while limiting his observation on the Angelus to a single paragraph (cf. MC 41). In this chapter we shall be commenting and reflecting further upon his teaching about the Rosary. A few words, however, should be said in reference to the very simple but profoundly rich devotion of the Angelus.

The simplicity of the Angelus is in its structure.[2] It consists of three versicles and responses, each of which is followed by a "Hail Mary," another versicle and response, and concludes with a short prayer as follows:

V. The angel of the Lord declared unto Mary,
R. And she conceived by the Holy Spirit. (Hail Mary, etc.)
V. Behold the handmaid of the Lord.
R. Be it done unto me according to your word. (Hail Mary, etc.)
V. And the Word was made flesh.
R. And dwelt among us. (Hail Mary, etc.)
V. Pray for us, O holy Mother of God.
R. That we may be made worthy of the promises of Christ.
    Let us pray. Pour forth, we beseech thee, O Lord, thy grace into
    our hearts, that as we have known the incarnation of Christ, thy
    Son, by the message of an angel, so by his passion and cross

we may be brought to the glory of his resurrection. Through the
same Christ our Lord. Amen.

The profound richness of the Angelus is found in its "biblical character, its historical origin which links it to the prayer for peace and safety,
and its quasi-liturgical rhythm which sanctifies different moments during the day, and because it reminds us of the Paschal Mystery. . ."
(MC 41). Its biblical character is clearly based upon the Annunciation
scene in Luke and the first part of the "Hail Mary," which is the
angelic salutation and part of Elizabeth's greeting of Mary at the Visitation.

Its historical origin is western and medieval (cf. TH 379). It has
been traditionally said three times daily, about 6:00 A.M., at noon, and
at 6:00 P.M., which is its "quasi-liturgical rhythm which sanctifies different moments during the day." This is akin to the *Liturgy of the
Hours*, which is designed to sanctify various parts of the day: Morning
Prayer, Midday Prayer, Evening Prayer, and Compline or Night
Prayer before retiring. The Office of Readings may be said at any time.
The reference to the paschal mystery is in the brief concluding prayer:
". . . so by his passion and cross we may be brought to the glory of his
resurrection." The morning custom of reciting the Angelus is connected with the monastic habit of saying three Hail Marys during the
little hour of Prime. The noontide recitation apparently originated with
the custom of recalling the Passion on Fridays and praying especially
for peace.

Pope Callistus III then extended it throughout the week for the
special intention of praying for victory over the Turks. The saying of
three Hail Marys in the evening at the tolling of a curfew bell in some
places, probably from the eleventh century, marks the beginning of reciting the Angelus at 6:00 P.M. This devotional prayer was stand-
ardized by the sixteenth century, and several of the popes have highly
recommended it during the past century. Its simplicity and spiritual
richness make it as a most attractive form of Marian devotion. The
Angelus is an excellent example of a private prayer permeated by the
spirit of the Scriptures, imbued with the great themes of the Christian
message, nicely harmonized with the liturgy, and completely Christocentric in its invocation of Mary's intercession.

The Structure of the Rosary and Its Historical Evolution

Pope Paul VI was particularly concerned with the renewal of the Rosary devotion which, he pointed out, has been called "the compendium of the entire Gospel" (MC 42). In the same context he refers to the fact that his predecessors often "recognized its suitability for fostering contemplative prayer . . . and recalled its intrinsic effectiveness for promoting Christian life and apostolic commitment." And his predecessor Pope St. Pius V ". . . explained and in a certain sense established the traditional form of the Rosary."

Let us look immediately at this "traditional form," which was the termination of a process that took several centuries to develop. It was established by St. Pius V, a Dominican Pope, in 1569, and has come to be known as the "Dominican Rosary." It is composed of fifteen decades of Hail Marys, each decade preceded by the Our Father, followed by the Doxology, and accompanied by meditation upon a mystery of our redemption. The complete Rosary consists of 15 mysteries: the five joyful, namely, the Annunciation, Visitation, Nativity, Presentation of the Lord in the Temple, and the Finding of the Christ Child in the Temple, all of which are clearly found in the Lucan infancy narrative, and which contemplate the beginnings of our redemption in the Incarnation; the five sorrowful, namely, the Agony of Jesus in the Garden, the Scourging at the Pillar, the Crowning with Thorns, the Carrying of the Cross, and the Crucifixion, all of which are found in the Passion accounts of the four Gospels concerning the redemptive sufferings and death of Christ; and the glorious mysteries, namely, the Resurrection, the Ascension, the Descent of the Pentecostal Spirit, the Assumption, and the Coronation of Mary as Queen of Heaven, the first three of which are explicit in the New Testament, and which contemplate the glorification of the Son and his mother as well as the bestowal of the fruits of the redemption in the sending of the Spirit to give birth to the Church.[3] Usually, whether the Rosary is recited in private or in common, five decades are said while meditating on one set of mysteries, which is what the Church requires to gain a plenary indulgence for this devotion on any given day.

The Psalter or book of 150 Psalms in the Bible is the primary liturgical source of the Rosary. It is the most important part of the Liturgy of the Hours and has been for centuries in the daily recitation of the Divine Office. A "psalter of the laity" developed with the intention of making available to the faithful the spiritual riches of the liturgy. It consisted of a series of prayers composed of one hundred fifty parts to match the number of psalms. The Irish Monks of the early medieval period were in the custom of dividing the psalter into three sets of fifty psalms each, and they brought this custom with them on their missionary journeys to the European continent. The Lay Brothers in the monasteries were required to recite fifty psalms or fifty Our Fathers for the soul of a departed member of their community. The practice of saying the Lord's Prayer in place of a psalm began to spread among the laity, and so the origins of the Rosary began to take root. In order to keep count of the prayers said, strings of beads were used, and these would gradually become our Rosary beads.

Devotion to Mary began to express itself in a psalter of 150 Hail Marys. Toward the end of the twelfth century, the first half of the Hail Mary as we know it today began to share the importance of the Our Father and the Creed as prayers that all the faithful should know, and another stage in the evolution of the Rosary was reached. Next, meditation began to develop with the addition to each psalm of a phrase referring to Jesus and Mary. Then the psalms were dropped and the phrases became little lives of the mother and Son extending from the Annunciation to their glorification. Dominic of Prussia, a Carthusian monk, helped to popularize the devotion by linking fifty Hail Marys with fifty such phrases sometime during the years between 1410 and 1439. This is the origin of the word "Rosary," since the series of fifty points of meditation was called a *rosarium* (rose garden). At the time the term *rosarium* was used to designate any collection of common content. As a symbol of joy, however, the rose was fittingly referred to Mary, and the name "Rosary" later became the title for the recitation of fifty Hail Marys, while "psalter" was retained for one hundred fifty Hail Marys. It is interesting to note that to this day the most common pair of Rosary beads consists of fifty Hail Marys. About the same time as Dominic of Prussia, another Carthusian, Henry Kalkar, contributed further to the traditional form by organizing the Hail Marys into decades with our Fathers before each decade (cf. TH 313-314).

The essential elements of today's Rosary are recognizable from the early fifteenth century. But it had to be simplified before becoming a practical form of prayer for all the faithful, and one that could be recited alternately in common. By 1480, Rosaries of fifty mysteries, one for each Hail Mary, were reduced to five, one mystery for each decade. In 1483, *Our Dear Lady's Psalter*, a Rosary book by a Dominican, makes mention of fifteen mysteries, all of which are the same as we have today except the final two glorious mysteries. He combined the Assumption and Coronation into a single mystery and made the Last Judgment the fifteenth mystery or fifth glorious mystery. The Dominican Alberto de Costello in 1521 was the first to use the term "mysteries" in reference to the meditations for each decade. He combined the old and the new by attaching a mystery to each of the fifteen Our Fathers and retained the series of one hundred fifty as sub-mysteries for each Hail Mary. But during the course of the sixteenth century, the rosary of fifteen mysteries gained in popularity. In 1470 there was a significant event in the spread of the Rosary devotion throughout the universal Church. That year at Douai in northern France, a Dominican, Blessed Alan de la Roche, founded the Confraternity of the Psalter of Jesus and Mary. This was the forerunner of the Rosary confraternities that would spring up throughout the Catholic Church of the West. When Pope St. Pius V issued his Bull of 1569, *Consueverunt Romani Pontifices* (often called the *magna carta* of the Rosary), he was truly establishing a form that had taken several centuries to evolve. The honor and privilege of spreading the Rosary devotion among all the faithful belong in a special way to him and the Dominican Order as a whole. St. Pius completed the harmonious combination of mental and vocal prayer that is the very substance of the Rosary. He made a lasting contribution to the real meaning of the devotion by requiring meditation on the mysteries for gaining the Rosary indulgences. This is still a necessary condition today and has preserved the essentially contemplative spirit of the Rosary.

*The Rosary as a Contemplative Form of Private Prayer
and the Eucharist*

Returning to Pope Paul VI's observations on the Rosary, we find that they are just as timely today as they were when they first appeared in print a little over a decade ago. Having reflected upon the many spiritual advantages of practicing the Rosary devotion, particularly as a "Gospel prayer" (cf. MC 44), of "the principal salvific events accomplished in Christ" (cf. MC 45), and a "prayer with a clearly Christological orientation" (cf. MC 46), he proceeds to consider the contemplative element of the Rosary:

> There has also been felt with greater urgency the need to point out once more the importance of a further essential element in the Rosary, in addition to the value of the elements of praise and petition, namely the element of contemplation. Without this the Rosary is a body without a soul, and its recitation is in danger of becoming a mechanical repetition of formulas and of going counter to the warning of Christ: "And in praying do not heap up empty phrases as the Gentiles do; for they think that they will be heard for their many words" (Matthew 6:7). By its nature the recitation of the Rosary calls for a quiet rhythm and a lingering pace, helping the individual to meditate on the mysteries of the Lord's life as seen through the eyes of her who was closest to the Lord. In this way the unfathomable riches of these mysteries are unfolded. (MC 47).

The essence of the Rosary devotion, its very heart and soul, is to ponder the mysteries of our redemption over and over again, as Mary herself did when they were actually unfolding before her contemplative gaze (cf. Luke 2:19, 51). The repetition of the vocal prayers, predominantly the Our Fathers and Hail Marys, is the "body" of the Rosary. And this is not unimportant for us human beings. By nature we are body-persons or embodied spirits. We are a marvelous unity of matter and spirit, of body and soul. Without our bodies we could not be present to our world. We could neither grasp it nor communicate with it. Because of "bodiliness," our spiritual life cannot be purely angelic. Our prayer life requires outward signs and bodily participation in order for our spirits to be sustained. As Pope Paul put it: ". . . a quiet rhythm and a lingering pace . . ." help us to meditate upon the mysteries of our redemption in the recitation of the Rosary. One might liken the vocal prayers, the "body" of this devotion, to good background music while we are reading. There does not have to be any conceptual connection between what we are reading and the theme of the music in order for it to help focus our concentration upon the poetry or prose in the book before us. So too the Our Fathers and the Hail Marys can help to deepen our gaze of loving faith and hope upon our Redeemer as we contemplate the mysteries of our salvation. As a form of prayer distinct from others, the Rosary combines the mental or interior and the vocal or external in a relatively relaxing manner. It is designed to be a good preparation for other forms of prayer, e.g., for the more intense participation in liturgical celebrations, or for the purely interior prayer of quiet contemplation.

Like every authentic Marian devotion, the Rosary is Christocentric. Our Blessed Mother is every gently but firmly focusing our prayerful attention upon her Son. Looking at Jesus "through the eyes of her who was closest to" him is a very apt way of epitomizing the whole Rosary devotion. Her presence to us is that of our spiritual mother who wishes us to be spiritually nourished and refreshed in our whole being as human persons. When we acknowledge her presence through explicit thoughts about her role in our redemption, she immediately wants us to behold her as one who mirrors Christ most faithfully. And she mostly wants us to gaze upon him directly as our sole Savior. If we become upset because our minds cannot cover all the images and ideas inspired by the mysteries, Mary reminds us that it is not important in prayer to cover everything. Prayer is not identical with study. We study primarily to know and grow in understanding. But we pray primarily to deepen our love of God and neighbor. And one idea can be enough to sustain us in that contemplative act of loving throughout an entire recitation of the Rosary.

With the inspiration and enlightenment that we can receive from Mary, the Rosary devotion should be a very effective way of preparing to participate in the liturgical celebration of the Eucharist with greater faith, hope, and love. Let us listen at length to the words of wisdom in Paul VI's teaching about this:

> Finally, as a result of modern reflection, the relationships between the liturgy and the Rosary have been more clearly understood. On the one hand it has been emphasized that the Rosary is as it were a branch sprung from the ancient trunk of the Chris-

tian liturgy, the Psalter of the Blessed Virgin, whereby the humble were associated in the Church's hymn of praise and universal intercession. On the other hand it has been noted that this development occurred at a time — the last period of the Middle Ages — when the liturgical spirit was in decline and the faithful were turning from the liturgy toward a devotion to Christ's humanity and to the Blessed Virgin Mary, a devotion favoring a certain external sentiment of piety. Not many years ago some people began to express the desire to see the Rosary included among the rites of the liturgy, while other people, anxious to avoid repetition of former pastoral mistakes, unjustifiably disregarded the Rosary. Today the problem can easily be solved in the light of the principles of the Constitution *Sacrosanctum Concilium*. Liturgical Celebrations and the pious practice of the Rosary must be neither set in opposition to one another nor considered as being identical. The more an expression of prayer preserves its own true nature and individual characteristics, the more fruitful it becomes. Once the preeminent value of liturgical rites has been reaffirmed, it will not be difficult to appreciate the fact that the Rosary is a practice of piety which easily harmonizes with the liturgy. In fact, like the liturgy, it is of a community nature, draws its inspiration from Sacred Scripture, and is oriented toward the mystery of Christ.

The commemoration in the liturgy and the contemplative remembrance proper to the Rosary, although existing on essentially different planes of reality, have as their object the same salvific events wrought by Christ. The former presents anew, under the veil of signs and operative in a hidden way, the great mysteries of our redemption. The latter, by means of devout contemplation, recalls these same mysteries to the minds of the person praying and stimulates the will to draw from them the norms of living. Once this substantial difference has been established, it is not difficult to understand that the Rosary is an exercise of piety that draws its motivating force from the liturgy and leads naturally back to it, if practiced in conformity with its original inspiration.

It does not, however, become part of the liturgy. In fact meditation on the mysteries of the Rosary, by familiarizing the minds and hearts of the faithful with the mysteries of Christ, can be an excellent preparation for the celebration of those same mysteries in the liturgical action and can also become a continuing echo thereof. However, it is a mistake to recite the Rosary during the celebration of the liturgy, though unfortunately this practice still persists here and there. (MC 48)

Reflecting upon the historical origins of the Rosary from the liturgy, Paul VI applies to this pious practice the general principles that he had laid down earlier regarding the way in which private devotions should be harmonized with the liturgy. There ought to be no conflict between them! The two attitudes that are to be changed here are: 1) that the Rosary should be suppressed to avoid its taking the faithful away from the more important liturgical worship; and, 2) to make the Rosary itself a part of the liturgical rites. Of course, as he clearly says at the end of the above paragraph, it is an abuse to recite the Rosary during the celebration of the liturgy, since one cannot both do that and participate actively and intelligently in the liturgical celebration itself. If, however, the devotion is allowed to remain what it has always been historically, a very effective way of meditating upon the mysteries of our redemption with Mary, then it "can be an excellent preparation for the celebration of these same mysteries in the liturgical action and can also become a continuing echo thereof." This is the way to harmonize the private devotion of the Rosary with the Church's official public worship in the liturgy, which is celebrated in a special way through, with, and in Christ, our eternal high priest, under the outward signs of sacramental symbols.

In complete accord with Pope Paul's inspiring and balanced harmonizing of the Rosary with the liturgy, I should like to propose one way of meditating upon the mysteries of this contemplative devotion in close connection with the celebration of the Eucharist. This is a practical application of his idea about making the Rosary devotion an effective way of entering more deeply into the spirit of the liturgical celebration as well as sustaining the special graces received from Christ in the Eucharist. The Rosary becomes both a preparation for a more fervent encounter with Christ in Holy Communion and also a "continuing echo thereof" afterward by helping inspire us to live in cooperation with the sacramental graces that we were given in the liturgy.

There is a parallel between the three sets of mysteries in the Rosary and the main aspects of the mystery of the Holy Eucharist. The joyful mysteries are especially related to the Real Presence. The sorrowful mysteries are appropriately associated with the Eucharist as a sacrifice. And the glorious mysteries are closely connected with the

Holy Eucharist as Holy Communion or the Blessed Sacrament of divine love.

Within the same framework, we may emphasize both the main Marian doctrines and the theological virtues of the Christian life: the Real Presence and the joyful mysteries, with faith and Mary's virginal motherhood of the Word made flesh; the Eucharistic Sacrifice and sorrowful mysteries, with hope and Mary's compassion; and, Holy Communion and the glorious mysteries, with love and Mary's Assumption as the consummation of her holiness begun in the Immaculate Conception.

Meditation upon the joyful mysteries of the Rosary is a wonderful way of deepening our faith in the saving truth that Jesus Christ, Son of God and Son of Mary, is really and truly present to us in the Holy Eucharist. At the Annunciation Mary received the grace to respond with loving faith to God's calling that she become the Virgin Theotokos, and her most chaste womb was made the "first tabernacle" of the Lord's presence as the Word incarnate. As we contemplate the joyful mysteries of our redemption with Mary in the setting of Luke's infancy narrative, it is clear that she was inspired by the Spirit of God from the very beginning to share her Son's saving presence with others. Even before the birth of her Child, Mary brought the Infant in her own womb to mediate that saving presence to Elizabeth and the child in her womb during the Visitation. After the Nativity, Mary and her husband, Joseph, showed him to the shepherds, who represent God's poor. During the Presentation of the Child in the Temple, Mary was granted by Simeon a prophetic glimpse into the sorrowful mysteries that she would share with her Son. Both she and Joseph grew in their faith through the experience of searching for the lost Child and finding him in the temple. They came to realize more fully that intimacy with him and his mission meant the suffering of making the sacrifices required by the Father's salvific will. Mary's own "Rosary" was pondering the mysteries of her redemption and ours as they unfolded before her (cf. Luke 2:19, 51). If we invite her to do so, Mary will help us believe with a deeper conviction of our faith that our saving God continues to dwell in our midst through his Real Presence in the Eucharist. Meditating over and over again with Mary and like Mary upon the joyful mysteries of the Rosary should help to deepen the redemptive grace of our faith in her Son's Real Presence as our Eucharistic Savior.

The contemplative recitation of the sorrowful mysteries beholds Mary's compassion with Christ's suffering and death. Contemplating his passion with her and like her is to share in his redemptive suffering. Through her example and inspiration, we learn how to behold him in his agony, not as mere onlookers but as his disciples called to take up our cross daily and follow him. Our hope is thereby strengthened, since we are more convinced that Jesus and Mary are with us to give our own sacrifices a redemptive meaning and value. We should be strengthened to enter into the spirit of the Sacrifice of the Mass with greater generosity and confidence. Through Mary's intercession and mediation, we grow better disposed to accept the graces of a more courageous hope about the sacrifices necessary to bear witness to Christ in a society that generally ridicules the values of his Gospel. We make such sacrifices a part of the one perfect sacrifice of our eternal high priest. In the Rosary devotion, our spiritual mother continually reminds us that we are saved only by living the Mass. As always, Mary directs our attention upon her Son as the sole Savior whose redemptive graces are offered to us in a most special manner in the holy Sacrifice of the Mass.

In meditating upon the glorious mysteries of the Rosary, we find a way of preparing to receive our risen Lord in Holy Communion with a more generous love in our hearts. Mary is the model and mediatrix of the graces that we continuously need to become better disposed to grow in love through the effects of the Eucharist as a sacrament. No human person ever responded more fully to God's love than she. Now she makes intercession for us that we too may encounter Christ more intimately in our lives of faith, hope, and love. The special sacramental grace of Holy Communion is that of actually growing in love of the Lord and of one another at the very moment of meeting Christ in the Sacrament of his divine love for us. By anticipation we share more fully, even here upon earth, in the life of eternal love of Jesus, Mary, Joseph, and all the saints in the heavenly Church.

Mary in Her Apparitions and Private Revelations
    Devotion to Mary, particularly in practices of popular piety, has

been very much influenced by her authenticated appearances, especially since the Apparition at Lourdes in 1858. Other apparitions of Our Lady that have been carefully investigated and approved by the Church as worthy of pious belief are Guadalupe, La Salette, the experiences of St. Catherine Labouré, and Fatima (cf. BYM 99). This does not necessarily imply that all other alleged appearances have been condemned, but that they do not yet have special ecclesiastical approbation. Even after such approval is officially bestowed by the Church, however, the event and the religious experiences associated with the visions remain in the realm of private revelation. This means that they are not being proposed to Catholics as objects of their divine faith and beliefs that are necessary for salvation. Only the mysteries and dogmas based upon divine "public" revelation are in that category.

Before briefly glancing at each one of these five authenticated appearances of Our Lady, let us make sure that we have a clear and balanced understanding of how they fit into Marian doctrine and devotion generally. Let us listen to our American bishops' teaching on the topic:

> These providential happenings serve as reminders to us of basic Christian themes: prayer, penance, and the necessity of the sacraments. After due investigation, the Church has approved the pilgrimages and other devotions associated with certain private revelations. She has also at times certified the holiness of their recipients by beatification, for example, St. Bernadette of Lourdes and St. Catherine Labouré. The Church judges the devotions that have sprung from these extraordinary events in terms of its own traditional standards. Catholics are encouraged to practice such devotions when they are in conformity with authentic devotion to Mary. Even when a "private revelation" has spread to the entire world, as in the case of Our Lady of Lourdes, and has been recognized in the liturgical calendar, the Church does not make mandatory the acceptance either of the original story or of particular forms of piety springing from it. With the Vatican Council, we remind true lovers of our Lady of the danger of superficial sentiment and vain credulity. Our faith does not seek new gospels, but leads us to know the excellence of the Mother of God and moves us to a filial love toward our Mother and to imitation of her virtues. (BYM 100)

If we view these apparitions of Mary along with the private revelations or special messages accompanying them in proper perspective, they can be spiritually enriching. It is in this spirit of seeing how they can inspire us to live up to our faith in her Son more fully that we very briefly take a look at these that have been officially declared worthy of our pious belief.

During December of 1531, the Blessed Virgin appeared twice to a Mexican Indian who had recenty been baptized Juan Diego. She came to him at Tepeyac near Mexico City with the instruction to tell the local bishop that a church should be built in her honor in that place. When he did as Mary had instructed him, roses fell from his mantle upon which a painting of Our Lady appeared as she had looked in the apparitions. Taking this as a miraculous sign, the bishop had a small church built in 1533 in accord with Mary's wishes, and a larger structure, started in 1556, was dedicated in 1709. Over the centuries there were additions. Today a new basilica, dedicated in the late 1960s, stands in Mexico City as the center of widespread devotion to Our Lady of Guadalupe. In 1945 Pope Pius XII named her patroness of the Americas. The proper opening prayer of her feast on December 12 in the American dioceses conveys the Gospel values of justice and peace, so crucial in ministries to the Hispanic peoples today, just as they were needed when Mary appeared to Juan Diego, who belonged to an oppressed class in his day. The prayer for this Marian memorial is: "God of power and mercy, you blessed the Americas at Tepeyac with the presence of the Virgin Mary of Guadalupe. May her prayers help all men and women to accept each other as brothers and sisters. Through your justice present in our hearts, may your peace reign in the world. We ask this. . . ."

On November 27, 1830, the most important of many visions of Mary to a Sister of Charity of St. Vincent de Paul took place. Since her canonization in 1947, she has been known as St. Catherine Labouré. In that vision within her convent chapel in the Rue du Bac at Paris, she saw Mary standing on a half-globe, with rays of light emanating from her fingers, surrounded by the words: "Mary conceived free from sin, pray for us who have recourse to thee." And then the same vision showed her a cross, the initial M, the heart of Jesus garlanded with thorns, and the heart of Mary pierced by a sword, all set about with twelve stars. A voice within her said to have a medal struck that would represent what she had seen in the vision, promising that all who wore it with devotion would receive great graces through the intercession of the Mother of God. Similar visions were repeated up to September, 1831. Sister Catherine followed her inspiration, and after investigation, the Archbishop of Paris permitted the medal to be struck. Fifteen hundred were issued in June, 1832. At the same time a book on the subject had huge sales in many languages, including Chinese. In 1838, a confraternity with the medal as its badge was founded at the church of Our Lady of Victories in Paris. Calling it the "Miraculous Medal" seems to be due to its origins, but the wonders of grace associated with the medal around the world are plentiful. As mentioned in Chapter VIII, it contributed greatly to the popular devotion and belief of the faithful in the Immaculate Conception defined in 1854.

On September 19, 1846, Our Lady appeared to two children who were watching cattle on a high mountain some miles from La Salette-Fallavaux in France. This was her only apparition to them. With tears she lamented the terrible irreligion of the people, mentioning servile work on Sunday and abusive language. Before departing she impressed upon them the need to make all she said known to her people. The children obeyed her. To look after the shrine built at the place of the apparition, a society of priests was organized and grew into the congregation of Missionaries of La Salette. When they first came to the United States in 1892, they found that devotion to Our Lady of La Salette had reached North America before them. In France there was apparently a connection between Mary's message to the two children and an organized effort to improve the observance of Sunday.

Between February 11 and July 16, 1858, Our Lady appeared to Bernadette Soubirous eighteen times in Lourdes in Southern France. Her family was very poor. The first apparition took place when she went to gather firewood with two younger children. She became separated from them on the bank of the River Gave, and her attention was drawn by the rustling of bushes at the mouth of a shallow cave or grotto in a rocky cliff. Then she saw a very beautiful girl, no taller than she, with a long Rosary hung over her arm. She seemed to Bernadette to be inviting her to pray. Bernadette knelt, took the Rosary from her pocket, and began to say it. The figure before her passed the beads through her fingers, but did not move her lips. Nothing was said, and at the end of five decades the figure smiled and disappeared. Another time Our Lady appeared to Bernadette was on the feast of the Annunciation, March 25, 1858. When Bernadette asked her name, the reply was: "I am the Immaculate Conception." The dogma had been defined just four years before. Her final apparition was on July 16, 1858, the feast of Our Lady of Mount Carmel. St. Bernadette was canonized in 1933. The feast of Our Lady of Lourdes is celebrated as an optional memorial on February 11. In the proper opening prayer, Mary is referred to as "the sinless mother of God." Today Lourdes is the shrine and center of pilgrimage with the widest international appeal. The apparitions are well documented. It has been the place where many miraculous cures have occurred. Popular piety and the liturgy are beautifully combined at Lourdes, which has inspired many people to devote themselves to the care of others. Mary and the Eucharist is a theme particularly evoked there (cf. TH 224-225).

Our Lady appeared to three children in Fatima, a scattered parish in mountainous country roughly in the middle of Portugal. She told them that she came from heaven, and asked that they return to the same place each month at the same hour of the same day for six months. She also told them to accept sufferings for the sake of sinners and to pray for peace. On June 13 she repeated the instructions. On October 13, she told the children that she wanted a chapel built there in her honor as the "Lady of the Rosary," which prayer she wished to be recited daily. She foretold the end of World War I. Then there took place the so-called miracle of the dancing sun, which seemed to rotate, emitting rays of brightly colored light, and then appeared to fall to the earth. Fifty thousand witnesses were seized with panic, thinking it was the end of the world. But things returned to normal after about ten minutes. Some people later reported seeing the extraordinary occurrences miles away. After seven years of examination, the local ordinary declared that the apparitions were worthy of credence and authorized the cult of Our Lady of Fatima. Two of the children died within three years of the apparitions, but Lucia entered a convent. She has revealed that Our Lady asked for the practice of penance, daily recitation of the

Rosary, and increased devotion to her Immaculate Heart. Over the years Sister Lucia manifested a number of other messages from Our Lady of Fatima, including her requests that Russia be consecrated to her Immaculate Heart and that the first Saturdays of the month be a time for Communions of reparation. Fatima, like Lourdes, has become a great center of pilgrimage. Among the many Fatima shrines in the United States is one at the Dominican Nuns' Monastery in Summit, N.J. An American Dominican priest, Father Thomas McGlynn, has sculpted the best statue of Our Lady of Fatima under the very careful supervision of Sister Lucia. It stands above the main door of the church at the shrine of Fatima, Portugal. Most importantly, concerning Fatima and all the apparitions and private revelations that we have been briefly considering, they have been providential happenings which have spread genuine devotion to Mary, whose message has always drawn people closer to her Son.

CHAPTER XIV

A Madonna for All Christians

JUST A little over two decades ago, on February 2, 1965, Pope Paul VI was expressing his hopes for the Fourth International Mariological Congress to be held in Santo Domingo, Dominican Republic, the following month. He conveyed his wishes that the participants would clarify the pure fonts of Marian devotion in sacred Scripture, the Fathers of the Church, the liturgy, the theological reflections of the masters, and in the traditional teaching of the Eastern and Western Church. And with Vatican II's Decree on Ecumenism fresh in his mind — it had been issued only a few months before on November 21, 1964 — he expressed his prayerful wish that Mary would help bring about the reunion of us all as "The Mother of Unity."

This final chapter of the book contemplates Mary as "The Mother of Unity." Having looked at the many Madonnas in the Catholic Tradition over the ages, from the New Testament to our own times, we now turn to see how Mary may be portrayed to our sisters and brothers in the other Christian churches. How can they come to recognize her as the "handmaid of the Lord" in Luke's Annunciation scene, or "the mother of Jesus" at Cana and the "woman" at the foot of the cross in John's Gospel, or the "New Eve" in the undivided Church of the early Fathers? Can they also venerate her as "The Mother of Unity" even though ecumenical difficulties remain regarding her and other important matters of our one faith in Christ? How much progress has been made on the path to the one Church of Christ, particularly in reference to the Marian question and since the day over twenty years ago when Paul VI prayed for reunion through Mary? Has she actually become more a help towards unity than a hindrance to our quest for it? We shall be addressing just such questions as these by taking inventory on what has been going on since Vatican II concerning Mary and the ecumenical movement, by reflecting upon the signs of hope and the difficulties remaining in the matter, and by proposing how Mary may become for us "The Mother of Unity," "A Madonna for all Christians."

Mary and the Ecumenical Movement

Since the International Mariological Congress at Santo Domingo in 1965, the theme of which was "Mary in the New Testament," there have been five more such congresses: 1967 in Lisbon; 1971 in Zagreb; 1975, during May of the Holy Year, in Rome; 1979 in Zaragoza, Spain; and 1983 in Malta. Each congress chooses a period in the Tradition to consider developments in Marian doctrine and devotion. Those of us who have participated can testify that the ecumenical aspects of the various themes have been carefully included. They have examined the many sources of Marian piety that the various Christian traditions hold in common. Theologians and pastors of the Orthodox, Anglican, and Protestant churches have been invited to deliver papers, and representatives from the different communions enter into special dialogues with a group of Roman Catholic theologians. An ecumenical statement resulting from these conversations has been an important part of these congresses.

Other efforts to include Mary in the quest for Christian unity on the international level during the past two decades began with the founding of the Ecumenical Society of the Blessed Virgin Mary (ESBVM). It was founded in London during 1967 to promote ecumenical devotion and the study at various levels of the place of Mary in the Church under Christ. In the almost twenty years of its existence, this society has given good reason for calling upon Mary as "The Mother of Unity." Started at a time when most Catholics considered it premature to involve Mary in the ecumenical dialogues, ESBVM has been able to help bring many Christians much closer together in England, especially Anglicans, Methodists, and Roman Catholics. It has sponsored international conferences on themes of Marian ecumenism on the average of every other year since 1971. Its founding father, H. Martin Gillet, was the first General Secretary and an inspiration to all of us members until his death in 1980. ESBVM has spread not only throughout England but to other countries as well, including the United States. The American society started in 1976 through special efforts centered at the National Shrine of the Immaculate Conception in Washington, D.C., and continues to meet twice annually. Like the English society which helped inspire its foundation, it places emphasis upon devotion as well as doctrine and always includes a prayer service at the meetings. Publications of the English ESBVM may be found in special issues of *The Way* (1975, 1981) and *One in Christ* (1979) as well as single pamphlets or review articles (cf. TH 382-383).

Also during the past two decades, the Mariological Society of America has devoted special attention to the scientific study of the ecumenical dimension of Mariology. *Marian Studies*, the proceedings of its annual national convention, contains a number of papers and presidential addresses showing the society's keen interest in and theological concern for Mary's indispensable role in the quest for the one Church of Christ. Each year since 1967 (except 1972), Father Eamon Carroll, outstanding member of our society over the years, has been giving a paper entitled "A Survey of Recent Mariology." He always includes a section on the ecumenical writings about Mary. It is an excellent way to keep updated on good reading regarding Marian doctrine and devotion.

More and more over the years, Mary has become a part of the ecumenical dialogues between the Roman Catholic Church and the other Christian communities. As a participant in three of these on the national level in our country, I can say from experience that the Marian issues help to concretize more fundamental ecumenical questions. As we have seen in this book, particularly in Chapters VIII and IX on the defined dogmas of our Catholic Faith concerning the Immaculate Conception and Assumption, the basic question of the relationship between Scripture and Tradition in the Church's teaching was concretely considered in explaining how they may be accepted as a part of divine revelation. The proper interpretation of Mary's free consent at the Annunciation also makes more apparent just what is at stake in the ecumenical conversations about the grace of redemption as a completely unmerited gift of God. In the next section of this chapter, we shall be discussing these and other issues of Marian ecumenism in greater detail.

Signs of Hope and Difficulties Concerning Mary and Ecumenism

Generally speaking, there are three hopeful signs as well as three roadblocks regarding Mary in our prayerful quest for Christian unity.[1] Of course, the very progress that has apparently been made in the matter during the past two decades or so is itself no small sign of hope. The difficult distance that we still must travel together, however, keeps us realistic regarding what has yet to be done in the dialogues. And we always remain prayerfully hopeful that the obstacles will be overcome in and through the Spirit of authentic unity.

Let us take a look at the three main difficulties first, since then we should be in a better position to assess the signs of hope. Appropriately enough, each one of these obstacles appears to be in opposition to one or another of the three basic principles of the Protestant Reformation, namely, the three *only*'s: *sola scriptura, sola fides,* and *solus Christus.* First of all, the *sola scriptura* principle, which prohibits the Church's proposing as a matter of faith or dogma necessary for salvation any belief or practice not explicitly contained in sacred Scripture, would seem to be violated by the Marian dogmas of the Immaculate Conception and Assumption. As we have considered in Chapters VIII and IX, there is certainly no clear revelation of them in the inspired word of God. The proposals made about the ways in which they might be implied in Holy Writ as divine suggestions or insinuations, contained in such a biblical theme as "Daughter of Sion," must be discussed in much greater depth in our ecumenical dialogues about Mary.

Secondly *sola fides,* or justification through faith alone, seems to be opposed by the traditional Catholic view of Mary as a model of our human cooperation with grace in performing good deeds as a part of working out our salvation. The interpretation of her *fiat* at the Annunciation as a meritorious act by Mary runs counter to the traditional Protestant understanding of our salvation as a completely gratuitous gift of God's redeeming love in Christ from our first grace at justification through our final perseverance. There seems to be no room for merit or cooperating with grace as deserving of growth in grace and of a heavenly reward, as there has been in the Catholic teaching on grace. And Mary comes across to our Protestant brothers and sisters as the outstanding example of this Catholic doctrine about salvation. In the course of this book, particularly when discussing Mary's free consent given at the Annunciation, we have tried to clarify that doctrine as in no way intending to detract from the complete gratuitousness of saving grace in Christ. It was pointed out that human freedom to cooperate with grace and so to merit God's pleasure and rewards is itself the result of grace. This basic ecumenical question, however, requires further discussion, especially as embodied in Mary's unique share in her Son's redemptive activity.

The third difficulty, which concerns devotion more than doctrine, at least directly, follows upon our interpretation of the "merits" of Mary and all the saints in glory (cf. Chapter XI). It is the practice of invoking or calling upon Mary and the saints. Ordinarily this pious practice of private devotion is called "praying to" Mary and the saints. When it is put that way, our Protestant sisters and brothers become especially suspicious about it. In fact, it might be wise, as with the term "Co-Redemptrix," not to use the phrase "pray to" except in our directly addressing the triune God and Jesus Christ. "Invoke" or "call upon" expresses the spiritual reality more clearly. Although, from the viewpoint of doctrinal differences, this particular obstacle is not the most profound problem, still it does have to do with a practice that deeply touches the religious spirit of our people generally. It appears to go against the third Protestant principle, *solus Christus*. Christ alone is the Mediator between God and us. Any other form of mediation on the part of Mary and the other saints is an intrusion. Invoking their intercessory prayer seems to be saying that the intercession that Christ, our one eternal high priest, is always making for us is not sufficient.

It would be helpful for us to realize why the great Reformers, Martin Luther and John Calvin, were evidently so concerned about this matter.[2] After all it had been a practice of both the Eastern and Western Church for more than a thousand years before their time, dating back to the martyrs and very early devotion to Mary, e.g., the *Sub Tuum* prayer (cf. Chapter XI). But Luther and Calvin were reacting against certain abuses that had crept into the practice over the centuries. The emphasis that emerged in popular piety during the Middle Ages was the image of Mary as the merciful mother pleading the cause of sinful people before the throne of Christ the just judge. So, in the popular religious imagination, she came to represent mercy tempering Christ's strict justice. One went to her with complete confidence, since the Son could not refuse the requests of his mother.

This unfortunate development was the result of a long and complex process in the worship of the Church, which had its adverse effect upon popular devotion. In brief, it seems to have resulted, at least in part, from the struggle of the Catholic Church to overcome the Semi-Arianism of the barbarian peoples who were converted to Christianity during late antiquity, especially the Visigoths. To counteract their denial of Christ's divinity, more and more the Christ of faith, in heaven, was looked upon as the second Person of the Holy Trinity, and the unique mediatorship of his risen humanity was lost sight of to a great extent in the pious practices of the faithful. The liturgical prayers and practices of the Church never intended that it should happen, but the strong affirmation of Christ's divinity in heaven led to a lessening of the significance of his glorified humanity. For instance, Sunday became less and less the Lord's Day, a little Easter celebrating the resurrection, and more and more Trinity Sunday. The liturgical renewal of our own times is trying to restore the early Church's Sunday celebration of the Lord's resurrection and the strong faith in the unique mediatorship of his glorified humanity. To fill the gap left during the Middle Ages by losing sight of the Lord's role as mediator, the mediation of Mary and the saints began to grow among the faithful. While this development had its good side, it did lead to abuses.

And so this attitude in popular devotion, which regarded it necessary to go to the mother in order to win the Son's mercy, introduced excesses into pious practices in the Church. It was one set of abuses that required reform. Unfortunately, Luther and Calvin, who started out to reform the Church from within and not to found new churches, did not succeed. And their legitimate protest against the excesses in popular devotion to Mary and other saints led toward the opposite extreme of minimalism, almost to the point of extinction, at least among their spiritual descendants. Their reduction of Marian feasts to a minimum led eventually to an absence of Mary from the Protestant faith generally. If faith is both expressed and nourished by worship, then it stands to reason that faith will be negatively influenced when a belief is no

longer celebrated regularly in the liturgy. Luther and Calvin themselves, however, did retain considerable faith in and devotion to Mary,
as we shall soon see in the third sign of hope for Mary and the quest for
one Church of Christ.

The first sign of hope has been the common study of the sacred
Scriptures by Protestant and Catholic biblical scholars. An outstanding
contribution in this respect, one that this book has made good use of, is
Mary in the New Testament. This book is the result of work done by
an ecumenical task force of New Testament scholars representing a
number of Christian traditions. Their joint study has made a specific
contribution to the whole issue of *sola scriptura* and possible developments of Marian doctrine in the tradition through their discussion
about "lines of development" out of the New Testament portrait of
Mary. A second sign of hope is seen in another attempt to return to our
common Christian patrimony, i.e., the study of the Fathers of the
Church. To a great extent, their witness to the apostolic faith took
place in the undivided Church of the first four ecumenical councils of
Nicea (325), I Constantinople (381), Ephesus (431), and Chalcedon
(451). As we know from our own study in this book, particularly in
Chapter V, "New Eve," the patristic Madonna was faithfully based
upon the New Testament portrait of Mary as the woman of faith and
the perfect disciple. This Marian emphasis helps us to approach the
sola fides principle with more mutual understanding.

The rediscovery of the Marian writings among the Reformers
gives us a third sign of hope about Mary and ecumenism. Outstanding
in this regard is Luther's magnificent commentary upon Mary's *Magnificat*. Calvin wrote his own commentary on the same canticle.
Zwingli expressed his belief in Mary's glorious Assumption. They all
wrote and preached extensively about devotion to Mary. It does appear
that a reexamination of their works in a much more ecumenical light
than was ever possible during the polemical period between Trent and
Vatican II should help us make some further progress along the path to
unity.

The Holy Spirit and Mary as "The Mother of Unity"
Within the bosom of the Holy Trinity, the Holy Spirit is the in-

finite Love between the Father and the Son. And so the Spirit is the bond of unity among the three divine Persons. Through Christ our redeemer, the same Pentecostal Spirit is the only bond of true Christian unity in the Church. The one Body of Christ is built up in love through the gifts of the Spirit. At the same time, the "Finger of God," as the third Person is called in the Tradition, touches each one of us in such a way that nothing good in our individual personality is suppressed. And so God's Spirit is one of a rich Christian diversity as well as a deep unity. Under the enlightenment and the inspiration of the Holy Spirit, however, our own personal gifts are always for the good of others and are not selfishly exploited for purely private gains. Similarly, the same Spirit is guiding our churches toward a truly "catholic" unity which leaves ample room for our special traditions in spirituality, liturgy, theology, governance, etc. The Spirit of Truth does call us to unity in the essentials of faith, worship, and Church structure, but confides to our creative freedom the varied ways in which we can express our faith, celebrate our liturgies, and perform our distinct but related functions in the daily life of the one Church of Christ.

However this Christian unity will be achieved, Mary must have a motherly role to play in its quest. The Spirit of God came upon her to make her the Theotokos, the mother of him who is the center of all Christian unity, Jesus Christ. As she exercises her spiritual motherhood to draw us closer to her Son, Mary cannot but be contributing to the cause of unity. To come closer to Christ must mean that we, both as individuals and as members of our different communions, are coming closer to one another in Christ. It is devoutly hoped that the different Madonnas portrayed in the course of this book will blend to become a "Madonna for all Christians."

Notes

Chapter I:

1. Pope John Paul II, "Call of the Extraordinary Synod," *The Extraordinary Synod — 1985: Message to the People of God* (Boston: St. Paul Editions, 1985), p. 20.
2. *Ibid.*, pp. 102-103.
3. *Vatican Council II — The Conciliar and Post Conciliar Documents*, Austin Flannery, O.P., Gen. Ed. (Northport, N.Y.: Costello Publishing Co., 1977). All translations of Vatican II documents and references to them in this book are taken from this edition.
4. Otto Semmelroth, S.J., "Chapter VIII — The Role of the Blessed Virgin Mary, Mother of God, in the Mystery of Christ and the Church," in *Commentary on the Documents of Vatican II*, Vol. I, Herbert Vorgrimler, Gen. Ed. (New York: Herder and Herder, 1967), p. 286.
5. Cf. Yves Congar, O.P., *Christ, Our Lady, and the Church: A Study in Eirenic Theology* (Westminster, Md.: Newman Press, 1957).
6. Quoted by Léon Cardinal Suenens, "Mary and the World of Today," in *L'Osservatore Romano*, English edition, June 15, 1972.

Chapter II:

1. Cf. Lucien Deiss, C.S.Sp., *Daughter of Sion* (Collegeville, Minn.: Liturgical Press, 1972).
2. *Early Christian Fathers*, Cyril C. Richardson, Ed. (New York: Macmillan Pub. Co., 1970), p. 21.

Chapter III:

1. Cf. *The Teaching of Christ: A Catholic Catechism for Adults*, Ronald Lawler, O.F.M. Cap., Donald W. Wuerl, Thomas C. Lawler, Ed. (Huntington, Ind.: Our Sunday Visitor, Inc., 1976), p. 110.
2. Cf. *Mary in the New Testament*, Raymond E. Brown, Karl P. Donfried, Joseph A. Fitzmeier, S.J., John Reumann, Ed. (Philadelphia: Fortress Press & New York / Ramsey, N.J. / Toronto: Paulist Press, 1978), pp. 9-12.
3. *The Jerome Biblical Commentary*, Raymond E. Brown, S.S., Joseph A. Fitzmeier, S.J., Roland E. Murphy, O. Carm., Ed. (Englewood Cliffs, N.J.: Prentice-Hall,

Inc., 1968), pp. 1-6, "Synoptic Problem," F. Gast, O.C.D., in Vol. II, *The New Testament and Topical Articles.*

4. *Mary in the New Testament, op. cit.*, pp. 77-83.
5. Raymond E. Brown, *The Birth of the Messiah: A Commentary on the Infancy Narratives in Matthew and Luke* (Garden City, N.Y.: Doubleday & Co., Inc., 1977), pp. 165-201.
6. *Mary in the New Testament, op. cit.*, p. 107.
7. Wilfrid J. Harrington, O.P., *The Gospel According to St. Luke: A Commentary* (Westminster, Md. / New York / Glen Rock, N.J. / Amsterdam / Toronto: Newman Press, 1967), p. 47.
8. *Ibid.*, p. 52.
9. *Mary in the New Testament, op. cit.*, p. 140.
10. *Ibid.*, p. 177.
11. René Laurentin, "Mary: Model of the Charismatic as Seen in Acts 1-2, Luke 1-2, and John," *Mary, the Spirit and the Church*, Vincent P. Branick, S.M., Ed., (New York: Paulist Press, 1980), pp. 28-39.

Chapter IV:

1. Cf. *Daughter of Sion, op. cit.*, pp. 209-216.
2. Cf. *The Jerome Biblical Commentary, op. cit.*, Vol. II, pp. 414-421.
3. *Mary in the New Testament, op. cit.*, p. 211.
4. *Ibid.*, p. 210.
5. *The Jerome Biblical Commentary, op. cit.*, Vol. II, p. 469.
6. *Mary in the New Testament, op. cit.*, p. 225.
7. *Mary in the New Testament, op. cit.*, p. 231.

Chapter V:

1. *Daughter of Sion, op. cit.*, p. 207.
2. *Early Christian Fathers, op. cit.*, p. 347.
3. *Daughter of Sion, op. cit.*, p. 204.
4. Cf. J. A. Ross Mackenzie, "The Patristic Witness to the Virgin Mary as the New Eve," *Marian Studies*, Vol. XXIX, 1978, pp. 67-78.
5. Cf. J. H. Newman, *The New Eve* (Westminster, Md.: Newman Press, 1952), pp. 61-62.

Chapter VI:

1. Frederick M. Jelly, O.P., "Mary's Virginity in the Symbols and Councils," *Marian Studies*, Vol. XXI, 1970, p. 87.
2. J. N. D. Kelly, *Early Christian Creeds* (N.Y.: Longman, Inc., 1972), pp. 74-75.
3. *Ibid.*, p. 89.
4. *Ibid.*, pp. 92-93.
5. *Ibid.*, p. 296.
6. Donald G. Daw, *From Dysfunction to Disbelief: The Virgin Mary in Reformed*

Theology (Washington, D.C.: Ecumenical Society of the Blessed Virgin Mary, 1977), pp. 8-9.

7. Cf. "Mary's Virginity in the Symbols and Councils," *op. cit.*, p. 91.

8. Karl Rahner, *Theological Investigations* 4 (Baltimore: Helicon, 1966), *"Virginitas in Partu:* A contribution to the problem of the development of dogma and of tradition," pp. 134-162.

9. John McHugh, *The Mother of Jesus in the New Testament* (Garden City, N.Y.: Doubleday & Co., Inc., 1975), pp. 223-233.

10. *Ibid.*, pp. 234-254.

Chapter VII:

1. J. N. D. Kelly, *Early Christian Doctrines* (New York / Evanston, Ill. / London: Harper & Row, Publishers, 1959), pp. 310-311.

2. *The New Eve, op. cit.*, p. 89. ¶3. *Early Christian Doctrines, op. cit.*, pp. 338-343.

4. Reginald H. Fuller, "New Testament Roots to the Theotokos," *Marian Studies,* Vol. XXIX, 1978, p. 46.

5. Cf. John C. Murray, S.J.., *The Problem of God* (New Haven: Yale University Press, 1964), pp. 40-53.

6. Frederick M. Jelly, O.P., "The Concrete Meaning of Mary's Motherhood," *The Way Supplement, Mary and Ecumenism,* No. 45, June 1982, p. 30

7. René Laurentin, *The Question of Mary* (New York: Holt, Rinehart and Winston, 1965), pp. 40-53, 142-143.

Chapter VIII:

1. *Papal Teachings: Our Lady* (Boston: St. Paul Editions, 1961), No. 32

2. Cf. Frederick M. Jelly, O.P., "Marian Dogmas Within Vatican II's Hierarchy of Truths," *Marian Studies*, Vol. XXVII, 1976, pp. 17-40.

3. Edward Schillebeeckx, O.P., "Exegesis, Dogmatics and the Development of Dogma," *Dogmatic Vs. Biblical Theology*, Herbert Vorgrimler, Ed. (Baltimore / Dublin: Helicon, 1964), p. 140.

4. *Ibid.*, pp. 115-145.

5. *The New Eve, op. cit.*, p. 62.

6. Karl Rahner, S.J., "The Immaculate Conception," in *Theological Investigations 1* (Baltimore: Helicon, 1961), p. 202.

7. Karl Rahner, S.J., "The Dogma of the Immaculate Conception in Our Spiritual Life," in *Theological Investigations 3* (Baltimore: Helicon, 1967), p. 140.

Chapter IX:

1. Kilian Healy, O. Carm., *The Assumption of Mary* (Wilmington, Del.: Michael Glazier, Inc., 1982), pp. 29-36.

2. *Ibid.*, p. 29.

3. Cf. *The New Eve, op. cit.*

4. Eamon Carroll, O. Carm., "Papal Infallibility and the Marian Definitions. Some Considerations," in *Carmelus*, Vol. 26, 1979, p. 227.

5. Karl Rahner, S.J., "The Interpretation of the Dogma of the Assumption," in *Theological Investigations 1* (Baltimore: Helicon, 1961), p. 216.
6. Karl Rahner, S.J., *Foundations of Christian Faith: An Introduction to the Idea of Christianity* (New York: The Seabury Press, 1978), pp. 436-443.
7. Kilian Healy, O. Carm., *op. cit.*, p. 35.
8. J. P. Kenny, S.J., "The Assumption of Mary: Its Relevance for Us Today," in *The Clergy Review*, Vol. LXIII, No. 8, August 1978. p. 290.
9. Kilian Healy, O. Carm., *op. cit.*, p. 39.

Chapter X:
1. Cf. T. R. Heath, O.P., *Our Lady*, Vol. 51 (3a., 27-30); St. Thomas Aquinas, *Summa Theologiae* (New York: McGraw-Hill Book Co., 1969), pp. 86-102.
2. Mark Jordan, "Mary the Mother of God in the Writings of St. Thomas Aquinas," *Notes & Commentary: The Center for Contemplative Studies in the University of Dallas*, No. 6, Fall 1983, p. 2.

Chapter XI:
1. Otto Semmelroth, S.J., *op. cit.*, pp. 280-281.
2. Cf. E. Schillebeeckx, *Mary Mother of the Redemption* (New York: Sheed and Ward, 1964), pp. 35-39.
3. Frederick M. Jelly, O.P., "Mary's Intercession: A Contemporary Reappraisal" in *Marian Studies*, Vol. XXII, 1981, pp. 83-87.
4. *The Teaching of Christ: A Catholic Catechism for Adults, op. cit.*, pp. 245-246.

Chapter XII:
1. Abbot Columba Marmion, O.S.B., *Christ in His Mysteries* (St. Louis: B. Herder Book Co., 1939), p. 161.
2. Frederick M. Jelly, O.P., "Mary's Intercession: A Contemporary Reappraisal," *op. cit.*, pp. 87-90.

Chapter XIII:
1. *Loc. cit.*
2. *The Teaching of Christ: A Catholic Catechism for Adults, op. cit.*, p. 579.
3. *Ibid.*, pp. 573-574.

Chapter XIV:
1. Eamon Carroll, O. Carm., *Understanding the Mother of Jesus* (Wilmington, Del.: Michael Glazier, Inc., 1979), pp. 43-47.
2. Robert E. McNally, S.J., *The Unreformed Church* (New York: Sheed and Ward, 1965), pp. 148-186.

Recommended Reading

The following list of books and articles provides some practical suggestions for further reading to those who may wish to pursue the various topics of this book in greater detail. It is, therefore, a selective and not a complete bibliography. After each entry, the chapters of this book to which the particular work pertains are given within italic parentheses. In those cases, however, where the readings refer to this book as a whole, then "All Chapters" will be added. In many of the writings, additional bibliographies are to be found. It is hoped that all who have read this book will be inspired to choose from the following titles those that they will find helpful for a deeper understanding of Mary's place in their spiritual life.

Allchin, A. M., *The Joy of All Creation: An Anglican Meditation on the Place of Mary* (London: Darton, Longman and Todd, 1984), *(Chapter XIV)*.

American Bishops' Pastoral Letter on the Blessed Virgin Mary, *Behold Your Mother: Woman of Faith* (Washington, D.C.: U.S. Catholic Conference, 1973), *(All Chapters)*.

Bearsley, P. J., "Mary the Perfect Disciple," *Theological Studies*, September 1980, Vol. 41, No. 3, pp. 461-504, *(Chapter III)*.

Bouyer, L., *The Seat of Wisdom* (Chicago: H. Regnery Co., 1965), *(All Chapters)*.

Braun, F. M., *Mother of God's People* (New York: Alba House, 1967), *(Chapter IV)*.

Branick, V., Ed., *Mary, the Spirit and the Church* (Ramsey, N.J.: Paulist Press, 1980), *(All Chapters)*.

Brookby, P., Ed., *Virgin Wholly Marvelous: Praises of Our Lady by the Popes, Councils, Saints, and Doctors of the Church* (Cambridge: The Ravengate Press, 1981), *(All Chapters)*.

Brown, R. E., et al., Ed., *Mary in the New Testament* (Philadelphia: Fortress Press & New York / Ramsey, N.J. / Toronto: Paulist Press, 1978), *(Chapters III & IV).*

Carroll, E. R., *Understanding the Mother of Jesus* (Wilmington, Del.: Michael Glazier, Inc., 1979), *(All Chapters).*

Congar, Y., *Christ, Our Lady, and the Church* (Westminster, Md.: Newman Press, 1957), *(All Chapters).*

Deiss, L., *Mary, Daughter of Sion* (Collegeville: The Liturgical Press, 1972), *(Chapters II-V).*

de Satge, J., *Down to Earth: The New Protestant Vision of the Virgin Mary* (Wilmington, N.C.: Consortium Books, 1976), *(Chapter XIV).*

Guardini, R., *The Rosary of Our Lady* (New York: P. J. Kenedy & Sons, 1955), *(Chapter XIII).*

Galot, J., *Mary in the Gospel* (Westminster, Md., 1965), *(Chapters III & IV).*

Healy, K., *The Assumption of Mary* (Wilmington, Del.: Michael Glazier, Inc., 1982), *(Chapter IX).*

Heath, T. R., Trans., Introd., Notes, Appendices, Glossary, *Our Lady*, Vol. 51 (III, qq.27-30, *Summa Theologiae*, St. Thomas Aquinas) (New York: McGraw-Hill Book, Co., 1969), *(Chapter X).*

Hinnebusch, P., *Mother of Jesus Present with Us* (Libertyville, Ill.: Prow Books, 1980), *(Chapters XI-XIII).*

Houselander, C., *The Reed of God* (New York: Arena Lettres, 1978), *(Chapters XI-XIII).*

Harrington, W. J., *The Rosary: A Gospel Prayer* (New York: Alba House, 1975), *(Chapters III, IV, & XIII).*

Jelly, F. M., "The Mother of Jesus" (Chapter 7) & "Mary, Mother and Model of the Church" (Chapter 15) in *The Teaching of Christ: A Catholic Catechism for Adults*, R. Lawler, D. Wuerl, T. Lawler, Ed., (Huntington, Ind.: Our Sunday Visitor, Inc., 1976 & 1983), *(All Chapters).*

_____"Marian Renewal Among Christians," *Homiletic & Pastoral Review*, May 1979, *(Chapters I & XIV).*

_____"The Mystery of Mary's Mediation," *Homiletic & Pastoral Review*, May 1980, *(Chapter XI).*

_____"Our Lady's Rosary and Her Eucharistic Son," *Our Lady's Digest*, Summer 1982, *(Chapter XIII).*

Laurentin, R., *The Question of Mary* (N.Y.: Holt, Rinehart and Winston, 1965), *(Chapters I & XIV).*

Maloney, G. A., *Mary: The Womb of God* (Denville, N.J.: Dimension Books, 1976), *(All Chapters).*

McHugh, J., *The Mother of Jesus in the New Testament* (Garden City, N.Y.: Doubleday & Co., Inc., 1975), *(Chapters II-IV).*

Newman, J. H., *The New Eve* (Westminster, Md.: Newman Press, 1952), *(Chapter V).*

Noone, P., *Mary for Today* (Chicago: The Thomas More Press, 1977), *(Chapter I)*.

O'Carroll, M., *Theotokos: A Theological Encyclopedia of the Blessed Virgin Mary* (Wilmington, Del.: Michael Glazier, Inc., 1982 & 1983), *(All Chapters)*.

Patsch, J., *Our Lady in the Gospels* (London: Burns & Oates, 1958), *(Chapters III & IV)*.

Perrin, J. M., *Mary: Mother of Christ and of Christians* (New York: Alba House, 1978), *(All Chapters)*.

Pope Paul VI, *Devotion to the Blessed Virgin Mary* (Boston: Daughters of St. Paul, 1974), *(Chapters XII-XIV)*.

Papal Teachings, *Our Lady* (Boston: Daughters of St. Paul, 1961), *(All Chapters)*.

Papal Teachings, *The Rosary* (Boston: Daughters of St. Paul, 1980), *(Chapter XIII)*.

Rahner, K., "The Immaculate Conception," in *Theological Investigations 1* (Baltimore: Helicon, 1961), *(Chapter VIII)*.

————"The Dogma of the Immaculate Conception in Our Spiritual Life," in *Theological Investigations 3* (Baltimore: Helicon, 1967), *(Chapter VIII)*.

————"The Interpretation of the Dogma of the Assumption," in *Theological Investigations 1* (Baltimore: Helicon, 1961), *(Chapter IX)*.

Second Vatican Council, *Dogmatic Constitution on the Church* (Nov. 21, 1964), Ch. 8 (on the role of Mary in the mystery of Christ and the Church), *(All Chapters)*.

Schillebeeckx, E., *Mary, Mother of the Redemption* (New York: Sheed & Ward, 1964), *(All Chapters)*.

Tambasco, A. J., *What are they saying about Mary?* (New York / Ramsey, N.J.: Paulist Press, 1984), *(All Chapters)*.

Vollert, C., *A Theology of Mary* (New York: Herder & Herder, 1965), *(All Chapters)*.1

Discussion Questions

Introduction (numbers following questions refer to pages)
1. What does it mean to say that there is only one Mary, but that there are many Madonnas? (1)
2. Although not necessary, why is it better to read the book in sequence? (3)

Chapter I "A Madonna for Catholics Today"
1. Why is it important to reflect upon Mary ecumenically in our time? (5)
2. What is meant by the "Christocentric" and the "ecclesiotypical" characteristics of Marian teaching? (7)
3. How are both these characteristics shown in the teaching of Pope John Paul II? (6)
4. How are these characteristics manifested in the very title of Chapter 8 of Vatican II's Dogmatic Constitution on the Church? (7)
5. What have been the doctrinal, devotional, and ecumenical advantages of the close decision at Vatican II to give the Council's teaching on Mary as part of the doctrine of the Church? (7-8)
6. How are both the ecclesiotypical and the Christocentric mutually complementary? (8)
7. What are Catholic theologians trying to do today both in Christology and in Mariology, and why should this be significant for your Christian faith? (7-10)
8. What are the special relationships between Mary and the other two Persons of the Blessed Trinity besides her Son, namely, the Holy Spirit and the Father? (9-10)
9. What is the connection between the renewal of Marian doctrine and devotion and the biblical, patristic, and liturgical renewals in the Church? (11-12)
10. How do you explain the spiritual, pastoral, and ecumenical emphases of Mariology in our time? (12-14)
11. What is the connection between Scripture, Tradition, and the Magisterium of the Church, expecially regarding Marian doctrine? (14-18)
12. What is the special role of parents in handing on the Tradition of Catholic faith? (17)

Chapter II "Daughter of Sion"
1. Why is it important to know the principal Old Testament themes

foreshadowing Mary's role in our redemption when we already have their fulfillment in the New Testament? (19-20)

2. In what way is the O.T. theme "Daughter of Sion" related to Mary?
(20-21)

3. What does it mean to say that the books of the O.T. were the inspired
Scriptures of the early Church? (21)

4. What does Vatican II teach about the O.T. in relationship to the
N.T.? (22)

5. How is Mary the "Daughter of Abraham, of David, and of the Father"? (22-25)

Chapter III "The Perfect Disciple — Mother of God's Son"

1. What does it mean to say that the N.T. composite portrait of Mary is
both Christocentric and ecclesiotypical? (26)

2. What are the three stages in the formation of the four Gospels, and
why is it important to know this in order to contemplate Mary in the N.T. revelation? (27-28)

3. How do you explain both the similarities and the differences among
the Synoptic Gospels? (30)

4. What does it mean to call the Gospels "confessional documents"? (31)

5. Do you see any connection between the theological purpose of Mark's
Gospel and the *apparently* negative view of Mary as the *mother* of Jesus? (31-32)

6. How did Matthew come to write his infancy narrative, and how does
it reflect his theological purpose in writing the Gospel? (33)

7. Why were the other four O.T. women included with Mary in Matthew's genealogy? (34)

8. Why do you think Joseph "resolved to send her [Mary] away quietly" according to Matthew? (34-35)

9. How does Matthew carefully avoid any connotation of pagan
mythology in his revelation of the virginal conception? (36)

10. Is Matthew 1:24-25 scriptural evidence against Mary's perpetual
virginity? (36)

11. How do you interpret the story of the Magi in connection with the
theological purpose of Matthew's Gospel and with the liturgical solemnity of
the Epiphany? (37)

12. How does Luke combine both the Christocentric and ecclesiotypical
emphases about Mary in his Gospel Madonna? (38)

13. How does Mary fit into Luke's theological purpose with the other
themes of his Gospel? (38)

14. How does Luke's infancy narrative link up with his Acts of the Apostles? (38)

15. What are the two parts of Luke's infancy narrative? (38)

16. How is the literary structure of Luke's Annunciation scene based upon the Annunciation patterns of the O.T? (40)

17. How do you describe the joy experienced by Mary at the Annunciation? (40-41)

18. Why did the greeting of Gabriel make Mary "greatly troubled"? (41)

19. How do you interpret the difficulty raised by Mary to Gabriel? (41-42)

20. What is meant by Luke's "Conception Christology"? (42)

21. What is the connection between Mary's difficulty and her virginity? (42)

22. What sign did Gabriel give to Mary that he was truly God's messenger? (43)

23. How does Mary's *"fiat"* ("yes") make her the first and foremost of her Son's disciples? (43)

24. What is the spiritual significance of Luke's "with haste" in the Visitation? (44)

25. What other themes of Luke's Gospel are shown in the Visitation scene? (44)

26. How is the first half of the "Hail Mary" directly from Luke? (45)

27. How did Elizabeth visit the first macarism (beatitude) upon Mary? (45)

28. What is the parallel between the O.T. Ark of the Covenant and Mary? (46)

29. What would it mean to hold that the *Magnificat* is an early Christian hymn? (46)

30. What is emphasized in the first part of the *Magnificat*? (47)

31. What does the second part of this canticle of Mary emphasize? (47-48)

32. How does this song place Mary on the boundary between the O.T. and the N.T.? (48)

33. Why does Luke refer to world history? (49)

34. Why is it significant for him to point out Bethlehem as Christ's birthplace? (49)

35. How does the lowliness of the conditions in which the Lord was born relate to the *Magnificat* and to the Gospel of Luke as a whole? (49-50)

36. Just how do the shepherds fit into Luke's Gospel as a whole? (50)

37. How can Luke use a title for Jesus as an infant that did not come into use until sometime after the Resurrection? (50)

38. Just what does Luke 2:19 tell us about Mary? (51)

39. What do Simeon's words to Mary mean in the Presentation scene? (51-51)

40. Was Christ's response to Mary in the Temple really a rebuke to his parents? (53)

41. In the context of the Finding in the Temple, how do you interpret Luke 2:51? (52)

42. How does Luke 11:27-28 bring together his Madonna as both "Mother of the Lord" and "Perfect Disciple"? (54)

43. What is the special meaning of Acts 1:14 for us at this time, expecially after Pope John Paul II announced a Marian Year beginning on Pentecost 1987? (55)

44. What are the three principal relations between Mary and the Holy Spirit in Luke's Gospel and in his Acts? (55)

Chapter IV "The Woman of Faith — Mother of God's People"

1. In what sense does John presuppose the teaching of the Synoptics about Mary? (56)

2. In his Gospel, what is the main conviction that John wishes to communicate? (57)

3. How is it possible to have more than one meaning in the symbols of John's Gospel without causing confusion and also contradicting its historical truth? (57)

4. What are the two "Books" of John's Gospel called, and why are they so called? (58)

5. Why is it important to know what John intends to symbolize by the Cana scene as a whole in order to grasp what he wishes to teach about Mary? (59-60)

6. Why does John use the word "sign" instead of "miracle" as used by the Synoptists?

7. Was Mary really asking for a "sign" at Cana? (60)

8. Is Jesus' reply to his mother really a refusal? (60)

9. Why does he call her "woman" instead of "mother"? (60)

10. To what does his "hour" refer? (60)

11. What might be the connection between the "woman" at Cana and Eve and the "woman" of Genesis 3:15? (61)

12. How do you understand the stage of Mary's growth in faith at Cana? (61-62)

13. What are the Christological and ecclesial symbolisms of the Cana scene? (62-63)

14. Who was the beloved disciple of the fourth Gospel? (63)

15. How does the "woman" on Calvary indicate a growth in faith compared to Cana? (63-64)

16. Just what is meant by John's "theology of the cross"? (64)

17. How does the beloved disciple represent all of us? (64-65)

18. Is Mary's spiritual motherhood over all of us really taught in John 19:26-27? (65)

19. What does it mean to hold that the scene of Mary at the foot of the cross is a literary creation of the evangelist, and would this affect our faith in her real role in our redemption? (65-66)

20. In what sense is Revelation 12 a symbolic reference to Mary? (67-68)

Chapter V "New Eve"

1. Why is the Eve/Mary comparison called antithetical parallelism? (69)

2. What is the connection between the Eve/Mary typology and the Mary/Church analogy? (69-70)

3. Just what is meant by the principle of "*recircumlatio*," a word that does not seem to have a single term equivalent in English, but one which we might translate as "recirculation" for purposes of discussion? (71)

4. In which of his works does St. Irenaeus make use of the "New Eve" image? (71)

5. Why is it important to understand the Christological context of St. Irenaeus's writings about the New Eve? (71-72)

6. What are the main biblical passages that inspired St. Irenaeus to contemplate Mary as the New Eve? (72)

7. How would you summarize both the similarities and the differences between Eve and Mary? (73)

8. What does the statement "Mary restores Eve" actually mean? (73)

9. How do you explain the saying among the Fathers of the Church, "death through Eve, life through Mary"? (74-75)

10. How does St. Bernard use the New Eve image? (76)

11. What does Cardinal Newman call the New Eve typology? (76)

12. What inspired Pope Pius XII to set the Eve/Mary analogy on Calvary? (77)

Chapter VI "Ever-Virgin"

1. What are the three principal parts of Mary's virginity? (78)

2. Where in the Liturgy is testimony given to the ancient Tradition that Mary is "Ever-Virgin"? (78-79)

3. Does "virgin birth" really mean the same thing as "virginal conception"? (79)

4. Where in the N.T. is the virginal conception revealed and how? (79)

5. What is the earliest patristic testimony to the virginal conception? (80)

6. How does the virginal conception come to be taught in the New Eve image? (80-81)

7. In what Creed is the doctrine of the virginal conception proclaimed? (81-82)

8. What do the American Bishops teach about the interpretation that the virginal conception is no more than a symbol without any historical basis as an actual fact? (82)

9. What has been taught to be its symbolism based upon its facticity? (82-83)

10. How is such symbolism both Christocentric and ecclesiotypical? (82-83)

11. How does such symbolism help remove the suspicion that it is based upon a negative attitude toward the marital act? (83)

12. What is the biblical basis for the Church's teaching on Mary's virginal parturition? (83)

13. Why did it take longer for this aspect of Mary's virginity to develop in the Tradition? (83)

14. What is the role of St. Ambrose in promoting this teaching? (83-84)

15. How does St. Augustine express the faith of the Church in the matter? (84)

16. How do the Fathers of the East and West differ in their interpretation of it? (84-85)

17. What is Karl Rahner's teaching about how it may be interpreted? (85)

18. Do you agree that our divine Catholic faith does not oblige us to take literally the genetic details in which the doctrine was often described by the Western Fathers? (85-86)

19. How were faith and devotion intimately joined in the development of the doctrine of Mary's perpetual virginity? (86)

20. What was St. Jerome's special role in defending this doctrine? (87-88)

21. How can the "brothers of the Lord" in the N.T. be interpreted in a way that is not contrary to Mary's perpetual virginity? (88-89)

22. Are Catholics called upon to believe in Joseph's perpetual virginity as in Mary's? (89)

Chapter VII "Theotokos: the Birth-Giver of God"

1. What is the earliest testimony to Mary's title "Theotokos"? (90)

2. Is the translation "Mother of God" the best one for "Theotokos"? (90)

3. What does it mean to say that the dogma defined at the Council of Ephesus that Mary is the "Theotokos" is primarily a Christological dogma? (91-94)

4. Does this mean that the dogma really doesn't say anything about Mary? (93)

5. What impact did the definition of this dogma have upon Marian devotion? (94)

6. How can we hold that the "Theotokos" is a dogma of our faith when it is not found explicitly taught in the New Testament revelation? (95-97)

7. What can we learn from our sisters and brothers in the Eastern Churches about this most glorious title of Mary? (97-98)

8. How is "Theotokos" also ecumenically helpful in our dialogues with the Anglicans and Protestants? (98-99)

9. Just how does "Theotokos" help us to preserve our true faith in Jesus Christ? (99)

Chapter VIII "Chosen by God to be the Holy Virgin Theotokos — the Immaculate Conception"

1. Just what is the close connection between Mary's being divinely called to be the "Theotokos" and her Immaculate Conception? (100-101)

2. Just what are the truths that we are called to believe in the defined dogma of the Immaculate Conception? (101-102)

3. How does this dogma still include Mary among those redeemed by her Son? (102)

4. Since its definition by Pope Pius IX in 1854, what have been some of the main references to the Immaculate Conception in the teaching of the Church? (102-103)

5. What are the main biblical references used to support this dogma? (104)

6. How is the New Eve image a possible explanation of the way this truth about Mary developed into a dogma of faith? (107-108)

7. What did St. Augustine hold regarding this doctrine and why? (108-109)

8. What did the Fathers of the East teach about this mystery toward the end of the patristic era? (109-110)

9. What was the witness of the devotion of the faithful in the liturgy? (110-111)

10. Who was Eadmer, and what was his teaching about the Immaculate Conception? (111-112)

11. Why was St. Bernard opposed to the doctrine? (112)

12. Why were Sts. Albert the Great, Bonaventure, and Thomas Aquinas opposed to it? (112)

13. Just what was the special contribution of Duns Scotus to the development of the doctrine of Mary's Immaculate Conception? (112-113)

14. What was the special contribution of Pope Alexander VII? (113-114)

15. How did the widespread devotion of the Miraculous Medal help to bring about the definition of 1854? (114)

16. Does this really mean that the dogma is based upon this private revelation? (114)

17. Just what was the response to Pius IX's encyclical *Ubi Primum*, and why may the Immaculate Conception of Mary be called more the "people's dogma than a "papal dogma"? (114-115)

18. What does this dogma teach us about our own redemption in Christ? (115-116)

Chapter IX "Mother and Son Reunited — Mary's Glorious Assumption"

1. Just what are we called to believe in the defined dogma of the Assumption? (117-119)

2. What are the biblical texts used by Pope Pius XII in the Papal Bull that promulgated the dogma? (119-121)

3. What might be the place of the New Eve image in the development of this dogma? (121)

4. What are the liturgical testimonies to the Assumption, and why are they so important in the development of the dogma? (121-122)

5. What is apocryphal literature, and how can it be influential in the development of doctrine? (122-123)

6. What can we learn about belief in the Assumption from the *Transitus Mariae*? (123)

7. Who was the great Doctor of the Assumption and what did he teach about it? (123)

8. What was the influence of the Pseudo-Jerome and Pseudo-Augustine upon the development of this dogma? (124)

9. What was the response to Pius XII's encyclical *Deiperae Virginis*, and how does it indicate that the dogma of 1950 as well as of 1854 was the "people's dogma"? (125)

10. What is the close connection between our faith in Mary's Assumption and in the Resurrection of her Son as well as our own? (125-127)

11. What do you hold about Mary's dying, and why? (127-128)

12. Where do you think Mary was buried, if you hold that she died, and why? (128)

13. Why is the opinion that Mary died not contrary to the Immaculate Conception? (128)

14. What do you hold about Mary's body decomposing, and why? (129)

15. What are the principal theological reasons behind the Assumption? (129-130)

16. How do you explain the historical fact that the solemnity of the Assumption was a holy day of obligation and that parish churches were named after this great mystery long before it was solemnly defined in 1950? (129-130)

Chapter X "Mary in the Theology of the Church's 'Common Doctor' "

1. Precisely why is St. Thomas Aquinas called the Church's "Common Doctor"? (131)

2. Where does his theology of Mary fit into this theological work as a whole? (130)

3. What is a *summa*, and why is it necessary to know where any part of it fits in? (131)

4. How is an article structured in the *Summa Theologiae*? (132)

5. Who was St. Thomas, and just what did he try to do in his theology? (132)

6. What are the two most significant references to Mary in the *ST*, and how do they epitomize Thomas's main teaching about her? (132-133)

7. How would you summarize his doctrine about Mary's sanctification, particularly explaining his problem with what would much later develop into the dogma of the Immaculate Conception? (134-137)

8. In his teaching on Mary's virginity, what are some of the theological reasons of fittingness that he uses to make this mystery about Mary more meaningful for believers? (137-139)

9. How does he explain the fact that the marriage between Mary and Joseph was a true marital union? (140)

10. How would you summarize his teaching about the appropriateness of the Annunciation? (141-142)

11. According to Aquinas, why can Mary be called "Mother of God" literally? (142-144)

12. How do you distinguish *latria, dulia,* and *hyperdulia?* (144-145)

13. How does Aquinas comment upon the wedding feast at Cana? (145-146)

14. Why is *ST* III, q. 2, a. 11, so significant ecumenically? (146)

15. Do you think that Aquinas eventually came to believe in what would much later be defined as the dogma of the Immaculate Conception, and why? (147)

Chapter XI "Mary and Joseph in the Communion of Saints"

1. What is the earliest testimony to the belief of the faithful about the power of Mary's intercession? (148)

2. How do you distinguish and relate "veneration," "intercession," "mediation," and "invocation"? (148-149)

3. Why is it important for our Marian devotion to see Mary as truly a member of the Communion of Saints? (149)

4. What does the article of the Creed "Communion of Saints" mean to you both doctrinally and devotionally? (150-155)

5. Who are included in the Communion of Saints? (150)

6. What does the technical theological term "eschatology" mean? (150)

7. Why is it so important to see the Pilgrim Church in relation to the Heavenly Church? (151)

8. How are all the members of the one Church in heaven, upon earth, and in purgatory actually united? (152)

9. What does the practice of invoking the saints in heaven do for the Pilgrim Church? (153)

10. What is a way of explaining the mystery of the intercession of the saints for us? (153)

11. How does our honoring of the saints give glory to God? (153-154)

12. Why are we so intimately united to the saints during the Eucharistic Liturgy? (154-155)

13. What does Vatican II teach about abuses in the veneration of the saints? (155)

14. How do you explain the unique role that Mary had in our redemption by her Son? (155-158)

15. Even though the universality of Mary's mediation has not been defined, is there a solid doctrinal foundation for believing that Mary has a mediating role in the distribution of all her Son's saving graces? (158-159)

16. How can Mary's mediation be understood so as not to interfere with the unique Mediatorship of Christ, who alone is our one eternal high priest? (162)

17. Do you think that Mary as Mediatrix of all graces should be defined, and why? (162)

18. How did devotion to St. Joseph develop in the Catholic Tradition? (163-165)

19. Why would the title "Virgin Father" for St. Joseph be better than that of "Foster Father"? (165-166)

20. What is most significant spiritually about our devotion to St. Joseph? (166)

Chapter XII "Mary in the Liturgical Year"

1. What is *Marialis Cultus*, and why is it so important for Marian devotion? (168-169)

2. What does Vatican II's Constitution on the Liturgy teach about Mary in the Liturgical Year? (169)

3. What are the liturgical celebrations concerning Mary during the Church Year? (169-170)

4. How would you summarize the beautiful teaching of *MC* about the close bond between Mother and Son throughout the Liturgical Year? (170-175)

5. How do you see Mary as the special Model for your life of worship in the Church? (175-177)

Chapter XIII "Mary in Private Devotions and Apparitions"

1. Why is it so salutary that the biblical and liturgical renewals have a profound influence upon Marian devotions, especially those practiced outside the Liturgy? (178-179)

2. What is "comprecation"? (179)

3. How is comprecation practiced in the Liturgy? (179)

4. Why is it helpful for us to practice comprecation in our private devotions? (179-180)

5. What is the historical origin of the Angelus, and why is it such an effective form of private devotion to Mary? (180-181)

6. How would you summarize the historical development of the Rosary, and what special part did the sons of St. Dominic play in spreading this great devotion? (182-184)

7. What did Pope Paul VI mean by calling the Rosary a contemplative form of prayer, and why does this not imply that the repetition of the prayers is unimportant? (184-186)

8. How would you summarize a good way of meditating upon the mys

teries of the Rosary in such a way as to let Mary show you how to deepen your devotion to her Son in the Blessed Sacrament? (186-190)

9. What are the five apparitions of Mary that have been especially approved by Rome? (191)

10. Does this mean that all other apparitions have been condemned? (191)

11. How do the American Bishops, in their Pastoral Letter *Behold Your Mother: Woman of Faith*, carefully give us a balanced appreciation for the spiritual significance of Mary's apparitions? (191)

12. Just why do Lourdes and Fatima *not* become an article of faith for us? (191)

13. What does the liturgical prayer for the memorial of Our Lady of Guadalupe tell us about the apparition to Juan Diego? (192)

14. What dogma is the apparition of Mary to St. Catherine Labouré associated with? (192)

15. What was Mary's special message at La Salette? (193)

16. How did Mary appear to St. Bernadette at Lourdes? (193)

17. How did Mary identify herself at Lourdes? (194)

18. Why do you think Lourdes has the widest appeal around the world of all the places of pilgrimage to Marian shrines? (194)

19. What was Mary's special wish at Fatima? (194-195)

20. What is the special connection between Fatima and world communism? (195)

Chapter XIV "A Madonna for All Christians"

1. Who called Mary the "Mother of Unity"? (196)

2. Just what "Madonna" does this final chapter of the book try to portray? (196-197)

3. How would summarize what has been happening during recent years regarding the special place of Mary in the ecumenical movement? (197-198)

4. What are the three main difficulties concerning Marian doctrine and devotion in our ecumenical dialogues with the Anglican and Protestant Churches? (199-202)

5. What are the three signs of hope about progress in our prayerful work for the one Church of Christ through the "Mother of Unity"? (202)

6. How would you compare each sign of hope with each difficulty, e.g., the common study of Mary in the Scriptures with the *sola scriptura* principle? (202)

7. What is the special relationship between the Holy Spirit and Mary in our quest for Christian unity? (202-203)